I0880051

VD
MA

LUTHERAN QUARTERLY BOOKS

Lutheran Quarterly Books will advance the same aims as *Lutheran Quarterly* itself, aims repeated by Theodore G. Tappert when he was editor fifty years ago and renewed by Oliver K. Olson when he revived the publication in 1987. The original four aims continue to grace the front matter and to guide the contents of every issue, and can now also indicate the goals of *Lutheran Quarterly Books:* "to provide a forum (1) for the discussion of Christian faith and life on the basis of the Lutheran confession; (2) for the application of the principles of the Lutheran church to the changing problems of religion and society; (3) for the fostering of world Lutheranism; and (4) for the promotion of understanding between Lutherans and other Christians."

For further information, see www.lutheranquarterly.com.

The symbol and motto of *Lutheran Quarterly*, VDMA for *Verbum Domini Manet in Aeternum* (1 Peter 1:25), was adopted as a motto by Luther's sovereign, Frederick the Wise, and his successors. The original "Protestant" princes walking out of the imperial Diet of Speyer in 1529, unruly peasants following Thomas Müntzer, and from 1531 to 1547 the coins, medals, flags, and guns of the Smalcaldic League all bore the most famous Reformation slogan, the first Evangelical confession: The Word of the Lord remains forever.

For the complete list of *Lutheran Quarterly Books*, please see the final pages of this work.

Stories from Global Lutheranism

— A Historical Timeline —

Martin J. Lohrmann

Fortress Press
Minneapolis

STORIES FROM GLOBAL LUTHERANISM
A Historical Timeline

Cover image: © iStock 2020; Tribal Motif by irinelle
Cover design: Laurie Ingram

Interior design and typesetting: PerfecType, Nashville, TN

Print ISBN: 978-1-5064-6457-2

eBook ISBN: 978-1-5064-6458-9

Dedicated to

my parents, John and Linda Lohrmann,

with love

Contents

Abbreviations

BC	*The Book of Concord: The Confessions of the Evangelical Lutheran Church.* Robert Kolb and Timothy J. Wengert, editors. Minneapolis: Fortress Press, 2000.
DHL 1	*A Documentary History of Lutheranism, Volume 1: From the Reformation to Pietism.* Eric Lund, editor. Minneapolis: Fortress Press, 2017.
DHL 2	*A Documentary History of Lutheranism, Volume 2: From the Enlightenment to the Present.* Eric Lund and Mark Granquist, editors. Minneapolis: Fortress Press, 2017.
DLLT	*Dictionary of Luther and the Lutheran Traditions.* Timothy J. Wengert, general editor. Grand Rapids: Baker Academic, 2017.
ELW	*Evangelical Lutheran Worship.* Minneapolis: Augsburg Fortress, 2006.
LW	*Luther's Works, American Edition,* 55 volumes. J. J. Pelikan, H. C. Oswald, and H. T. Lehmann, editors. Philadelphia: Fortress and St. Louis: Concordia, 1955–86.
TELC	*The Encyclopedia of the Lutheran Church,* 3 volumes. Julius Bodensieck, editor. Minneapolis: Augsburg, 1965.

INTRODUCTION

Living Stones and Faith Rocks

Come to him, a living stone, though rejected by mortals yet chosen and precious in God's sight, and like living stones, let yourselves be built into a spiritual house, to be a holy priesthood, to offer spiritual sacrifices acceptable to God through Jesus Christ. (1 Pet 2:4–5)

With this talk about living stones and spiritual houses, we might say: faith rocks!

Biblical images of living stones and solid rocks can invite us to think of several different aspects of Lutheran history that will appear in this book. First, in today's way of speaking, "Faith rocks!" can mean that faith in God is beautiful, awesome, and exciting. Why does faith rock so much? As the reformer Martin Luther wrote in *The Freedom of a Christian*, faith receives God's promised grace, healing, forgiveness, and freedom, it honors and trusts God alone, and it unites the soul with Christ.[1] Faith—the experience of living by trust—looks to a loving Lord for life and receives all the good things that the Holy Spirit is ready to give us. This original Reformation idea that faith alone reconciles us with God, each other, and ourselves has provided the foundation for five centuries of Lutheran preaching, living, and serving. The deep trust in God that Lutherans call faith sends us into an awesome adventure of courage, resilience, and love. Faith totally rocks.

Second, "faith rocks" also refers to the people and movements that make up Lutheran history. The people are the rocks and living stones! While it may seem strange to describe people as rocks, it turns out that rocks and stones can serve as powerful images of what it means to belong to God and to each other in Christian community. The stones of a building support each other, fit well together, and offer shelter and safety. Sometimes they crumble and need maintenance; they can be moved and rearranged to serve new and upbuilding purposes.

Rocks—and church traditions—move and change more than we might think. For example, when I was working on a history of the congregation I served in Philadelphia, I learned that in the early years of that church (around the 1870s), the congregation had a rock wall surrounding the property that was made of the beautiful local stone called Wissahickon schist. As pretty as the rocks were, that wall was always hard to maintain because of the sloping ground it was on. When the congregation later decided it wanted to build a parsonage, people had the good sense to tear down the crumbling wall and reuse the rock in the construction of a new home: same stones, new purpose and place. Whether by time, water, wind, earthquake, eruption, construction, or other acts of nature and people, rocks and stones certainly can change and move. Just like that, church history tells stories of how people of faith have moved and changed, relocated and been dislocated, and experienced themselves being torn down and built up by powerful forces of time, place, and—dare we trust—the Spirit of God. In this way, the people are living stones who help share the gospel story.

Third, Jesus Christ himself is *the* rock on which all faith is built. As 1 Peter says, he is the original living stone, the one foundation on which all the church's other living stones are built. This interpretation of Jesus as the rock of faith was one of the major early points of the Lutheran tradition.[2] The **Reformation** got its start in the late Middle Ages of Europe, a time when the institutional church and its leaders—especially the popes in Rome—saw themselves as the fulfillment of Jesus's words, "And I tell you, you are Peter, and on this rock I will build my church, and the gates of Hades will not prevail against it" (Matt 16:18). Because St. Peter was supposedly the first bishop in Rome, this passage was used by those in authority to say that the popes who followed him were likewise the rock on which the church was founded.

Early in his conflicts with the church, however, Martin Luther "came to the conclusion that the word 'rock' meant 'faith' . . . faith had to be the rock upon which Christ had built His church."[3] Jesus had promised Peter that the church would be built upon the power of Peter's confession of faith, against which the gates of hell themselves would not prevail. Later in the Reformation, explaining this view of the church and the rock of faith, Luther's colleague Philip Melanchthon wrote, "The church is not built upon the authority of a human being but upon the ministry of that confession Peter made, in which he proclaimed Jesus to be the Christ, the Son of God."[4] The Lutheran church's rock of faith is not an institution or church structure; neither is it the most up-to-date evangelism strategy or latest trend in spiritual guidance. Instead, the rock is Jesus himself, whom we know one day at a time through the risky trust that is **faith**: entrusting our entire bodies and souls to his goodness and care. Jesus is the rock.

Fourth, "faith rocks" can help us consider the painful sides of church history. Rocks can become obstacles that get in the way of following Jesus, the living stone. Old buildings and structures can outlive their purposes and get in the Holy Spirit's way. People of faith can themselves become stumbling blocks to the life of God and life with God. Indeed, shortly after making his beautiful confession of faith, Peter rebuked Jesus for saying that the messiah must suffer and die. At that time, Jesus "turned and said to Peter, 'Get behind me, Satan! You are a stumbling block to me; for you are setting your mind not on divine things but on human things'" (Matt 16:23).

In addition to telling stories of courage and hope, this book also looks at what has happened in Lutheran history when hard-headed and hard-hearted people have strayed from God and done terrible damage to the lives of those around them. Many parts of this history are challenging, controversial, or downright sinful and shameful. They are stumbling blocks to faith. They are the broken ruins of dead or misguided faith. The possibility that human faith might obscure Christ rather than lead people to him appears already in

1 Peter 2:4, where the line "rejected by mortals" has been used by Christians to blame others for the problems around them, as seen in long and ugly Christian history of persecution against Jews, fights against Muslims, and hurtful conflicts about differing worldviews.

Painful as they can be, these, too, are important parts of the story, just like Jesus's strong words against Peter in Matthew 16. Considering Luther's participation in the history of Jewish persecution, we can hear Jesus say, "Get behind me, Luther! For you are setting your mind not on divine things but on human things." While it may seem like the godliest of things to do, using our beliefs to condemn or hurt others is a form of setting our mind on human things. Jesus himself laid down his life not for a few pious friends but for everyone, as John the Baptist announced: "Here is the Lamb of God who takes away the sin of the world!" (John 1:29). In a similar way, looking at the horrors of colonialism and slavery, Jesus tells white Christians who haven't thought twice about building their church on racist and colonizing foundations, "Get behind me, Satan! You are a stumbling block to me!" Seeing the devastation of climate change and our reluctance to face it for the sake of the world that God so loves, Jesus continues, "If any want to become my followers, let them deny themselves and take up their cross and follow me. For those who want to save their life will lose it, and those who lose their life for my sake will find it. For what will it profit them if they gain the whole world but forfeit their life? Or what will they give in return for their life?" (Matt 16:24–26).

Amid such deep sin and hurt, the Lutheran teaching about **"law and gospel"** provides a helpful framework for dealing with the good, the bad, and the complicated of Christian history. For Lutherans, God's word speaks to our souls by telling the truth about sin and the truth about grace. In the words of the prophet Samuel's mother Hannah, "The Lord kills and brings to life; he brings down to Sheol and raises up" (1 Sam 2:6). God's word is a hammer that breaks hard hearts and calls sin what it is in order to turn people to the loving voice of the good shepherd who calls the sheep by name.

By listening to God's word in this dynamic "law and gospel" way, Lutherans have clear standards to which they can hold themselves accountable: namely, to ask whether faith in God has ruled their hearts and whether love of neighbors has guided their actions.

If the answer is yes, then we give thanks for the goodness in our lives and get back to it, one day at a time. If the answer seems to be no then the Spirit helps us turn around and pray to God for new wisdom and strength to follow where Jesus leads. When it comes to self-reflection about our place in the world, Luther said that Christians should daily ask God to "give, preserve, and increase in us faith and the fulfillment of the Ten Commandments and remove all that stands in our way and hinders us in this regard."[5]

By such measures, the Lutheran tradition offers good guidance for not only learning its history but thinking critically about it. Lutherans have done well when their lives and communities have been built upon the crucified and risen Christ. Lutherans have missed the mark—which is the meaning of "sin" in Greek—when they have made other things like culture, dogma, and control more important than trusting God and loving their neighbors. This book provides abundant examples of both the stumbling blocks that get in the way of faith and the strong foundations that come from living in the Spirit of God.

Fifth and finally, the image of faith rocks and living stones means that this book is like a mosaic. A mosaic is a work of art that consists of many different stones that are arranged to create a unified image. In the same way, this book sets many short stories next to each other in order to depict a collective history of global Lutheranism. The fifty stories in this book, therefore, are individual living stones and faith rocks, which together make a single large picture, a mosaic of Lutheran history.

Building a mosaic is different than the usual way I study and write history. My favorite method of research is to dig deep in some original sources and see what treasures I can unearth, as if I were taking part in an archeological dig. In this mosaic of a history, however, I am more like a museum collector than an archeologist. In most cases, I am gathering together stories that other researchers have dug up, so that I can rearrange them here to share a new picture of Lutheran history.

Creating this new picture allows us to see many of the "faith rocks" of Lutheran history in a way that honors the foundations, changes, challenges, and promise of this living Christian tradition in the twenty-first century. With more than seventy-five million

A cross made of stones, forming the center of a labyrinth. Photo by Martin Lohrmann, used with permission.

members in about one hundred countries, Lutherans today are a diverse expression of the global church. This matches the expansive view of the church that the Lutheran reformers held when they presented the *Augsburg Confession* to a gathering of the **Holy Roman Empire** in 1530. As Melanchthon put it, the church "consists of people scattered throughout the entire world who agree on the gospel and have the same Christ, the same Holy Spirit, and the same sacraments, whether or not they have the same human traditions."[6] In both its consistency and change, global Lutheranism portrays a picture of people "scattered throughout the entire world," who are nevertheless united in the body of Christ through the work of the Holy Spirit.

While Lutheranism first grew and spread in central and northern Europe, some of the most vibrant Lutheran communities are now in Africa and Asia. There are about as many Lutherans in Tanzania as in Sweden, and more Lutherans in Indonesia than in Norway.[7] The single largest Lutheran church body in the world is the Ethiopian Evangelical Church Mekane Yesus, a community of over eight million members that focuses on caring for the whole person in both body and soul. Namibia—a country with a million Lutherans among its total population of about two million people—is the only country outside of Europe with a majority Lutheran population. In the early twenty-first century, Lutheran members of the global body of Christ have much to learn from and share with one another.

To borrow a phrase from biblical poetry, sharing this history as a mosaic truly makes this "a time to gather stones together" (Eccles 3:5). As a collector of stories, I owe deep debts of gratitude to the many writers and scholars who have unearthed such gems through their dedication and research. This includes the authors of essays in journals like *Lutheran Quarterly* and of books like *Black Christians: The Untold Lutheran Story*, *Abundant Harvest: Stories of Asian Lutherans*, and *The Future of Lutheranism in a Global Context*. Recent contributions to the great fruitfulness and continuing importance of this subject have also appeared in the book *Global Lutheranism: Vitality and Challenges*, edited by Peter Vethanayagamony and F. Volker Greifenhagen. New reference works like *A Documentary History of Lutheranism* and *Dictionary of Luther and the Lutheran Traditions* have proven themselves to be outstanding resources for further exploration. This book will also provide readers with a good historical complement to a recent theological introduction by Kirsi Stjerna, *Lutheran Book: Orientation and Sources*. Wonderful works like these have provided much of the rich material gathered here. I sincerely hope to honor such scholarship and represent these sources well in this book. I apologize for omissions, errors, and other shortcomings. Writing even a little book like this one has shown me how much I still need to learn, how many inspiring stories there are yet to hear, and how much fascinating historical and theological work remains to be done.

Beyond the stories told here, many others could and ought to be told. This book does not intend to present the definitive history of global Lutheranism. Just because many stories are not included here does not mean that they do not have a place in the mosaic. I know from the outset, for instance, that this book could provide more examples of young people's experiences, study the roles of gender and identity in greater detail, and spend more time on the rich local histories of Lutherans around the world, from Asia to the Americas and from the equator to the poles. I am sorry that this short book only scratches the surface and that there is still much more historical mining to do. To that end, I encourage readers to keep their own lists of topics they want to learn more about and explore with others. There are so many great stories in the Lutheran tradition that deserve to be discovered and shared. The stories that you and your communities will add to this mosaic are truly essential to the whole.

A great way to describe this unique global witness to Christ has come from the church in China, where Lutherans in the early twentieth century became known as the *Xinyi Hui*: the faith-righteousness church.[8] Lutherans continue to believe that people fully receive the great love, mercy, and grace of God simply by trusting the God who promises such riches: in this church, God's righteousness comes through faith. This book shows the history of Lutherans around the world by studying people, places, beliefs, stumbling blocks, and developments, aware that all the individual pieces fit into a larger story of what is now a vibrant branch of global Christianity. Five hundred years after Martin Luther started the Reformation by pointing to Christ as the rock of faith, Lutherans have continued to uncover new gems, explore deep layers of meaning, and create inspiring expressions of life with God in their times and places. Faith still rocks!

The Structure of This Book

Each chapter of this book covers a hundred years of Lutheran history, focusing on ten moments or movements that highlight major themes facing the church in those years. Introductions to each chapter set the stage for the stories that follow and connect each episode with wider historical and religious topics. Questions at the end of each chapter invite further reflection for individuals and groups who are interested in thinking about historical issues in contemporary ways. Because Christian history includes many words and concepts that are not always common knowledge, some terms that are especially significant for the Lutheran tradition will appear in bold print in the text. Readers will find explanations of those terms in the glossary near the end of the book. The book also uses endnotes, so that readers can dig into the sources for themselves.

The first chapter focuses on the Reformation era. Because many of these stories have already been told in numerous books and resources (including professional documentaries and feature films!), this chapter primarily seeks to connect Lutheranism's early years with themes and traits that would continue to shape later centuries. For instance, why did Martin Luther's ideas make such strong and lasting impressions on Christianity? How did an institutional Lutheran church develop? What kinds of social attitudes and spiritual traits would continue to be found in Lutheran communities? What did diversity look like for Lutheranism in its first several decades? These topics set a framework for interpreting the centuries that follow.

Although most of the history of Lutheranism in the 1600s (the focus of the second chapter) is set in Europe, Lutherans were already part of global movements of people and ideas by the middle of that century. Within two hundred years of the start of the Reformation, Lutherans had established lasting communities in North America and the Caribbean, and translated the New Testament into Tamil in southeastern India. Many of these efforts took place in the context of European colonization around the world, requiring readers today to study and reflect upon the damaging legacies of racism and exploitation that came with colonialism. While honest acknowledgment of the hurtful past can be difficult, it is essential for understanding that Lutheranism is not primarily a cultural or ethnic tradition but a living expression of the Christian gospel of freedom and grace.

Chapter 3 covers most of the 1700s, a time heavily influenced by the Age of Enlightenment. Important themes in this section include questions about faith and reason, church and state, tradition and change. Lutherans contributed to the beautiful music of the era, participated in the founding of the United States as a constitutional democracy, and engaged in public reflection on how to use reason for the common good. At the same time, significant challenges arose in matters of war and exile, popular piety and social reform, Christian freedom and human bondage. Far from being a time disconnected from our own, these years show that Lutherans have been wrestling with key questions about life and truth for a long time: some successful past movements to foster faith and serve neighbors can continue to provide inspirational witness, while clear failures to practice the faith and love Lutherans preached stand as stark reminders for people today of how directly our beliefs and actions impact the well-being of people around us.

If many issues facing people around the world today have clear roots in the Enlightenment, even more of our contemporary blessings and curses have direct origins in the nineteenth century. The era stretching from 1817 to 1917, the focus of the fourth chapter, reveals an increasingly global Lutheran church, with stories from Africa, Asia, the South Pacific, Europe, and the Americas showing the good that can come as faith gets shared and lived out in new contexts. It is not too simple to say that missionary efforts blossomed in places where local cultures were respected and embraced, while colonial approaches that sought to impose European ways often brought terrible and lasting damage. Around the globe, Christians continued to struggle with the relationship between change and tradition in worship, theology, and social roles.

Lutheranism's most recent century, and the focus of the fifth chapter, reflects a truly worldwide community. Theological and social liberation movements have continued to push Christians to practice the gospel freedom they preach. The roles of women in church leadership, as well as ecumenical and interfaith cooperation with other communities, have also had major effects on Lutherans. At the same time, Lutherans were impacted by the violent wars of the twentieth century, the Cold War between capitalist and communist governments, and the complicated international politics that accompanied the transition of many nations from colonies to independent states. Whether eagerly or reluctantly, Lutherans have drawn upon the best of their tradition when they have met the world around them with faith in God and love of neighbors.

Acknowledgments

The idea to use key episodes to tell the story of Lutheranism first came as I was putting together a "Timeline of Global Lutheranism" for the journal *Lutheran Quarterly*. I thank *Lutheran Quarterly* editor Paul Rorem and managing editor Virgil "Bud" Thompson for supporting that project; Dr. Rorem also provided many helpful suggestions for the book and its journey toward publication. The original timeline, related essays, and other multimedia resources can be viewed through either *Lutheran Quarterly*'s website or through Johns Hopkins University Press.[9] I also thank Scott Tunseth, Marissa Wold Uhrina, and Jennie Wojciechowski of Fortress Press for their efforts to help this book come to print.

Much of this material developed in courses on Christian history and mission that I have taught with Dr. Kristine Stache at Wartburg Seminary. I am thankful for the way Dr. Stache consistently reminded our classes that sharing the gospel always starts with paying attention to the work of the Holy Spirit. Similarly, our students have kept me on my toes and have contributed to this book through their questions, insights, and typographical corrections. The first people to read a full draft of this book were my brother Rev. Marcus Lohrmann and former Wartburg Seminary student Rev. Daniel Quest, who each provided helpful written feedback. Doctoral student Denise Rector and teaching assistant Lillian Brondyke also read a later draft and made valuable contributions. I thank my wife Carrie and our children Hilde, Jonah, and Theodore for being on this journey of faith and life with me.

As mentioned above, I owe a great debt of gratitude to the many scholars from whose work I have learned. I hope I have represented such research accurately and faithfully. Because even the encyclopedias, dictionaries, and the internet itself cannot tell all the stories there are to discover, I hope this book serves as a starting point for further adventures in faith, hope, and love, as seen in and through Lutheran witnesses. I dedicate this book to my dear parents, John and Linda Lohrmann, with deep appreciation for how they have shared the Christian story with me and many others through their life together. With the words of Psalm 22, I commend this book to future generations who will cherish the Christian freedom that is theirs in faith.

Indeed, all who sleep in the earth shall bow down in
worship;
all who go down to the dust, though they be dead,
shall kneel before the Lord.
Their descendants shall serve the Lord,
whom they shall proclaim to generations to come.
They shall proclaim God's deliverance to a people yet
unborn,
saying to them, "The Lord has acted!"[10]

Martin J. Lohrmann
Wartburg Theological Seminary
Dubuque, Iowa
Season of Easter, 2020

CHAPTER ONE

1517–1617

Introduction to Lutheranism in Its First Century

Lutheranism began as a reform movement within the Roman Catholic Church of the late Middle Ages in Europe. Previous centuries had seen their share of church reforms: people like Bernard, Hildegard, Francis, Clare, and Dominic brought inspiring change to their local communities and to the wider church based on renewed emphasis on faith in Jesus Christ and service to neighbors. Teaching theologians like Anselm of Canterbury, Peter Abelard, Peter Lombard, Albert the Great, Thomas Aquinas, William Ockham, and Catherine of Siena similarly opened new worlds of thought through creative and provocative writings. While these medieval church leaders found ways to work within the mainstream church, other leaders who advocated for reform like Peter Waldo in France, John Wycliffe in England, and Jan Hus in Bohemia were condemned and their teachings repressed.

Far from being a time of stagnation or conformity, the political, social, and church structures of the late Middle Ages were constantly changing. A great diversity already existed within the **Christendom** of late-medieval Europe, which stemmed from the challenging work of thinkers like those named above and from dramatic changes in the church itself. Institutionally, a "Western Schism" in the 1300s

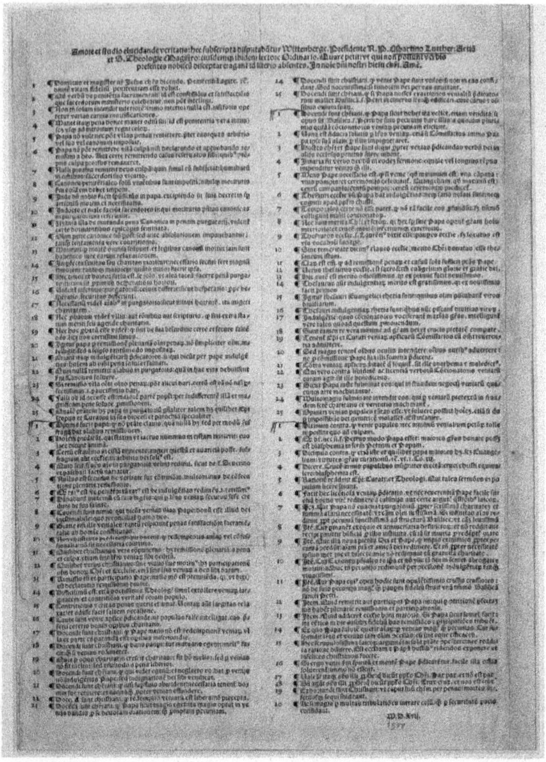

1.1 The *Ninety-Five Theses* of Martin Luther printed in one page by Hieronymous Hotzel, Nuremberg, 1517. Wikimedia Commons.

occurred when several popes moved the papacy to Avignon, France, and then a rival pope was elected in Rome. One church council of the early 1400s deposed two competing popes and installed a new one, with the result that there were three popes for a time. When unity finally came again in 1417, it seemed as if the church of western Europe might be governed more by international councils than by a single head. Even though a strong papacy survived those challenges, such questions about church leadership were still simmering in the early 1500s.

Relationships between church and state were similarly diverse. The Avignon papacy had grown from close ties between popes and the kings of France. By contrast, the English—who were in a Hundred Years' War with France in the 1300s and 1400s—valued more local control of their churches and maintained some independence from Rome. Quite apart from the later Reformation in northern Europe, Spanish monarchs Ferdinand and Isabella launched a renewal of the church in Spain in the late 1400s through a combination of theological reform and the forced conversion of Muslims and Jews, overseen by the scholarly Cardinal Francisco Jiménez de Cisneros. People in Bohemia (the area around Prague) continued to follow the teachings of Jan Hus and practiced their faith in defiance of the Church of Rome, even when that meant that their kings were excommunicated and threatened with invasion. By Luther's time, both the common people and local political authorities were often eager to redefine their connections with Rome.

Finally, the religious ideas and practices of the late Middle Ages also differed across regions, monastic orders, and schools of thought. Monastic communities like the Benedictines, Franciscans, Dominicans, and Augustinians competed for both local support and intellectual influence. University theologians could either align themselves with thinkers like the Dominican Thomas Aquinas or the Franciscan William of Ockham or—nearly as controversially—seek out a blended position. With their special affinity for St. Augustine (often called the Doctor of Grace), the medieval Augustinian order to which Luther belonged developed unique ways of talking about and living out their faith in light of the radical grace of God. Adding to this complex mix, Renaissance **humanists** started to bypass traditional authorities by reading classical works of philosophy and theology—including the Bible—in their original languages, which gave them new perspectives on old sources. Far from a time of stability and uniformity, therefore, the early 1500s were marked by adaptation and energy even before an unknown professor named Martin Luther shared some new ideas with his monastic, educational, and congregational communities in the autumn of 1517.

From these late-medieval roots, Lutheranism would grow into a significant branch of global Christianity. As a reform movement, Lutherans wrestled from the beginning with questions of continuity and change, political power and social justice, unity and difference. As we will see, responses to these themes shaped early Lutheran communities and set patterns of thought and action for generations to come.

October 31, 1517: Luther's *95 Theses*

Why Martin Luther? How did a young theology professor at a new university in a small town in central Europe change Christendom and world history? In a word: **faith.**

As a member of the Augustinian monastic order, Brother Martin was surrounded by religious practices that kept faith in God central to his daily life. Scripture and prayer filled his days, with Bible readings at mealtimes, worship, and personal devotion time. With clear gifts for advanced study, Luther's Augustinian order—especially his mentor Johann von Staupitz—prepared him for leadership by encouraging him to begin graduate school and earn a doctorate. Ordained a priest in Erfurt in 1507, installed as a professor in 1512, and assigned local pastoral duties in 1514, Luther came to know the beliefs and worries of all kinds of people by teaching in the university, taking on leadership roles with his monastic brothers, and participating in the worship life of parishioners in the Wittenberg City Church.

While these experiences were common enough for a late-medieval priest and professor, Luther uniquely combined his spiritual life with academic study: in the classroom he gave scholarly attention to the religious faith he was living out in the monastery and the local congregation as he gave his first sets of lectures on the Psalms and Paul's letter to the Romans. Throughout his career, Luther's theological work remained closely connected to his pastoral focus on daring to trust Christ with one's whole life.

1.2 An early image of Martin Luther in three-quarter view by Lucas Cranach the Elder, 1520. Wikimedia / Source/ Photographer, YAF8QqkEOdJdvg at Google Cultural Institute.

Why Luther? By spending his formative years praying, studying, and observing what it means to be saved by Jesus Christ, he came to see that people receive God's good news of salvation not by being holy enough, humble enough, or spiritually serious enough, but simply by trusting in God for all things. As he explained in his 1515/16 lectures on Romans, "to believe in Christ is to reach out to Him with one's whole heart and to order all things in accord with Him."[1] Faith simultaneously includes risk and confidence: risk, because it means admitting that we are not holy on our own; confidence, because God is faithful, trustworthy and loving, beyond human sin, doubts, and unworthiness.

In the fall of 1517, Martin Luther applied this conviction about faith's saving power to the church's use of indulgences. Of relatively recent origin in the Middle Ages, indulgences had become one of the ways people could pay the debt of their sins and get right with God. Indulgences were not the same thing as buying salvation. People in the medieval church knew that God alone forgives sin. But it was thought that when people sinned, they then needed to do something good to make up for the wrong they committed. The medieval church taught that God forgives the spiritual guilt of sin, but people still need to work off an earthly penalty. To that end, the church encouraged spiritual practices like making religious vows, praying, doing good works, going on a pilgrimage, fasting, joining a crusade, giving alms to the poor, sponsoring a mass, making donations to the church, and (yes) buying indulgences as ways to reduce the penalty of sin, in whole or in part.

In Luther's time, the theology of indulgences was still in the process of being developed; for instance, the idea that an indulgence could be applied to the soul of someone who had already died only started to appear in the later 1400s.[2] In keeping with university practice, young Dr. Luther drew up 95 theses—points for discussion and debate—about the meaning and practice of indulgences. Because the *95 Theses* are about indulgences and other penitential practices, some scholars believe that Luther was not yet "**Lutheran**" or "**evangelical**" by that time in 1517. But throughout the text, Luther's underlying concern was about how people get right with God, the key theme of his entire career. Because an indulgence was being preached and sold in towns near Wittenberg in those days, the topic of indulgences was a good contemporary issue to identify as one that invited reflection on larger theological themes of sin and grace, **justification** and reconciliation.

The introduction to the *95 Theses* shows that Luther was indeed using a discussion of indulgences to talk about bigger issues: "Out of love and zeal for the truth and the desire to bring it to light, the following theses will be publicly discussed at Wittenberg under the chairmanship of the reverend father Martin Lutther, Master of Arts and Sacred Theology and regularly appointed Lecturer on these subjects at that place."[3] Luther's "love and zeal for the truth" launched a Reformation. The first thesis opens with a big-picture reference to the start of Jesus's preaching ministry (Matt 4:17) and what it means to be a Christian. It states, "When our Lord and Master Jesus Christ said, 'Repent,' he willed the entire life of believers to be one of repentance."[4]

Because the theology of indulgences was relatively new, Luther's questions about them were not automatically controversial. The topic could have still been up for open debate. As the *95 Theses* spread, however, people noticed the deep questions about sin, grace, and church authority that they contained. In these 95 points for discussion, Luther had clearly criticized medieval theology, contemporary church practices, and the wealth of the church and Pope Leo himself, as seen here:

> 65. Therefore the treasures of the gospel are nets with which one formerly fished for men of wealth.
> 66. The treasures of indulgences are nets with which one now fishes for the wealth of men . . .
> 86. Again, "Why does not the pope, whose wealth is today greater than the wealth of the richest Crassus, build this one basilica of St. Peter with his own money rather than with the money of poor believers?"[5]

These larger themes caught people's attention and resonated with concerns about corruption in the church, distrust of powerful figures in distant Rome, and interest in the spiritual life of the common people. Within months, the indulgence controversy became a debate around Europe about church authority and about the possibility of reforms based on the free gift of grace given through faith in Christ. Because of the dramatic debates and events that followed their publication, the *95 Theses* are rightly considered the beginning of the Reformation.

Did Luther really post the *95 Theses* to the door of the Castle Church in Wittenberg on October 31, 1517? The accuracy of this central Reformation image remains debated among historians.[6] Whether or not he used a hammer, Luther did mail them to Archbishop Albrecht of Mainz on that day, which makes "posting" an accurate word to use. It would have been customary for Luther to put an announcement like this on the Castle Church door, which served as a campus kiosk or bulletin board, but neither Luther nor any other potential eyewitness left any direct description of this event. Regardless, Luther's *Disputation on the Power and Efficacy of Indulgences* from October 31, 1517—better known as the *95 Theses*—accurately represents the start of a new era in Christianity. The risky trust in God that Luther called "justification by faith alone" changed the world.

August 29, 1518: Philip Melanchthon Arrives in Wittenberg

As the indulgence controversy continued to heat up, Luther responded with several important writings and presentations. Early in 1518, his *Sermon on Indulgences and Grace* was published, giving readers a simpler summary of the scholarly ideas first presented in the *95 Theses*. Already well known across Germany by then, Luther was invited to share his thoughts with a gathering of Augustinians in Heidelberg that April. In this *Heidelberg Disputation*, Luther described a theology of the cross in the following theses:

19. That person does not deserve to be called a theologian who looks upon the invisible things of God as though they were clearly perceptible in those things which have actually happened [Rom 1:20].
20. That person deserves to be called a theologian, however, who comprehends the visible and manifest things of God seen through suffering and the cross.
21. A theology of glory calls evil good and good evil. A theology of the cross calls the thing what it actually is.[7]

Luther further developed this **theology of the cross** in his *Explanations of the Ninety-Five Theses* (published later that spring), claiming that God works not through human ideas of righteousness and holiness but through "the crucified and hidden God."[8] Then and now, Luther's conviction that God works in lowly ways challenges dominant views about who is holy and how people get holy: Christ's holiness consisted in personally "becoming sin" and bearing it himself on the cross rather than avoiding it, in order to bring back to life people who are otherwise inescapably overcome by sin and suffering.[9] Later in the year, Luther was summoned to Augsburg, where he met Cardinal Cajetan. In his *Proceedings at Augsburg*, Luther summarized the frustrations of his time with Cajetan, who was under instructions from Rome to get Luther to recant rather than have the open discussion and mutual conversation that Luther and many others longed for.[10]

1.3 Engraving of Philip Melanchthon in 1526 by Albrecht Dürer captioned, "Dürer was able to draw the living Philip's face, but the learned hand could not paint his spirit" (translated from Latin). Wikimedia Commons.

Amid such key moments in Luther's life and work, Philip Melanchthon arrived to teach at the University of Wittenberg in the summer of 1518. Melanchthon would be Luther's valuable colleague for decades to come, as together they taught their gospel-centered theology and put church reforms into practice. Among the sharpest minds of the sixteenth century, Melanchthon was only twenty-one years old when he started teaching in Wittenberg. With a great gift for languages and for clarity of thought, Melanchthon had earned his Bachelor of Arts degree in Heidelberg at age fourteen and his master's degree from the University of Tübingen at age seventeen. He came to Wittenberg with ambitious goals to reform school, church, and society by going back to the sources—*ad fontes*—of classical learning and biblical wisdom.

Within a few years, Melanchthon was doing just that. His 1521 *Loci Communes* became the first theology book of the Lutheran Reformation. In it, Melanchthon interpreted Paul's Letter to the Romans as a summary of what believers need to know about the gospel of Jesus Christ, as it walks people through topics like sin and grace, faith and good works, and other important key points (*loci communes*) of Christian life like service to the neighbor. Melanchthon taught that faith in Christ is not just learned by the head but received in the heart and lived out every day, as he wrote, "to know Christ means to know his benefits."[11] With this theological study of Romans, Melanchthon planted Lutheran teaching in the Bible, showing readers how to learn and share a gospel theology that has its roots directly in the grammar, logic, and rhetoric of scripture alone.

Melanchthon attended the Leipzig Disputation in the summer of 1519, where Wittenberg professors Andreas Bodenstein von Karlstadt and Martin Luther debated the Dominican theologian Johann Eck on topics like indulgences and church authority. When Luther went into exile at Wartburg Castle after the 1521 **Diet of Worms**, Melanchthon was one of the few people who was able to keep in touch with Luther through letters. The next year, Melanchthon helped Luther finalize his 1522 translation of the New Testament from Greek into German.

Later generations, however, would come to view Luther's time at Wartburg Castle as an early sign of weakness in Melanchthon's leadership abilities. As we will see more in the next section, changes in Wittenberg continued under the leadership of Dr. Karlstadt while Luther was away. These reforms (which Luther supported) included the marriage of priests, the voluntary disbanding of the Augustinian monastery, and giving the cup to laypeople during Holy Communion.[12] When three self-proclaimed prophets came to town and university students started rioting, Melanchthon communicated these events to Luther and asked for advice. Excitement about the prophets soon fizzled out and the three men moved on.

When Wittenberg's city council passed new laws about church reform in January 1522, the political and religious situation grew more chaotic. Luther returned from exile in early March to help restore order in the town. Although Luther's return has often been seen as an indication of Melanchthon's supposed timidity, historian Heinz Scheible has refuted that view, showing that the young Melanchthon:

> had no office that would have given him any influence. Luther and a portion of the townspeople would gladly have enlisted him as preacher in the city church, but, since Melanchthon was not ordained, the provost, [Justus] Jonas, did not yet want to take responsibility for such a move. Thus, Melanchthon was, so to speak, a private individual, albeit not a completely normal one, but instead a rather young, but nevertheless intellectually superior professor who had championed Luther's theology orally and in writing. He was also the one who, together with some students, received **both kinds** in the Lord's supper as the first laypersons. Moreover, he sat on some commissions, where with Jonas and von Amsdorf he represented a moderate position. And he was a faithful liaison for Luther and, through Spalatin, for the elector's government.[13]

On this moment and others in Melanchthon's life, Scheible's work has shown Melanchthon to be a leader of integrity, who took courageous principled stands throughout his career, both before and after Luther's death in 1546.

In addition to his *Loci Communes*, Melanchthon shaped the early Reformation by reorganizing schools in Germany. He developed models of early childhood education that focused on reading, writing, and clear thinking. Building on these primary skills, Melanchthon wrote instructions for the first *Gymnasium* (high school) in Germany. Established in Nuremberg in 1526, this new school emphasized math and music, critical thinking, clear communication, and reading Greek and Latin classics in their original languages. Hebrew was also offered for students who might pursue a career in theology. A reformation of the medieval liberal arts tradition, this model became hugely influential for education in Europe. In his lifetime, over fifty cities asked Melanchthon to help create similar schools for them.[14]

Philip Melanchthon's addition to the University of Wittenberg in 1518 marked the beginning of a fruitful partnership that lasted over a quarter of a century. As we will see later in this chapter, Melanchthon's work was crucial to the spread of the Lutheran Reformation. He is rightly remembered for his work with Luther, his faithful service to the gospel, and the love of learning that earned him the name *Praeceptor Germaniae*, the teacher of Germany.

June 13, 1525: War and Marriage

The so-called "Wittenberg Unrest" that took place when Luther was at Wartburg Castle raised challenging questions about how much and how fast to reform society. Politically, the 1521 Diet of Worms affirmed the pope's excommunication by making Luther's teachings illegal in the **Holy Roman Empire**. Enforcement of this **Edict of Worms**, however, was left to local officials.

In **Electoral Saxony** where Luther lived, Frederick the Wise decided to protect the reformer and not enforce the imperial edict. In nearby Ducal Saxony, though, Duke George banned the printing of Luther's 1522 translation of the New Testament and advocated an empire-wide military enforcement of the edict against Luther.[15] Enforcement of the Edict of Worms in the northern land of Pomerania led Johannes Bugenhagen—a priest and teacher who had moved to Wittenberg in 1521—to write his first Reformation tract, a letter of consolation to fellow reform-minded clergy in his homeland.[16] In the Netherlands, many Lutheran preachers went into exile or were arrested. This led to the Reformation's first martyrdoms, the execution of Augustinian brothers Heinrich Voes and Johann Esch, who were burned at the stake in Brussels on July 1, 1523. Their execution inspired Luther's first published song, a ballad in honor of the martyrs entitled "A New Song Here Shall Be Begun."[17]

While princes and city governments were dealing with the Edict of Worms in their spheres of influence, the people of central Europe were also responding to the call for reform of church and society at grassroots levels. In 1520, Luther had written that all Christians share equal spiritual status through baptism: "All Christians are truly of the spiritual estate, and there is no difference among them except that of **office** . . . This is because we all have one baptism, one gospel, one faith, and are all Christians alike; for baptism, gospel and faith alone make us spiritual and a Christian people."[18] Luther's call for spiritual equality matched longstanding grievances among peasants and merchants, who wanted more legal, economic, and social rights. In previous decades, these social movements had led to peasants' revolts, especially in southern Germany. Fighting broke out again in the mid-1520s, as groups of peasants stormed castles, chased monks out of monasteries, and demanded social changes from their rulers.

Luther had responded to the Wittenberg Unrest by emphasizing faith and love: faith trusts God and receives Christ's promises, while love looks to the good of the neighbor, which sometimes means taking things slow in matters of reform. While this approach defused a volatile situation in Wittenberg, it also did not answer questions about who gets to decide when it's time to make a change or go slow. In Luther's view, community leaders like ruling monarchs and city councils should oversee such decisions, because they have already been entrusted with positions of leadership in matters of justice, good governance, and public order. But what if these rulers were the same people who kept justice from happening? Using his own story as an example, Luther described how he had taken a stand for truth without taking up arms, because—while extreme measures might seem warranted—a revolution that creates new physical and social harm likely hurts people more than it helps them. As he put it, insurrection "always results in more damage than improvement, and verifies the saying, 'Things go from bad to worse.'"[19]

Radical preachers like Thomas Müntzer, however, connected the spiritual liberation of the Reformation with the social and economic complaints of the peasants. To Luther, this combination of religious zeal and social upheaval was dangerous. His tracts from that period grew increasingly harsh against rebellious factions, as he called for ruling authorities to suppress uprisings by any means necessary. Not needing Luther's blessing to use military force, in May 1525 the armies of Philip of Hesse and Duke George of Saxony killed thousands upon thousands of peasants at the Battle of Frankenhausen, while their soldiers only suffered casualties in the single digits. It was a slaughter of peasants by the nobility, one of whom favored the Reformation (Philip) and one of whom was against it (George).

From Luther's perspective, the tremendous suffering of the Peasants' War confirmed the concerns he had voiced about rebellion and revolution. Because he sided with the authorities rather than the common people while a slaughter was taking place, however, Luther has been seen as betraying his own call for liberation and reform. The great theologian of black liberation, James Cone, for instance, asserted that Luther's "ethic of the status quo" put him and other reformers like him on the wrong side of scripture and history.

> They were wrong *ethically* because they were wrong *theologically*. They were wrong theologically because they failed to listen to the bible—with sufficient openness and through the eyes of the victims of political oppression. How ironic it is that he who proclaimed *sola scriptura* as one of the guiding lights of his reformation did not really hear the true meaning of that proclamation. For to hear the message of Scripture is to hear and see the truth of God's liberating presence in history for those who are oppressed by unjust social structures.[20]

Critiques like Cone's raise serious, essential questions about how religious faith informs Christian engagement in matters of political and social injustice. Throughout the Reformation era and into the present, questions about how to work for and support peace, justice, and liberation rightly challenge faith communities to prayer, reflection, and action. Although these are hard issues to address, in his book *Do No Harm* theologian Stephen Ray has encouraged Christians to keep at it: "What I am contending is not that we can never get it quite right, but that, with care, we might not get it so wrong."[21]

Living amid such turbulent times, Luther supposedly said, "If I knew the world was ending tomorrow, I would still plant a tree today." Although that phrase is often attributed to Luther, there is no evidence he actually said it. However, confronted with struggles like his excommunication, the Edict of Worms, the Peasants' War, and the recent death of **Elector** Frederick the Wise, Luther did believe that the Last Days were at hand.

Instead of responding to the possible end of time by planting a tree, Luther got married. To him, marriage was an affirmation of life. He married Katharina von Bora, a runaway nun who seems to have belonged to an impoverished noble family.[22] Since her flight from a convent on Easter Day, 1523, Katharina had been working in the household of the Wittenberg artist Lucas Cranach. After other marriage plans for her had not worked out, Katharina herself suggested the match with Martin Luther. Pastor Bugenhagen presided over the small private wedding of Martin and Katharina on June 13, 1525. A public ceremony followed some days later.

1.4 Katharina von Bora (Luther) by Lucas Cranach the Elder, 1528. Wikimedia Commons.

The marriage of priests was obviously a change for men in ministry. But it also changed social life for women in many ways. In the Middle Ages it was not uncommon for priests to have families, but the women in those relationships had no rights because neither they nor their children had any of the legal status that often comes with marriage. Giving legal sanction to married pastors, therefore, brought new protections for women and children, including pastors' widows. In some cases, marriage could bring increased public recognition and influence to women, as seen in the life of Katharina von Bora. After her marriage, Katharina (whom Martin often called Käthe, or Katie) ran a sizable family business that involved overseeing room and board for students and guests, running a farm, managing the finances, brewing beer, and buying a second piece of property. In his will, Luther defied the Saxon law that said women could not own property by leaving his estate to her rather than to a male guardian or to their children.[23] Indeed, Katie Luther was a formidable public figure and highly effective manager.

Although their marriage appears to have taken place quite suddenly, Martin and Katharina developed strong bonds of love. Most of what we know about their life together comes from letters written by Martin to his wife; Katharina's letters have mostly not survived. Despite this scarcity of sources, the evidence reveals a relationship of mutual respect and love. Martin and Katharina had six children together, four of whom lived to adulthood. The early deaths of two daughters, Elisabeth at age one in 1528 and Magdalena at age thirteen in 1542, brought great sorrow to their parents and made them "partners in calamities."[24] More than just a personal side of life that he kept to himself, being a husband and parent impacted Luther's theology. His family experiences deepened his understanding of the Bible and of God as a loving parent. Amid chaotic times like the Peasants' War, Martin and Katharina turned to each other for love and companionship, providing a stirring example of how complex social times can impact family life, and vice versa.

Like Katharina von Bora, another influential woman in the community, Elisabeth Cruciger, fled a monastery, moved to Wittenberg, and married a professor. Elisabeth wrote a hymn called "Herr Christ der einig Gottes Sohn" (The Only Son from Heaven).[25] It was published in one of the first Lutheran hymnals—the *Erfurt Enchiridion* of 1524—and was translated into Swedish, Danish, and English within the decade; it has remained in many Lutheran hymnals ever since.[26] Elisabeth Cruciger provides another good example of how women actively shaped the early Reformation.

The Lutheran reformers supported basic education for girls both to serve their spiritual life and give them practical skills for daily use. Despite this new emphasis on female education, gender roles in church and society remained quite traditional: educating girls was of secondary importance compared to the education of boys, and it largely existed to advance women's domestic work rather than provide an alternative to it. Even with the growth of female literacy, religious and legal barriers prevented women from full leadership roles and equal rights in society, including in Lutheran communities, for centuries to come.

Escape from convents or the disbanding of monasteries brought advantages and disadvantages to women. In many cases in the late

Middle Ages, young women had not chosen to enter monastic life themselves but had been sent to convents by their families. For such women—including Katharina von Bora—leaving the monastery was a first step toward new opportunities. However, convents had also long served as important centers of women's education and independence.[27] Women like Caritas Pirkheimer in the Lutheran city of Nuremberg loved life in the cloister and fought to retain it.[28] As much as the Reformation might have opened some doors for women, no institution arose in the sixteenth century to fill the important role that convents had served in women's lives.

June 25, 1530: Presentation of *Augsburg Confession*

Although Martin Luther had been excommunicated by the papacy and condemned by the imperial Edict of Worms early in the 1520s, his case continued to create political and legal waves. In Luther's homeland of Electoral Saxony, Frederick the Wise dealt with the Edict of Worms by not enforcing it. When Frederick died in 1525, his brother John pursued a similar strategy upon becoming the elector. Other lands like Hesse, Prussia, and Schleswig-Holstein, along with cities like Nuremberg and Magdeburg continued to adopt Lutheran reforms as official religious policy.

Emperor Charles V, however, remained opposed to the Reformation. One of the most powerful individuals in world history, Charles was at once the king of Spain, ruler of Spanish colonies in the Americas, Holy Roman Emperor of the German Nation, and the leader of the Austro-Hungarian **Hapsburg dynasty**, which also ruled over Belgium and the Netherlands. He was frequently at war with France, the Ottoman Empire, or both at once. For their part, popes often aligned themselves with France because Charles's power threatened their independence and strategic interests, too. In the summer of 1527, a battle between France and Charles's imperial troops in northern Italy spread southward, with the result that unruly and underpaid imperial soldiers invaded Rome and took Pope Clement prisoner.

Amid this complicated foreign policy, German taxes and soldiers were essential resources for the emperor's wars. German rulers who supported Luther's reforms, therefore, had some leverage in their negotiations. At an imperial diet in Speyer in 1526, pro-Reformation leaders convinced Charles's brother King Ferdinand of Austria to suspend the Edict of Worms. Legally, this created a new opportunity to institutionalize church reforms. In Electoral Saxony, this led to the Saxon visitations, in which theologians like Luther and Melanchthon traveled with political representatives to visit local parishes, evaluate the preaching, and examine church finances and administration.

These visits advanced Lutheran reforms. Melanchthon wrote *Instructions for the Visitors of Parish Pastors in Electoral Saxony* to serve as a template for the theological and institutional reform of congregations. Pastor Bugenhagen traveled to Braunschweig and Hamburg to write Lutheran **church orders**, which were church constitutions that guided the reform of parishes, schools, and public welfare programs. Luther's experience with the visits led him to publish his **catechisms** as a preaching resource for clergy and as a spiritual guide for parishioners and their children. These works—especially Luther's *Small Catechism*—put Reformation ideas into everyday language in ways that have shaped Lutheranism ever since.

The political situation, however, remained perilous. At a second Diet of Speyer in 1529, King Ferdinand (again representing his brother Charles) reinstated the Edict of Worms. In response, a group of German princes and city officials lodged a *protestatio*, a legal appeal; this is the origin of the name **Protestant**. In the following months, Emperor Charles invited the Protestants to explain their teachings and reforms at another upcoming imperial diet in Augsburg. The two main items on the agenda were the religious debates of the Reformation and war against the Ottoman Empire. These items are more related than they might appear: the war against the Muslim Turks kept Charles from using military force against his German Protestant subjects. For that reason, it is fair to say that Lutherans owe part of their existence to Islam. In the words of an old Austrian saying: "The Turk is the Lutherans' lucky star."[29]

In preparation for the upcoming meeting in Augsburg, the Wittenberg theologians refined their written statements of faith and practice. In October 1529, Philip of Hesse called theologians like Luther, Melanchthon, Johannes Brenz, and Andreas Osiander to meet in Marburg with Swiss and South German reformers Martin Bucer, Huldrych Zwingli, and Johannes Oecolampadius so that they might present a united Protestant position. The theologians agreed on fourteen of fifteen points, with the lone disagreement on the **real presence** in Holy Communion. Luther and his colleagues insisted that Christ is truly present in Holy Communion on the basis of Jesus's words "This is my body" (Matt 26:26). Although Zwingli and Oecolampadius believed that Communion was important for Christians as a remembrance of Christ and a sign of Christian unity, they would not affirm that Christ was physically present in the bread and wine. Despite many common convictions, this impasse led to a division between **Lutheran** and **Reformed** Protestants in the decades and centuries that followed.[30]

Before working on those fifteen Marburg Articles, the Wittenberg colleagues had already written a summary of their beliefs known as the Schwabach Articles. (As with the later *Augsburg Confession* and *Smalcald Articles*, it was typical for these writings to be named after the towns in which they were composed or presented). A third text came together in April 1530 when Luther, Melanchthon, Bugenhagen, and Justus Jonas gathered in Torgau to draft an explanation of reforms like priestly marriage and **communion in both kinds**. Part three of Luther's 1528 *Confession concerning Christ's Supper* provided a similar personal summary of the reformer's faith.

Because Luther was under the condemnation of the Edict of Worms, he spent the summer of 1530 near the southern edge of Saxony, at Coburg Castle. He and Melanchthon exchanged letters regularly, with Luther giving feedback on drafts. Melanchthon became the primary author of the document presented in Augsburg. Other reformers like Jonas, Brenz, Osiander, Urbanus Rhegius, and Johannes Agricola were also with him.

Rather than simply revise the previous theological statements, the Lutheran group discovered that they would need to write an even more direct statement of their faith. This was because Catholic theologian Johann Eck had gathered 404 supposedly heretical quotations from a variety of reform-minded writers. Some of his points accurately reflected controversial statements by people like Luther and Melanchthon; others were taken out of context or were meshed with the views of leaders with whom the Wittenberg theologians disagreed like the more radical reformers Hans Denck and Balthasar Hubmaier.

For this reason, Melanchthon's first goal at Augsburg was to show that the Lutherans were Christian. He therefore stressed continuity between the reformers and a common Christian faith that streteched across the centuries. The first part of the ***Augsburg Confession***—as this document came to be called—contains twenty-one articles showing the biblical and historical roots of Lutheran teachings, even as it clearly presents Lutheran views of debated topics like original sin, justification, good works, the sacraments, and invocation of the saints. Building especially upon the Torgau Articles, the second part of the *Augsburg Confession* explains the reasons for the practical reforms that Lutherans had made.

On June 25, 1530, Saxon chancellor Christian Beyer read the German text in a booming voice that could be heard by people outside the hall.[31] As a document explaining religious policy, it was presented and signed not by theologians but by political leaders:

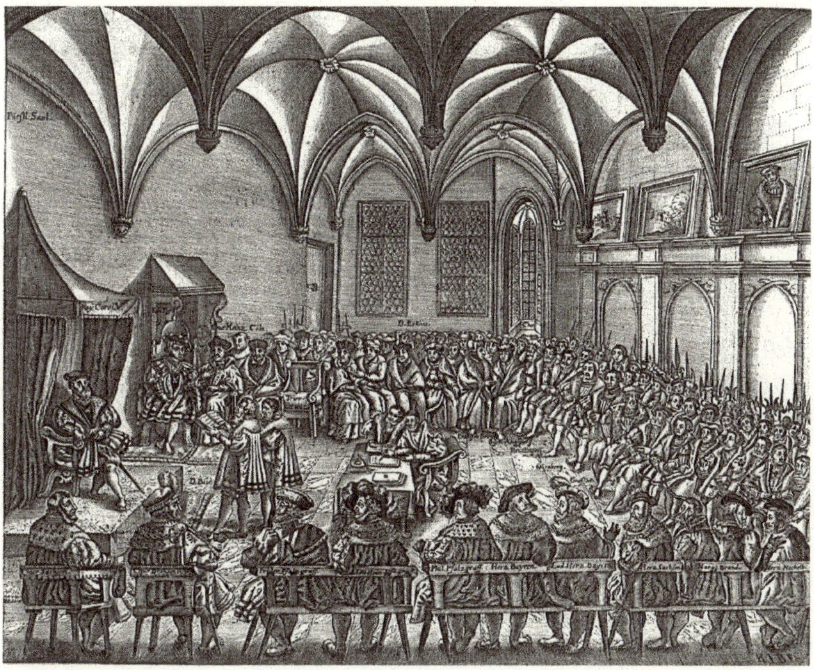

1.5 Saxon chancellor Christian Beyer presents the *Augsburg Confession* before Emperor Charles V at the Diet of Augsburg, 1530. Wikimedia Commons.

six princes and two city councils. Duke Albrecht of Brandenburg-Ansbach reportedly said that he would give his head in defense of these teachings, exemplifying the public witness of both princes and their people in the *Augsburg Confession*.[32]

As seen in its direct appeal to Emperor Charles, the *Augsburg Confession* aimed to show that Lutheran reforms had firm biblical, historical, and pastoral foundations. It asked not for victory over opponents but for tolerance to teach and practice the faith in these ways. Upon the recommendation of his theological advisers, however, Charles rejected the *Augsburg Confession* and demanded that the Protestants return to the Roman Catholic Church. Upset that the *Augsburg Confession* had not received a fairer hearing, Melanchthon wrote a defense of it, called the *Apology of the Augsburg Confession*, which he finished in Wittenberg the following year. Defending and clarifying the doctrines of the *Augsburg Confession* would continue to be a major task of both Lutheran theology and public policy.

In addition to these theological responses, the Protestants also began to prepare a political strategy in case Emperor Charles might decide to force them back to the Church of Rome militarily. Named after the town where these political leaders met, the **Smalcaldic League** was founded in 1531 for the sake of mutual defense. Worried that religion might become a convenient excuse for wars of self-interest within the empire, Luther and Melanchthon asserted that theological agreement with the *Augsburg Confession* should be required for membership.

Within a few years, the *Augsburg Confession* became the standard explanation of Lutheran faith, along with Melanchthon's *Apology* (defense) and Luther's catechisms. For a 1537 gathering of the Smalcaldic League, Melanchthon wrote his *Treatise on the Power and Primacy of the Pope*. It functioned as an appendix to the *Augsburg Confession*, which had remained silent on the issue of the papacy. Around 1540, Melanchthon was asked by Saxon Elector John Frederick to revise the *Augsburg Confession* for new rounds of theological dialogue. Uncontroversial in its time, that text—called the *Variata*—later became suspect among Lutherans because it was being used by Swiss reformers to support a symbolic presence of Christ in the sacrament of Holy Communion. For that reason, Lutheran communities ever since have affirmed the *Unaltered Augsburg Confession* that was first presented in 1530.

The *Augsburg Confession* remains the central statement of faith for Lutherans around the world. Its care for unity within the one church of Christ has made it an effective document for **ecumenical** dialogue, even as its emphasis on justification by faith alone has continued to provide a gospel foundation for Lutheran teaching and preaching across the centuries.

September 1534: Publication of the German Bible

Luther's translation of the Bible began with his project to translate the New Testament from Greek, which he started while he was in exile at Wartburg Castle. After returning to Wittenberg in March 1522, Luther and Melanchthon worked on revisions. The German New Testament appeared in two editions later that year, with illustrations provided by the workshop of the artist Lucas Cranach. In the years that followed, Luther continued to publish translations of the Old Testament in separate volumes. These included the Five Books of Moses, the Psalms, the first books of the Prophets (such as Joshua and Judges), and Isaiah.

Although a handful of other Bible editions had previously been printed in German, Luther's translations were the first to use the new tools of humanist scholarship to translate from Greek and Hebrew sources rather than Latin. In addition to Melanchthon's expertise in Greek, Luther built upon the *Novum Instrumentum* (1516) by Erasmus of Rotterdam as he translated the New Testament. He also benefited from recently published Hebrew grammar books produced by northern European scholars like Johannes Reuchlin and Konrad Pellikan. Luther's translation of the entire Bible included regular meetings with fellow Wittenberg scholars Melanchthon, Caspar Cruciger, Johannes Bugenhagen, Justus Jonas, Matthäus Aurogallus, and Georg Rörer. Although there is one description of Luther sitting at a table translating the Bible with his colleagues and "the rabbis," this referred to the group's use of medieval Jewish commentaries and not the personal presence of rabbis, as the influential historian Philip Schaff later thought in the 1800s.[33] Rather than working together as a translating committee or team, Luther's colleagues seem to have functioned more often as a consulting group, so that the name "Luther Bible" aptly describes the reformer's tremendous personal effort to share the scriptures in German.

Delayed by war, illness, political tensions, and challenging sections of Hebrew (especially in the book of Job), the Luther Bible was published in 1534. As with previous translations, it included images from the Cranach workshop to add visual aids and attractiveness. Although Luther did not believe that the books known as the Apocrypha were essential for saving faith, he included translations of them in his publication of the entire Bible. His famous description of the Epistle of James as a "letter of straw" did not mean a rejection of James. Instead, it recalled 1 Corinthians 3:12, in which St. Paul described various building materials like gold, stone, wood, and hay. By calling James "an epistle of straw," Luther was saying that it is weak material for building a faith based on God's grace alone. Far from rejecting this New Testament letter, he referred to the Epistle of James positively in his catechisms and many other places.

Rather than revealing a highly subjective view of scripture and of translating the gospel, these words about James show a consistent approach that keeps salvation by grace alone through faith alone in Christ alone at the heart of the Bible's message. Lutheran biblical interpretation emphasizes who God is and what God does to love and save a fallen creation. This remains a distinct way to read the Bible, especially when contrasted to both purely linguistic studies of the text and to modern **fundamentalist** quests for biblical inerrancy. Amid so many options for how to read the Bible, Luther focused on a God who loves creation to death and beyond: "There you have it. The gospel is a story about Christ, God's and David's Son, who died and was raised and is established as Lord. This is the gospel in a nutshell."[34] This is the scriptural starting point from which Lutherans interpret the Bible and live out their faith.

While Luther believed in the importance of regular people having access to the word of God, he did not assume that scripture was always clear in its meaning or that people would automatically know how to read it well. For that reason, Luther wrote prefaces to each book of the Bible to describe the main points at hand. From his conflict with Andreas Karlstadt (who wanted to apply the laws of Moses to Christians), Luther learned the importance of acknowledging that not everything in the Bible pertains directly to contemporary Christians.[35] Believing that the historical **creeds** of the church were not additions to scripture but summaries of biblical teaching about God and salvation, he wrote catechisms and preaching aids to keep the heart of the gospel clear: "I believe that Jesus Christ, true God, begotten of the Father in eternity, and also a true human being, born of the virgin Mary, is my LORD."[36] More than a rulebook, Luther saw the Bible as the place where we get to know Jesus. Connecting God's word with the humble surroundings of Jesus's birth, he wrote:

> We heard earlier that the angel gave a sign to the shepherds [Luke 2:12]; but to Mary or Joseph or to any other man, however pious they may have been, he gave no sign except the swaddling clothes in which he was wrapped, and the cradle into which he was laid, that is, the Scripture of the prophets and the law. In these he is enclosed, they possess him, they speak of him alone and witness to him and are his sure signs, as he says himself, in John 5[:39]: "Search the scriptures, because you think that in them you have eternal life; and it is they that bear witness to me."[37]

Luther cared passionately about both grammatical precision and sharing God's liberating message in personally meaningful ways. He translated with an ear for how the Bible's words would sound when read in worship.[38] To that end, his translation observed the rhythms of German speech and used its idioms to tell the good news. This led to the Luther Bible's lasting place as a monumental achievement in the history of the German language. The *Hochdeutsch* (High German) dialect that Luther used refers not to a higher class or social status, but to the language of the relatively hilly region around Saxony, especially in comparison to the *Plattdeutsch* or *Niederdeutsch* (Flat German or Low German) spoken in the low-lying coastal lands further north. Thus, the labels High and Low German describe geography rather than social class. Affirming the importance of regional variation in language and customs, Bugenhagen quickly oversaw a Low German translation of the Luther Bible.

Luther's translation of the Bible was among his most revolutionary, world-changing accomplishments. It challenged the Church of

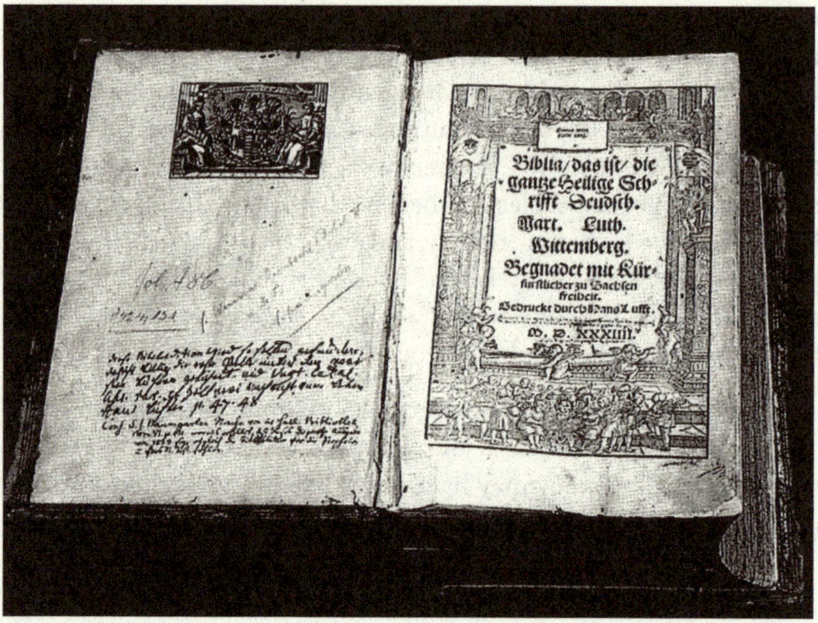

1.6 Luther's German Bible, 1534. Wikimedia Commons / Torsten Schleese.

Rome's control over the Latin Bible, gave individuals and communities access to God's word in their native tongues, and provided a foundation for modern German. Early Bible translations in other languages across Europe—including English, Finnish, French, Slovak, and Swedish—benefited greatly from Luther's example. The English reformer William Tyndale, for instance, likely visited Wittenberg in the 1520s and incorporated many of Luther's insights into his 1526 English New Testament. Most important of all, Luther's translation of the Bible stemmed from his great confidence that the word of God does things: it creates faith in God and love of neighbors through the power of the Holy Spirit working in those who hear and read it; as Isaiah 55:11 says, "so shall my word be that goes out from my mouth; it shall not return to me empty, but it shall accomplish that which I purpose, and succeed in the thing for which I sent it."

February 18, 1546: Death of Martin Luther

The counts of Mansfeld—the noble family ruling Luther's homeland around Eisleben—had been fighting among themselves for several years. In previous months during the mid-1540s, Luther and Melanchthon traveled there to help resolve the dispute, but to no avail. Still recovering from an illness, Melanchthon could not attend the next round of discussions. Although his wife Katharina worried about his health, Luther left Wittenberg on January 23, 1546 with a small group that included his sons and an assistant named Johannes Aurifaber. The group stopped in Halle, where they were joined by longtime friend and colleague Justus Jonas. Luther's letters to Katie from these days include words of comfort, such as "Pray, and let God worry."[39]

Deliberations in Mansfeld seemed to make progress, but Luther sometimes had to leave the discussions because of poor health. Over the years, he had come to suffer from kidney stones, gout, vertigo, earaches, headaches, heart problems, and an elective wound in his leg that was used for blood-letting and was prone to infection.[40] In addition to participating in the talks with the nobility, Luther preached some sermons at St. Andrew's Church in Eisleben, the last of which he ended early because he was not feeling well.

On February 17, Luther again felt ill and spent most of the day in an upstairs bedroom. He came down briefly in the evening before going back to bed. Suspecting the worst, Luther's sons and friends like Jonas stayed with him. Luther prayed and said psalms. Jonas heard his confession, announced the gospel to him, and asked if Luther was prepared to die in the same faith he had preached, to which Luther said yes. The previous day, Luther had written:

> Nobody can understand Vergil [*sic*] in his *Bucolics* and *Georgics* unless he has first been a shepherd or a farmer for five years.
>
> Nobody understands Cicero in his letters unless he has been engaged in public affairs of some consequence for twenty years.
>
> Let nobody suppose that he has tasted the Holy Scriptures sufficiently unless he has ruled over the churches with the prophets for a hundred years. Therefore there is something wonderful, first, about John the Baptist; second, about Christ; third, about the apostles. "Lay not your hand on this divine Aeneid, but bow before it, adore its every trace."
>
> We are beggars. That is true.[41]

In these last reflections, Luther brought the wisdom he learned from classical writers like Cicero and Virgil to the wisdom he had still only begun to taste from the prophets and the apostles. The final line—"We are beggars. That is true"—connected Luther with both the start of his career in the Augustinian monastery and the radical grace of his Reformation message. Luther died before dawn on February 18, 1546.

Although the counts of Mansfeld wanted Luther to be buried in Eisleben—where he had been born and died—Elector John Frederick insisted that Luther be buried in Wittenberg. After funeral sermons by Jonas and court preacher Michael Coelius in Eisleben, Luther's body was taken to Jonas's church in Halle, where crowds gathered to pay their respects. After another day's journey to Bitterfeld and Kemberg, the procession was met in Wittenberg by a crowd including the elector, Melanchthon, Bugenhagen, and Katharina Luther. From the eastern Elster Gate, the assembly processed across town to the Castle Church, where the reformer was buried in front of the pulpit. Bugenhagen delivered a funeral sermon commending the congregation to trust the message of repentance and faith that Luther had preached so powerfully for decades. Melanchthon then gave a classical eulogy, in which he compared Luther's death to the prophet Elijah's being taken into heaven (2 Kings 2). He prayed for mercy and faith in what might prove to be challenging days ahead.

Indeed, troubles soon multiplied. Although Luther had worked with an extensive network of church leaders and reformers—especially the Wittenberg theological faculty—his unique personality and leadership were irreplaceable. In the years ahead, the Wittenberg faculty would continue to play a strong role in church leadership, but other factors soon arose that fragmented Lutherans in Saxony and around Germany.

Unrelated to the timing of Luther's death, Emperor Charles V had finally settled conflicts with France and the Ottoman Empire. For the first time in decades, Charles could militarily suppress German Protestantism. Although more will be said in the next section, the ensuing Smalcaldic War (1546–1547) left Lutherans extremely vulnerable. Questions about the right interpretation of Luther's legacy also spurred conflict among Luther's surviving coworkers and their younger colleagues, inaugurating the frequently asked question: "What does it mean to be Lutheran?"

The war similarly took a toll on Luther's family. Luther had written a will leaving his estate to Katie. The will was honored, but the lengthy siege of Wittenberg during the war despoiled the family's farms and property and forced Katie and her children into exile. After this, she relied on the assistance of noble patrons like the king of Denmark and friends like Melanchthon and Bugenhagen to support her family. An outbreak of the plague caused Katie to flee Wittenberg for Torgau in 1552, where she died from injuries sustained in a wagon accident. Troubles continued for the Luther family, as one of the Luthers' four adult children, Martin Jr., died in his thirties from complications of alcoholism.[42] More positively, Hans and Paul Luther enjoyed careers in law and medicine, respectively, while their sister Margarethe started a family with a Prussian nobleman.[43] As Luther wrote in his *Small Catechism* and as he and his family experienced firsthand, life on earth can truly be a "vale of tears," leading people to cry out to the Lord alone for deliverance and blessing: "We are beggars. That is true."

September 25, 1555: The Peace of Augsburg

Ever since the 1521 Edict of Worms condemned Luther and his teachings, Lutherans in the Holy Roman Empire had been in violation of imperial law. Although Lutheran political leaders formally protested this edict at the 1529 Diet of Speyer, Emperor Charles V upheld his decrees against Luther by siding with the Roman theologians at the Diet of Augsburg the following year. After this, Lutheran lands formed the Smalcaldic League as a way to provide mutual self-defense in case Charles would militarily enforce his imperial religious policy. Because Charles was occupied by conflicts with France and the Ottoman Turks in the 1530s, he established a temporary settlement with the German Lutherans, making it possible for church reforms to continue in those years.[44]

Around the time of Luther's death, Charles had finally established peace on his borders and could turn his attention to the religious divisions within the empire. In preparation for war against the two leading states in the Smalcaldic League (Electoral Saxony and Hesse), Charles reached neutrality agreements with Lutheran leaders like King Christian III of Denmark, Elector Joachim II of Brandenburg, and Moritz of Ducal Saxony.[45] At the 1546 Diet of Regensburg, Charles offered Moritz the electorship (the right to vote for emperor)—along with a verbal promise not to make religious changes—in exchange for Moritz's neutrality in the coming war.[46] Pursuing a "divide and conquer" strategy, Charles based the war not on religion but on personal charges against Elector John Frederick of Saxony and Philip of Hesse: the two had gone to war against a Catholic duke and Philip had broken imperial law by taking a second wife (bigamy was a capital crime).[47] In the Smalcaldic War that followed, the Lutheran Duke Moritz switched from neutrality to alliance with Charles and Charles's brother, King Ferdinand of Austria.

Although Charles started at a disadvantage, he won the decisive Battle of Mühlberg in April 1547. John Frederick and Philip of Hesse became Charles's prisoners. The victorious emperor entered Wittenberg with his troops on May 25. An account of those days by Pastor Bugenhagen reported that although the townspeople were worried about the city being pillaged and Luther's grave being desecrated, Charles and his entourage acted honorably. The emperor was even upset to learn that worship services at the Castle Church had been suspended since his arrival; he requested that services carry on as they had before. In those days, Bugenhagen preached to the imperial soldiers on the Acts of the Apostles and asked that they honestly report the faith they had seen and heard in Wittenberg.[48]

For siding with Charles, Moritz received control of Wittenberg and the Saxon electorship. He reopened the University of Wittenberg, which had closed during the war. Assured that Elector Moritz would allow them to teach and practice according to their Lutheran faith, Melanchthon and Bugenhagen remained with the people, churches, and university in Wittenberg that they had served for decades.[49] By staying in Wittenberg in times of trouble, they believed they were following biblical leadership values and Luther's teachings.

Charles had given Moritz a verbal promise that the religious situation of his lands would not change after the Smalcaldic War. At the 1548 Diet of Augsburg, however, Charles went back on that

1.7 Matthias Flacius Illyricus (Matija Vlačić; 1520–1575), theologian, woodcut by Theodor de Bry (1528–1598). Wikimedia Commons.

word. In a document that came to be called the **Augsburg Interim,** he proposed a temporary (interim) religious policy that would suspend most of the Lutheran reforms in Germany until the **Council of Trent**, which was then underway, settled them more decisively. This Interim was enforced militarily across much of Germany, causing many Protestant church leaders there to go into hiding or exile. Through a censorship clause, the Interim also made it a crime to publish critiques against it.[50] Having received an early draft of the document from Moritz, Melanchthon and his colleagues were the first to write against the Interim that spring.[51]

In the months that followed, the city of Magdeburg became a center for refugees and for protests against the Interim. Lutherans in Magdeburg like Nicholas von Amsdorf, Nicholas Gallus, and Matthias Flacius Illyricus combined their theological objections to the Augsburg Interim with a strong dislike for Elector Moritz, whom they viewed as a traitor for siding with Charles in the war.[52] This anger was also directed at Wittenberg theologians like Melanchthon who continued to work with the traitorous Moritz, giving rise to new quarrels between Lutherans.

For protesting the Augsburg Interim so vociferously, Magdeburg earned the wrath of Emperor Charles. Beginning in 1550, Charles paid his ally Moritz to conduct a siege for him. Because Moritz was besieging their city on behalf of the Catholic emperor, the people of Magdeburg felt further justified in their continued resistance to Moritz and the Wittenberg theologians.

At the same time, it had become clear to many in Europe that winning the Smalcaldic War had given Charles too much power. Quietly, Moritz began to organize a new coalition against Charles. This resistance plan grew stronger when it was joined by King Henry II of France, who was always glad to weaken his greatest rival. In this way, the Siege of Magdeburg allowed Moritz to keep an army to use against Charles, which was being paid for by the emperor himself. In early 1552 Moritz and his allies attacked Charles at an imperial residence in Innsbruck and forced him to retreat over the Alps. The ensuing treaty of Passau gave temporary legal rights to churches of the *Augsburg Confession*, a status later enshrined in the **Peace of Augsburg** signed by Charles's brother King Ferdinand in 1555.[53]

While the Magdeburgers could take pride in their strong resistance to the imperial religious policy, these events also vindicated the position of the theologians in Wittenberg. They had faced a real threat of further war, either by provoking the emperor into battle or by encouraging the local people to rebel. Instead, the Wittenberg theologians had helped Moritz buy time to pursue a different course of action. Moritz's plan resulted in a new day for Lutheran communities and a milestone in the history of religious tolerance. Unfortunately, Moritz himself did not live to see this: an eager warrior, Elector Moritz had died in battle in 1553. He was succeeded by his brother August, who became a major Lutheran political leader for decades.

The Peace of Augsburg gave territories within the Holy Roman Empire the right to practice Christianity either by keeping communion with the Church of Rome or by sharing the faith of the *Augsburg Confession.* For the first time, Lutheranism was legal. On the principle of ***cuius regio, eius religio*** (whose region, their religion), local governments could choose to embrace Reformation teachings and practices. Although this "religious policy from above" gave the nobility strong control of local church life, the possibility of rebellion added some incentive for political leaders to listen to their people, as we will see in the events surrounding the Thirty Years' War (discussed in chapter 2).

After the Peace of Augsburg became the law of the land, an immediate threat of war based on the Reformation had disappeared for a time. Nevertheless, complicated issues of faithfulness and resistance, church and state, doctrine and practice, as well as the interpersonal and theological conflicts that developed in the wake of the Smalcaldic War, would continue to challenge Lutherans for decades—and even centuries—to come.

Later 1500s: Lutheranism across Europe

By the later 1500s, Wittenberg-style church reforms had spread far beyond German lands. In some cases, Luther's thinking influenced movements that then charted their own course, as was true of the English Reformation. In Denmark and Sweden, however, entire kingdoms were reorganized around Luther's catechisms, the *Augsburg Confession*, and Lutheran church orders. In still other places like the Netherlands, Slovenia, and Austria, smaller Lutheran communities developed without the approval or protection of political authorities. As diverse as these situations were, they each took root because people cared enough to live out their faith and share it with those around them.

In England, several reform-minded priests had connections with Luther. Robert Barnes, for instance, was an Augustinian brother like Luther, who spent some time in Wittenberg and promoted reform of the English church. He was executed by King Henry VIII in 1540 for publicly disagreeing with the king's religious policies and for preaching justification by faith alone.[54] William Tyndale, the great translator of the Bible into English, also visited Wittenberg and benefited from Luther's German translations before he was arrested and killed in Antwerp in 1536.

Working for a time in Nuremberg, soon-to-be English archbishop Thomas Cranmer married Margaret Osiander, the niece of Lutheran reformer Andreas Osiander. Although the English Reformation eventually followed Calvin more than Luther after the 1530s (especially after an influx of Reformed theologians took refuge in England to escape the Augsburg Interim), its early phases and several of its leaders had worked closely with Lutheran reformers, a relationship that peaked with the 1536 Wittenberg Articles, a statement of shared faith signed by Lutheran and English theologians including Luther, Melanchthon, and Barnes.

The Danish Reformation started through the efforts of local priests like Hans Tausen, who developed their own reform movements even as they supported Luther's teachings. With the end of the Danish Civil War in 1536, King Christian III called together reforming priests like Tausen and started to reorganize the church according to Lutheran principles. Danish theologians drafted a **church order**, which they sent to Wittenberg for editing.

Pastor Bugenhagen then went to Copenhagen, where he crowned the new king and queen, installed Lutheran **superintendents (bishops)**, and helped the University of Copenhagen reopen based on the educational program developed by Melanchthon and the Wittenbergers. Peder Palladius, who had just completed a doctoral degree at the University of Wittenberg, was made the "first among equals" as superintendent of Zealand, the island that makes up most of Copenhagen. He visited local congregations, oversaw their transition to Lutheran forms of worship, and helped produce a Danish translation of the Bible in 1550.[55] The Reformation in Denmark brought together a complex mix of popular reform—led by Tausen and others—and the top-down action of the monarchy and church officials like Palladius.

At the time, Norway and Iceland were **colonies** of Denmark. The Reformation was therefore initially experienced as a colonial imposition in those lands. Catholic bishops were expelled; one Icelandic bishop who led an uprising was beheaded.[56] It took the patient and dedicated work of leaders like Gudbrandur Thorláksson in Iceland and Jörgen Eriksson in Norway in the later 1500s for most people to start to identify with the new teachings. Thorláksson completed an Icelandic translation of the Bible in 1584. In Norway, the Danish liturgy was used for a century, and the Danish Bible was used until 1814.

Itself newly independent from Denmark in 1523, Sweden's first encounter with the Lutheran Reformation came through students returning from Wittenberg. Influenced by Luther's teaching, the brothers Olavus (or Olaus) and Laurentius Petri found favor with King Gustav Vasa. They began a gradual reform of the Church of Sweden by promoting clerical marriage, sermons and worship in Swedish, and the translation of the Bible. The Swedish bishops of the time became Lutheran, with the result that Swedish Lutheranism maintained the apostolic succession of bishops going back to the early church known as the **historic episcopate**. Despite generally having the support of their king, Olavus and Laurentius had to fight to keep Gustav Vasa from using the Reformation as a cover for simply taking church properties and funds for the crown.

The Swedish kingdom included the Finnish people to the east, whose language and culture differ significantly from other Nordic peoples. Beyond a general Swedish influence on church life in Finland, a major reform occurred when a Wittenberg graduate named Mikael Agricola translated much of the Bible into Finnish, becoming "the father of Finnish literature and written Finnish."[57]

The Lutheran Reformation also spread to the eastern end of the Baltic Sea, especially through the influence of Duke Albrecht of Prussia. Albrecht supported a Lutheran church order already in 1525, written by local reforming bishops and Luther's early colleague Paul Speratus. In 1544, a university modeled on Wittenberg was founded in the capital city of Königsberg (now Kaliningrad, Russia). Prussian—and later Swedish—influence over the modern-day countries of Estonia and Latvia also led to the establishment of lasting Lutheran churches in those countries. Because Duke Albrecht belonged to the same Hohenzollern dynasty that ruled Brandenburg, "Prussia" later came to signify not just the smaller territory on the Baltic but the larger land of Brandenburg with its capital in Berlin.

Lutheranism also spread into Poland, Silesia, Slovakia, Austria, Hungary, and Slovenia. Ethnic Germans in Transylvania (now part of Romania) embraced the Reformation in their communities already by the 1540s. In these places, Lutherans were usually minority communities living in tenuous political situations, which came to include strong coordinated efforts against Protestantism from ruling dynasties like the Hapsburgs and the kings of Poland. Nevertheless, many committed leaders pushed for Lutheran worship reforms and the translations of the Bible, as seen in the witness of Primus Truber.

Exiled from his homeland in modern-day Slovenia for his Reformation views, Truber found refuge in Nuremberg and then served as a pastor in Rothenburg ob der Tauber. While there, he began writing a Slovenian grammar and translating the New Testament.[58] Following a brief return to Ljubljana, he was again exiled and went to Württemberg in southwestern Germany, where he continued his translation projects and served as a pastor until his death in 1586.[59] Sometimes in trouble with Lutheran authorities for his good relationships with Reformed theologians, Truber's life shows a personal commitment to church reform that included experiences of exile, an openness to international Protestant dialogue, and a dedication to translating the faith.

In the absence of a single overarching figure like a pope, what made a person or community "Lutheran"? In places like Denmark, Sweden, and Prussia, Lutheran reforms of teaching and practice—especially as established in texts like the *Augsburg Confession*, Luther's catechisms, and local church orders—provided the legal foundation for religious life, whether the majority of people wanted these reforms or not. This included lands like Iceland, Norway, and Finland, where local communities developed distinct church cultures under colonial rule.

In other places like Poland, Transylvania, and Slovakia, communities found ways to live out their Reformation faith as minority groups for centuries. Later German Lutherans who settled in the Volga region of southern Russia in the mid-1700s similarly endured the challenges of war, exile, imprisonment, and mass emigration over the centuries. Descendants of those early Volga Germans are now part of the Evangelical Lutheran Church of Russia and Other States, which includes churches in Georgia, Kazakhstan, Kyrgyzstan, Ukraine, and Uzbekistan.

From Finland and the Baltic to Slovenia, Transylvania, and the Volga, Lutherans in the eastern part of Europe have long been engaged in ecumenical dialogue with Orthodox, Catholic, and Muslim neighbors. Whether state churches or minority communities, a theology of justification by faith alone, liturgical reform, clerical marriage, and a commitment to share the gospel in local languages and cultures provided common Lutheran experiences.

June 25, 1580: Publication of the *Book of Concord*

Lutherans have never had a single person or group to serve as an ultimate church authority. Instead, from the beginning of the Reformation, Lutherans promoted regional variation in church policies and practices. While Luther himself had a unique role in shaping the church during his lifetime, he also worked as part of a university faculty and team of reformers. On a practical level, he and his colleagues supported the rights of local governments like Wittenberg's city council or rulers like the elector of Saxony or the king of Denmark-Norway to provide legal foundations for Lutheran church life. They viewed this as part of the government's basic duty to support beneficial social structures. Unlike the English Reformation, in which the monarch became the personal head of the church, the Lutheran ideal for governments that embraced the Reformation was was more like a partnership: the state would provide the structures and guidelines for healthy religious life, while the church would see to it that love of God and service to the community remained at the heart of local teaching and practice. Although this ideal was certainly open to abuse or neglect, this pattern helps explain why Lutherans have allowed for many different ways to organize their churches and relate to local governments. Unlike other denominations that have focused on church structures—whether papal, episcopal, presbyterian, or congregational—as key signs of faith and unity, Lutherans have tended to focus on points of doctrine rather than church structures when they talk about what it means to be Christian together.

The reformers' idea that Christianity always includes diversity across time and place had provided an early basis for Lutheran appeals to Rome for the right to make sensible reforms for the sake of local communities. But who gets to decide how much flexibility is appropriate and which reforms are either acceptable or too far afield? In Luther's lifetime, people could write to him and his Wittenberg colleagues and receive responses for how to address such questions. Already in the late 1540s, however, the Smalcaldic War led to major fights between Lutherans themselves.

The first controversy after Luther's death was precisely over which parts of the faith are negotiable and which are not. It was called the adiaphoristic controversy, from the Greek word ***adiaphora***, which refers to matters that scripture leaves open. In previous decades, for instance, Lutherans had decided that things like church governance, the use of images and music in worship, clerical vestments, feasting and fasting were secondary matters in comparison to the core commitment to preach the good news and share the grace of the sacraments in ways that matched the New Testament witness. In such secondary issues, Christians should practice freedom and tolerance. Because Melanchthon and his colleagues drew upon this view of secondary matters in their discussions with Catholic leaders after the Smalcaldic War, their opponents pushed them on the important question of when negotiation needed to end and a clear stand for the gospel be taken.

Another controversy of the time grew out of a saying by Wittenberg theologian Georg Major that "good works are necessary for salvation." The problem here was that "necessary" can mean two very different things: it can mean a precondition for salvation—making works a requirement before salvation and thereby negating justification by faith alone—or it can mean a natural consequence, such that good works "necessarily" or naturally follow God's free gift of justification. It took decades for theologians to clarify this debate and find mutually acceptable terminology about the relationship between faith and good works. Similar debates revolved around how God's righteousness dwells in people, how deeply original sin had corrupted humanity, and what Lutherans mean by "free will."

Other controversies developed in opposition to John Calvin's teachings about Christ's presence in the Eucharist and about predestination. Lutherans insisted on the **real presence** of Christ in Holy Communion, because God promised to be with people in the flesh; their Reformed counterparts (those who agreed more with Zwingli or Calvin) emphasized the spiritual meanings of the Lord's

Supper and thought that Lutherans had retained too much medieval superstition regarding the sacrament's physical elements. Regarding predestination, Calvin thought it was both biblical and logical to teach that God had destined some people for damnation. Understanding his reasoning, Lutheran theologians nevertheless believed that this teaching was unhelpful when it came to sharing the gospel.

In the absence of a single authority, these internal and external debates took on lives of their own, with no end in sight. A particularly embarrassing episode occurred in 1557, when Lutherans and Catholics were called together for dialogue in the city of Worms. Aware of the intra-Lutheran controversies, Catholic theologians exploited these differences, watched the Lutherans fight amongst themselves, and concluded that it was impossible to discuss theology with a church whose own members could not agree on their beliefs.

In these years, the main factions among Lutherans generally followed the lines drawn by the adiaphoristic controversy. Theologians associated with Philip Melanchthon came to be known as "Philippists," who had supposedly strayed from Luther in their preference for Melanchthon's teachings. Another party came to be called "Gnesio Lutherans," a label which means Genuine or True Lutherans. These were most devoted to following what seemed like Luther's plainest meaning, apart from the theological influence of Melanchthon. Additionally, a "Flacian" party developed around the teachings of Matthias Flacius Illyricus, who pushed more radical views of sin, grace, and the importance of true doctrine than other Gnesio Lutherans. These controversies did not abate with Melanchthon's death in 1560 but continued to divide Lutherans across Germany.

Tired of the social and political damage caused by these theological divisions, territorial rulers commissioned Jakob Andreae, who was a theologian at the University of Tübingen and a church leader in the southwest German region of Württemberg, to craft a unifying document. Andreae started with a collection of sermonic commentaries on Luther's catechisms. This first effort was too vague to satisfy many colleagues. In his next attempt, Andreae stated both what Lutherans believed and what they viewed to be out of bounds. This created a middle space for dialogue and difference. He then sent his text to colleagues in different parts of Germany for feedback.

Martin Chemnitz and David Chytraeus served as two key collaborators with Andreae in the document that became the *Formula of Concord*. Chemnitz was a highly regarded leader among the Gnesio Lutherans, and Chytraeus was a respected representative of Melanchthon's views. Together they effectively addressed the theological challenges of the day. Chemnitz took the lead on issues close to the Gnesio Lutherans like original sin and righteousness, while Chytraeus offered moderating approaches to controversies related to the Philippists like free will, good works, and the real presence of Christ in the Lord's Supper. Joined by Saxon theologian Nicholas Selnecker and Brandenburg theologians Andreas Musculus and Christopher Koerner, these authors submitted the *Formula of Concord* for the approval of pastors and politicians in 1577.

Previously satisfied with the Melanchthonian theology of his territory, Elector August of Saxony had not initially supported Andreae's project. His support grew, however, when he learned that some of his Wittenberg theologians were secretly teaching his wife a Calvinist view of the Lord's Supper and saying that this had been Luther and Melanchthon's real teaching. Elector August imprisoned those theologians and lent his formidable influence to a clear, common statement of Lutheran teaching and unity.

Thus, the *Formula of Concord*—which could be rephrased from the Latin *Formula Concordiae* as a "blueprint for harmony"—attempted to provide not only theological unity but social and political stability, as well. In the years after its composition, pastors and politicians were required to sign their agreement (or risk losing their jobs), making the Formula the official religious policy of most German Lutheran states.

To further solidify such **confessional** standards, Andreae and Elector August led a drive to publish the ***Book of Concord.*** This collection of Reformation writings would stand as a single summary of Lutheran doctrine. Published on the fiftieth anniversary of the presentation of the *Augsburg Confession*—June 25, 1580—the *Book of Concord* contained works by Luther and Melanchthon, as well as the *Formula of Concord* in two versions: the theological text called the Solid Declaration and a shorter summary, the Epitome, which Andreae had written for politicians who did not want to read so much theology.

The *Book of Concord* begins with a preface written by these second-generation reformers but signed by politicians, showing its dual religious-political goals. It then affirms three ecumenical creeds common to the Western Christian tradition: the Apostles' Creed, the Nicene Creed, and the Athanasian Creed. The next writing is the *Unaltered Augsburg Confession* (1530), which was more widely accepted than the 1540 revision that Elector John Frederick had asked Melanchthon to make. Melanchthon's *Apology of the Augsburg Confession*, which had long stood as the primary interpretation of the *Augsburg Confession*, comes next in the *Book of Concord*, followed by Luther's *Smalcald Articles* (1537) and Melanchthon's *Treatise on the Power and Primacy of the Pope*. The *Treatise* is followed by Luther's *Small* and *Large Catechism* and the two versions of the Formula mentioned above.

Thus, rather than a single pope, archbishop, church structure, or prayer book, Lutherans organized themselves around texts that point to a shared interpretation of the gospel. In its time, the *Book of Concord* provided religious and political unity for the majority of German Lutherans. While doctrinal controversies continued, they did not generate the same kind of internal division as before. Instead, Lutherans could present a more common witness in their conflicts with Reformed Protestants and Roman Catholics. While those debates often had academic and political aspects, the Lutheran emphasis on "true doctrine" (*die reine Lehre*) was rooted in the pastoral concern that people know and live into gospel freedom. For Lutherans, good doctrine means taking care that the good news of Jesus Christ truly stands at the heart of Christian life and witness.[60]

Because these debates largely occurred within German lands, the *Book of Concord*, as a whole, has played a more prominent role in traditions with roots in German Lutheranism. In Nordic lands, by contrast, the *Augsburg Confession* and Luther's catechisms provided sufficient religious unity. Lutherans around the world continue to view this confessional tradition in different ways. Even so, Lutherans are relatively unique among Christians in thinking of the faith in terms of shared confessional statements rather than church structures, patterns of worship, or other Christian values.

30185

CONCORDIA.

יהוה

Christliche,

Widerholete/einmütige Bekentnüs

nachbenanter Churfürsten/ Fürsten vnd Stende
Augspurgischer Confession/ vnd derselben zu ende
des Buchs vnderschriebener Theologen
Lere vnd glaubens.

Mit angeheffter/in Gottes wort/ als der einigen Richtschnur/ wolgegründter erklerung etlicher Artickel/ bey welchen nach D. Martin Luthers seligen absterben/ disputation vnd streit vorgefallen.

Aus einhelliger vergleichung vnd

beuehl obgedachter Churfürsten/ Fürsten vnd Stende/ derselben Landen/ Kirchen/ Schulen vnd Nachkommen/ zum vnderricht vnd warnung in Druck vorfertiget.

it Churf. G. zu Sachsen befreihung.
reßden. M. D. LXXX.

1.8 Title page to a 1580 edition of the *Book of Concord*, belonging to Wartburg Theological Seminary. Photo by Martin Lohrmann, used with permission.

1599: Philip Nicolai Publishes the "King and Queen of Chorales"

Congregational singing quickly became a hallmark of Lutheran worship, with early Reformation hymns composed already in the 1520s by reformers like Elisabeth Cruciger, Justus Jonas, Paul Speratus, and Luther himself. The Wittenberg **cantor** Johann Walther also became an important Wittenberg colleague, writing choral versions of new Reformation hymns. As hymnwriters and musicians,

Lutherans developed their choirs and musical gifts not to replace congregational singing but to support it.

Early Lutheran hymnwriting built upon several sources. In some cases, the reformers would adapt existing Latin hymns or chants, translating them and revising the text to highlight gospel-centered theology, as happened with *Veni Redemptor Gentium* ("Savior of the Nations, Come"), a hymn attributed to fourth-century bishop Ambrose of Milan and reworked by Luther. Other early Lutheran hymns were paraphrases of the Psalms or other biblical texts, as in Luther's version of Psalm 130—"Out of the Depths I Cry to You" and Jonas's hymn setting of Psalm 124—"If God Were Not upon Our Side."

Drawing on the German Meistersinger tradition that combined poetry and folk songs, Lutheran musicians felt free to compose their own melodies and lyrics for use in worship, as seen in hymns like Cruciger's "The Only Son from Heaven" and Luther's "From Heaven Above to Earth I Come." This stood in contrast to other Protestants, for whom the only songs allowed in worship were those with explicitly biblical texts and instrumentation. With the teaching about adiaphora allowing them to view worship music and instruments as matters of freedom, Lutherans embraced the pipe organ as a valuable aid for congregational worship, while other Protestants excluded the organ because it does not appear in the Bible.

It is worth correcting the common misconception that Luther wrote hymns based on songs he heard at the pub. While Luther sometimes adapted popular melodies or wrote his own tunes, a likely reason for this false impression may come from a confusion about the phrase "bar songs." In music history, the "bar form" refers to a pattern of how words and music fit together to create a melodic line.[61] Since the bar form was common in Luther's time, it is correct to say that Luther wrote "bar songs," but not in the way people might commonly think today: the songs do borrow from local folk music traditions, but not actual pub tunes.

With a high regard for its use in and out of worship settings, Martin Luther valued music as a blessed part of life. In his view, music was both a tool for sharing the gospel and a gift of God in itself. As Robin Leaver has put it, "because music comes from God as a gift . . . it has dimensions of meaning, power and effectiveness that far exceed any human art or science. Music is not an *inventio*, a work of humankind, but a *creatura*, a work of God."[62] This means that music does not need to be "Christian music" to be godly. While it can be as misused as other things like religion, language, and scientific knowledge, music serves God through enjoyment, artistry, and as participation in God's good creation.

The love of music has nurtured a rich musical culture in the Lutheran tradition across the centuries. Among the gems of this musical heritage are two hymns by the pastor Philip Nicolai (1556–1608). A survivor of war, controversy, and epidemics, Nicolai published a pastoral work for plague survivors in 1599, concluding it with two hymns: *Wachet auf, ruft uns die Stimme* ("Wake, Awake, for Night Is Flying") and *Wie schoen leuchtet der Morgenstern* ("O Morning Star, How Fair and Bright"), honored respectively as "the king and queen of chorales." Written amid times of deep pain and loss, these hymns have long given voice to faith in God, love of neighbor, and the spiritual power that accompanies the cross of Christ.

Frequently sung in the season of Advent, *Wachet auf* draws on the parable of the ten bridesmaids (Matt 25:1–13) to send believers to seek Christ the bridegroom. Even more personally, *Wie schoen leuchtet der Morgenstern* expands on the language of the bridegroom of the soul—used by Luther in his 1520 tract *The Freedom of a Christian*—to ponder the intimacy of living, dying, and rising again with Christ. Nicolai's stirring words and lively music intimately blend New Testament teachings, Lutheran convictions, and personal faith. Nicolai wrote his own grief and hope into the text, as each of the seven stanzas of *Wie schoen leuchtet* begins in German with a letter naming a student of Nicolai's who had died of the plague: *Wilhelm Ernst, Graf und Herr zu Waldeck* (William Ernest, Count and Lord of Waldeck).

Over the centuries, Nicolai's hymns provided the basis for works by musicians like Dietrich Buxtehude, Johann Sebastian Bach, Felix Mendelssohn-Bartholdy, Max Reger, and Paul Manz. They also contributed to a Lutheran spiritual tradition in which both instrumental and vocal music give voice to feelings and faith, grief and grace.

Music and hymnody are major ways in which Lutherans around the world have taken part in and enriched the Christian

1.9 First edition of Philipp Nicolai's *Wachet auf, ruft uns die Stimme*, 1599. Wikimedia Commons.

tradition, the arts, and spiritual experience as they continue to make music that expresses the faith for their times and places. Luther commended singing as part of a great start to any day, as he wrote in the Morning Blessing section of his *Small Catechism*: "After singing a hymn perhaps (for instance, one on the Ten Commandments) or whatever else may serve your devotion, you are to go to your work joyfully."[63]

Questions

1. Martin Luther took a stand. What was he standing on? How did he test his foundations? What are your foundations? What do you stand on and what do you stand up for?
2. The Lutheran Reformation can be both celebrated for its emphasis on freedom and criticized for a moderate or slow

approach to social change. What values steered the reformers' concerns for liberation and social stability?

3. What do you think of Luther's response to the Peasants' War or Melanchthon's response to the Smalcaldic War? What would you do in such a situation?
4. People from the sixteenth century to today have criticized Luther for not going "far enough" in his reforms, especially in matters of worship or social change. What do you think of those critiques? What changes seem most important to you today?
5. Lutherans in the Reformation era had significant conflicts over theological teachings. Which doctrinal debates seem most serious to you, and why? What doctrinal principles inspire you to faith and action, even if those principles might bring conflict with others?
6. With so many regional variations, what did it mean to "be Lutheran" in the 1500s? What do you think this means today?
7. Do you think it would be a good idea for Lutherans today to write new statements of faith like the *Augsburg Confession* or *Small Catechism*? Why or why not?
8. What role did music and the arts play for early Lutherans? How do the arts impact your religious faith and spirituality?

CHAPTER TWO

1617–1717

Introduction to Lutheranism in Its Second Century

In the autumn of 1617, Lutherans commemorated the hundredth anniversary of the Reformation with popular literature, plays, sermons, and illustrated pamphlets.[1] While some of these works were grounded in local pride and heritage, international politics also supported this burst of religious energy. Struggles for power and influence at the highest levels of society continued to shape life across Europe. For that reason, it was a **Reformed** prince, Elector Frederick V of the Palatinate (an influential territory along the Rhine River), who most publicly called for Protestant celebrations of a Reformation centennial. A leader of the military alliance known as the Protestant Union, Frederick would shortly thereafter get embroiled in the devastating conflict that became known as the Thirty Years' War.

Lutheranism was not merely a pawn in international power politics. As this chapter will show, Lutherans continued to nurture rich theological and spiritual cultures, as well as contribute to the arts and sciences. Lutheran music continued to develop, especially as seen (and heard!) in the works of Johann Sebastian Bach, whose job as a church cantor included teaching theology and composing pieces for Sunday worship. While not alone in their support of what became the Scientific Revolution, Lutheran universities in this period promoted the study of Nicholas Copernicus's theory that the earth revolves around the sun. Supported by both Lutheran and Catholic patrons, the Danish astronomer Tycho Brahe and his younger German colleague Johannes Kepler continued to explore these important ideas in the natural sciences. And although later Lutheran artists did not surpass the fame of Lucas Cranach the Elder (1472–1553) or his son Lucas Cranach the Younger (1515–1586), a vigorous culture of religious art and architecture endured into the 1600s, as the visual arts continued to add depth to Lutheran communities and congregational worship. As art historian Margit Thøfner has written, "Lutheran worship became a complex ritual choreography set in a richly furnished church interior."[2]

The rise of **Lutheran Pietism** later in the 1600s included active attention to social welfare, even as it came into conflict with the

2.1 *Loci communes theologici* by Johann Gerhard (1582–1637). Photo by Martin Lohrmann and used by permission.

concerns and methods of **Lutheran Orthodoxy**. Building on devotional and spiritual traditions that stemmed back to Luther himself, early Lutheran Pietists emphasized personal faith, fruits of the Holy Spirit, and living out one's faith in daily life for the good of the community. This raised objections from other Lutherans that salvation might once again be defined by works rather than faith alone. While these movements have often been set against each other and regarded as opposites—belief versus works; objective theology versus personal piety—they can also be seen as two sides of the same Lutheran coin: people who have been reconciled with God freely through faith do good works of love with no strings attached, just as good trees bear good fruit. Both Lutheran Pietists and Lutheran Orthodox theologians had strong biblical and Reformation bases for their convictions, which led to new expressions of the faith in their times and places.

For this history of a global movement, it is also important to notice that Lutheranism was spreading beyond Europe already in the 1600s and early 1700s. A Danish quest to find a Northwest Passage through North America to East Asia brought the first Lutheran worship services to that continent, as the ship's pastor Rasmus Jensen held services and celebrated communion in late 1619 before he died in the following months. In the mid-1600s, European **colonialism** brought enduring settlements of Lutherans to Dutch New Amsterdam, to the colony of New Sweden in the Delaware Valley, and to Danish and Dutch colonies in the Caribbean. A Lutheran duke of Courland (a region of western Latvia) made three unsuccessful attempts to start a colony and mission field on the Caribbean island of Tobago.[3] Danish colonies in India also resulted in the establishment of lasting Lutheran communities in southeastern India in the early 1700s.

In these efforts, Lutherans were not absent from international missionary efforts, as many histories of Christian mission claim. Instead, they were often at the forefront of European mission work, in both the positive sense of actively sharing the gospel with people around the world and in the negative aspects of connecting evangelism with Eurocentric, racist, and colonial systems. European sharing of the gospel of Jesus Christ often went hand-and-glove with the harsh treatment of local peoples and of inhumane participation in the Atlantic slave trade. These challenging realities will be addressed in this and following chapters.

Amid powerful local and international pressures, many people still wanted to do what was right and live out their faith in God by showing concern for the well-being of those around them. Such commitment to God and neighbor appeared amid the violence of the Thirty Years' War, the upheavals caused by colonization, and the social and religious uncertainty that came with new philosophical and scientific ways of thinking. Using the Lutheran "law and gospel" lens for reading history—both telling the truth about sin and claiming the truth about God's love to save the lost—it is possible to study such complicated times with some clarity. We can be honest about the inhumane, ungodly, and unjust actions of the past, give thanks for grace, faith, and liberation where it appeared in people's lives, and let these stories inspire our efforts to recognize and address the sinful circumstances we live with today, many of which have precedents in histories like these.

Early 1600s: The Rise of Lutheran Orthodoxy

With the publication of the *Book of Concord* in 1580, Lutherans across Germany had largely settled the internal controversies that arose after Luther's death and found a common basis for preaching and teaching. Signed by heads of state—including powerful princes like Elector Ludwig of Palatine on the Rhine (the Palatinate), Elector August of Saxony, Elector Joachim Frederick of Brandenburg, and the dukes of Ernestine Saxony—the *Book of Concord* provided a legal foundation for religious life in the territories that accepted it. Rather than viewing this combination of doctrine and law as a problematic mixing of church and state, Lutheran politicians and pastors believed that secular authorities had a duty to promote good religious teaching, which in turn would benefit individuals and communities both spiritually and socially.

This blending of religious teaching with state law gave rise to a period that can be described as the time of Lutheran Orthodoxy, which lasted approximately from the late 1500s to the early 1700s. Depending on their perspectives, later Lutherans have viewed this as either a golden age of Lutheran teaching or as a rigid period devoid of spirituality, social concern, and open-mindedness. By getting better acquainted with Lutheranism in the age of orthodoxy, we might begin to appreciate the more nuanced ways people of the time lived out their faith and addressed the challenges they faced.

The word *orthodoxy* comes from Greek and means "right teaching" or "correct doctrine." Although such a concept may suggest an almost obsessive attention to theological detail, the emphasis on right teaching came from a very pastoral concern: if the gospel of Jesus Christ truly sets people free and promises life with God, then a clear understanding of what the gospel is and what it does matters immensely. More than a purely intellectual exercise, knowing Christ's gospel impacts people's relationships with God, self, neighbors, worldviews, and daily actions. For these next generations of Lutherans, concern for right doctrine very much included care for the whole person and for the wider community.

Lutherans knew that there were several ways to be Christian in western Europe, a reality that historians now describe as an age of **confessionalization**. Some neighboring lands had embraced the Reformed Protestantism influenced by leaders like Huldrych Zwingli and John Calvin. Just as the *Augsburg Confession* and the *Book of Concord* defined religious policy for Lutheran lands, confessional writings like the *Heidelberg Catechism* (1563) and the *Second Helvetic Confession* by Heinrich Bullinger of Zurich (1566) helped give instruction and set religious policy for Reformed areas. Other nearby territories like Bavaria and cities like Salzburg and Bamberg remained Roman Catholic. Catholic territories, of course, valued their connection with the pope in Rome and affirmed the Council of Trent, which had met in three phases between 1545 and 1563. More than simply representing partisan options for how to live out one's Christian faith, these religious "confessions" influenced international politics, local laws, worship, spiritual practices, and everyday culture.

It is possible to criticize this age of orthodoxy and confessionalization for its potentially troubling mix of religious conformity and socio-political coercion. With the benefit of hindsight, however, we might more generously wonder what it was like to live amid such powerful forces and to wrestle with these big-picture issues as members of local Christian communities. For Lutherans, teaching the gospel meant sharing the message of God's gift of pure grace to a fallen world, which is received through faith and lived out in service to the neighbor. As a spiritual tradition, this Lutheran approach created a different religious culture than the Reformed emphasis on God's sovereignty and Christian discipline. It varied from more radical reformers who rejected civil society and traditional religious practices. And it was distinct from Catholic views of the sacraments, the priesthood, and the use of Latin as the primary language of the Bible and worship. For all of its conflicts and shortcomings, this era saw the blossoming of rich and frequently inspiring ways to live out Christian faith.

Early experiences had heightened Lutherans' concern about the importance of their views of right doctrine for faith and life. They had seen how radical preaching played a role in the Peasants' War of 1524/25. They had strong pastoral and biblical reasons for disagreeing with the Reformed teaching that Christ is present spiritually but not physically in Holy Communion. They had lived for decades under both the threat and reality of war from Catholic leaders who wanted to bring Protestants back to the Church of Rome by force.

Lutheran theologians like Johann Gerhard (1582–1637) worked to explain the faith in such a way as to clarify and defend a Lutheran approach to gospel preaching and living. Best known for his massive theological textbooks, Gerhard also wrote devotional works for Christians to use as part of their daily spiritual practice. While his contributions to Lutheran Orthodoxy have earned him a place alongside Luther, Melanchthon, and Chemnitz in the Lutheran theological tradition, Gerhard had been influenced early in life by Pastor Johann Arndt (1555–1621), with whom he maintained a good relationship over the decades. Arndt wrote the book *True Christianity*, which remained a classic of Lutheran devotional writing and influenced the Lutheran Pietism movement that started later in the century. Although Arndt was accused of spiritualism—of promoting subjective and unbiblical spiritual ideas—the faculty of the University of Wittenberg judged his teaching to be sufficiently orthodox.[4] The centuries-long popularity of *True Christianity* testifies to the important balance of head and heart that this work offered in an age of orthodoxy. Like his mentor Arndt, Gerhard valued works of spiritual devotion that spoke to the lives of regular people.

In addition to Gerhard, other notable scholars of Lutheran Orthodoxy included Aegidius Hunnius (1550–1603), Polykarp Leyser (1552–1610), Abraham Calov (1612–1686), and Johann Quenstedt, all of whom taught at the University of Wittenberg. Caspar Brochmann (1585–1682) was an important orthodox leader of the Danish Lutheran church in the seventeenth century. As with other writers like Philipp Nicolai and Gerhard, many theologians of the Lutheran Orthodox period published devotional works, hymns, sermons, and Bible commentaries, sharing a faith that would make sense outside of the lecture hall.

Because Lutheran Orthodoxy often centered around universities and **consistories** (local parish offices of church governance), the contributions of women can be harder to find in this era than in the earlier history of the Reformation. The historical record is largely dominated by male activities and publications, so that further scholarly research in this area is truly needed. Women had more opportunities to contribute to the frequently grassroots movements of Lutheran Pietism than the decidedly patriarchal structures of Lutheran Orthodoxy.

In their doctrinal writings, Lutheran Orthodox scholars followed the point-by-point theological method that Philip Melanchthon had developed in his *Loci Communes*, as they carefully examined individual biblical concepts to teach the main points of Christian faith. Because this *loci* method is full of detail, these works can appear dry and overly intellectual, especially when contrasted to Luther's frequently fiery, free-flowing style. Over time, this issue of style became a point that inaccurately represented a major difference between Luther and Melanchthon. Post-Reformation movements could then be judged positively as faithful to the passionate faith of Luther or negatively attached to the supposedly dry and soulless methods of Melanchthon. Such historical perspectives arose in the mid-twentieth century, for instance, in influential works like Franz Hildebrandt's short book *Melanchthon: Alien or Ally?* and Richard Caemmerer's essay "The Melanchthonian Blight."[5] From such perspectives, many scholars have evaluated Lutheran Orthodox theologians on this artificial Luther-Melanchthon spectrum, with Orthodox theologians applauded for their heroic dedication to Luther's pure doctrine, even as their

Melanchthonian commitments to precision and method are portrayed as nearly fatal flaws.[6]

As seen in the previous chapter's discussion of the relationship between the two reformers, these generalizations are not accurate. Luther had great capacity for extended works of theological detail, as seen in *Bondage of the Will* or the voluminous Genesis lectures that he delivered during the last decade of his life. For his part, Melanchthon was a conscientious writer and teacher, who cared not only about what he said but how he said it. Like Luther, he could write about the faith of the heart and the inexpressible mysteries of God in passionate and poetic ways. Later generations of Lutherans had many good theological and rhetorical examples to choose from as they composed works that addressed the needs of their day.

Rather than an era of Lutheran history in which the head won out against the heart, the story of Lutheran Orthodoxy becomes much more compelling when we ask why theologians wrote the way they did. They cared about theological precision because they lived in a world in which theological truth was public policy, impacting everything from what people heard in their local congregations to high-stakes issues of international politics. Their academic writings were thus one part of larger efforts in pastoral care for souls and social welfare. If their methods for discerning truth differed from those of later centuries, such thinkers nevertheless shared with Lutherans before and after them the same "love and zeal for the truth" that first inspired Luther's reforms.

1618: Outbreak of the Thirty Years' War

No one calls a war a "Hundred Years' War" or a "Thirty Years' War" while they are in it. These labels come long after the fighting has ended and conflicts that seemed so uniquely intense come into view as belonging to a larger single story. For instance, in the Hundred Years' War of the 1300s and 1400s, generations of French and English nobility and soldiers fought for land and titles in France, costing countless lives and bleeding into a long English civil war. The Thirty Years' War of the seventeenth century similarly developed from a convoluted mix of local political struggles, religious conflicts, and powerful dynasties that people at the time could not entirely recognize. Regardless of its complex factors, this war resulted in devastating loss of life and destruction of communities across central Europe.

The 1555 Peace of Augsburg had resolved the political side of the Reformation with its principle of ***cuius regio, eius religio***. In this model, local areas would follow the religion that their nobility or city council embraced; the common people's views counted only insofar as rulers wanted to avoid provoking rebellion through unpopular religious policies. Such popular uprising against religious change at the highest level did, in fact, happen in Brandenburg, where the people refused to follow their rulers' Reformed beliefs and practices.[7] On more individual levels, people who wanted to practice a religious tradition other than the one promoted by the government were given time to put their affairs in order and move elsewhere.

Although the Peace of Augsburg largely brought an end to religiously motivated warfare in the 1500s, it contained some built-in shortcomings. First, Reformed Protestants who followed the teachings of reformers like Zwingli or Calvin had no legal rights in the Holy Roman Empire. This led to major social and political challenges, as Reformed teachings continued to spread among both the nobility and common people in prominent areas like Brandenburg and the Palatinate on the Rhine.

Second, some German city-states like Cologne, Würzburg, and Bamberg had long been ruled by prince archbishops. The Peace of Augsburg had not addressed the question of who would have the power to appoint future archbishops, especially in Protestant-leaning cities like Cologne. In the 1580s, Catholic leaders reasserted their rights to appoint the prince archbishop of Cologne, leading to a war that the Catholic rulers won. Würzburg and Bamberg similarly become more strongly Catholic than they had been in previous decades; at the same time, Protestants lost influence in the northwest German territory of Cleves when the formerly Lutheran prince Wolfgang William converted to Catholicism in 1613.[8] In the wake of such conflicts, a Protestant Union and a Catholic League were each formed within the Holy Roman Empire for military purposes. Even so, the religious lines of these groups were never entirely solid, as Lutheran Saxony did not join the Protestant Union and the Catholic Hapsburg dynasty never endorsed the Bavarian-led Catholic League.

Third, the goals and policies of the Hapsburg family added international fuel to local fires. Before he stepped down in 1556, Charles V had ruled (directly or indirectly) over Spain and its American colonies, Hapsburg lands including Belgium, the Netherlands, and Austria-Hungary, and the Holy Roman Empire of the German Nation. After the reign of Charles V, Hapsburg leaders divided their Spanish and Austro-Hungarian lands from each other, but dynastic connections and shared interests kept longstanding bonds intact, including a strong commitment to Roman Catholicism. Behind the scenes, therefore, the rise of the future Emperor Ferdinand II—a Hapsburg who had exiled thousands of Lutherans from his Austrian lands around the year 1600—came with Spanish support for Ferdinand's attempts to consolidate power in central Europe.[9] Spanish troops in Belgium and the Netherlands also gave Ferdinand military support on the western edge of the Holy Roman Empire.

These local conflicts came crashing together when the Austrian Hapsburgs attempted to make Ferdinand the king of Bohemia, thereby installing an ambitious Catholic over a largely Protestant territory, against the objections of local people and leaders. This led to the defenestration of Prague in May 1618, when two Catholic diplomats were thrown out of a castle window.[10] War broke out after the local Protestant nobility elected the Reformed Elector Frederick V of the Palatinate as king of Bohemia. Reasserting Ferdinand's claim to the throne, the Catholic League mobilized and quickly defeated the Protestants around Bohemia, while Spanish troops from the Netherlands brought the war to the Palatinate and western Germany. By the early 1620s Elector Frederick was deposed, his electorship was transferred to King Maximilian of Bavaria, and the Protestant Union was disbanded.[11] In the next several years, Emperor Ferdinand's armies had won victories across northern Germany. He issued an Edict of Restitution that aimed to undo the Peace of Augsburg's religious settlement and bring most of Germany back to Catholicism.[12]

As happened in the Princes' Revolt of the early 1550s, however, the increased power of the Hapsburgs brought strong reactions from many sides. To protect its southern border, the Lutheran kingdom of Denmark entered the war in the later 1620s with the support of Catholic France. Though this Danish effort proved unsuccessful, another set of alliances changed the course of the war when King Gustavus Adolphus of Sweden landed in northern Germany. A capable military leader and committed Protestant, King Gustavus Adolphus had recently extended Swedish power across the Baltic Sea. With support from France and Electoral Saxony, Gustavus Adolphus led his armies across northern and central Germany. At the peak of his strength, however, his alliances started to fracture and he died in battle in 1632. Remembered as a Protestant hero for his efforts, Gustavus Adolphus was nevertheless unable to bring a decisive end to the fighting.

The last phase of the Thirty Years' War was characterized by even more violence and chaos, as the various armies "swept back and forth through the empire, destroying buildings, plundering the populations, and spreading terror, disease, and death."[13] In these years, the French fought the Spanish, the Danes fought the Swedes, and Germans fought each other. Neither the Lutheran Swedes nor the Catholic Hapsburgs could establish themselves as the dominant power in central Europe. Eventually, smaller peace negotiations between warring factions led to the 1648 Peace of Westphalia.

This treaty reestablished the *cuius regio, eius religio* policy in the Holy Roman Empire, with the important addition that Reformed Protestantism would finally have legal standing; groups like Mennonites with roots in the more radical side of the Reformation, however, remained vulnerable to persecution. After all the fighting, the Peace of Westphalia largely restored lands back to their 1624 borders and religious confessions. German Protestantism had barely survived its greatest military threat since the Reformation era and Sweden found itself in a newly powerful position.[14] Also, after nearly a century of struggle, the Netherlands gained independence from Spain. Born amid religious and political conflict, the Netherlands established Reformed Protestantism as its state church but extended religious **tolerance** to other groups, including Jews, Catholics, Lutherans, Mennonites, and English Puritans.

For most people in central Europe, the war had been disastrous. The common use of armies full of underpaid mercenary soldiers led to robbery, rape, and destruction. Unsanitary conditions brought

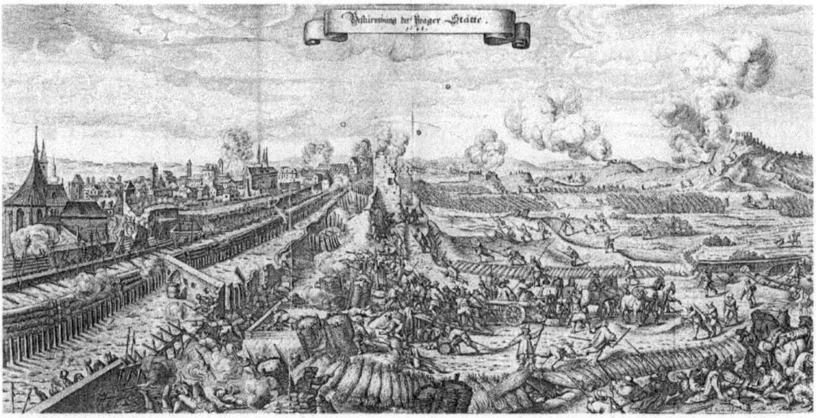

2.2 Scene from the Thirty Years' War: "The Swedish Siege of Prague," 1648. Wikimedia Commons.

increased outbreaks of the plague and other diseases. One particularly horrific moment took place in the city of Magdeburg, which was then a relatively large city of about 20,000 inhabitants. As historian Hajo Holborn described it:

> On May 20, 1631, imperial [Hapsburg] troops had broken into the city and dealt with its citizens in the most savage fashion, till fire destroyed the whole city with the exception of its old cathedral. Two thirds of the inhabitants, together with many of the plundering soldiers were caught in the holocaust. The behavior of the soldiers in the early Swedish [phase of the] war had already been incredibly cruel on both sides, but the destruction of Magdeburg brought the hatred of the two parties to a fever pitch.[15]

While exact numbers of the war's casualties are impossible to know, a general estimate suggests that several million people died during the war, roughly a quarter or a third of the population of central Europe at the time.[16]

Had this devastation been the result of a "religious war"? Yes and no. In the early conflicts, religion was certainly an issue. The people of Bohemia stood up for their religious rights and convictions as they resisted Hapsburg attempts to reimpose Catholicism. Leaders like Emperor Ferdinand II and King Gustavus Adolphus held genuine commitments to their respective faith traditions.

Military leagues like the Protestant Union, the Catholic League, and the later alliance between Sweden and Saxony certainly sought to provide mutual protection to co-religionists.

At the same time, ever since the Peace of Augsburg, religion had served as one socio-political marker among many. The defenestration of Prague was as much an objection to Hapsburg interference in local politics as a religious statement. In the first phase of the war, leaders in Saxony and Brandenburg did not come to the aid of their fellow Protestant ruler, Elector Frederick. France supported Lutheran armies in order to undermine the power of fellow Catholic rulers in Spain and Austria. By the end, the war had very little to do with religious faith and nearly everything to do with power. Even so, because of its role as a tool of mighty nation states, religion came to be seen by the social thinkers and political leaders of the **Enlightenment** as a problem that reasonable people needed to overcome rather than as a resource for responsible governance and civil society. Whatever one's views of the role of religion and politics in the Thirty Years' War, this history shows how quickly a series of passionate local conflicts could cascade into acts of terrible violence and destruction.

1620s: Baroque Lutheranism

Spanning the early 1600s to the later 1700s, the Baroque period has come to describe the art, architecture, music, and literature that followed the Renaissance. It is characterized by complexity, sensuality, and grandeur. Religiously, Baroque works offered artistic alternatives to the **iconoclasm** of Reformed and Radical Protestantism and provided an escape from the brutality of the Thirty Years' War. Intellectually, the period stood between the new humanist learning of the Renaissance and the rationalism of the Enlightenment. In this time, physicists like Johannes Kepler and Isaac Newton pursued theories of cosmic harmony, theologians examined detailed questions of faith and nature, and religious poets imagined a more just society.

The Baroque era brought new attention and methods to scientific inquiry. By the early 1600s, Lutheran lands had long been friendly to work of the Polish astronomer Nicholas Copernicus, who proposed that the earth orbits the sun. Although Luther and Melanchthon dismissed these ideas when they first heard them as being far-fetched, Copernicus's famous *De revolutionibus orbium coelestium* (On the revolutions of heavenly bodies) had been promoted by a Wittenberg professor of mathematics and theology named Georg Joachim Rheticus and was eventually published in Nuremberg under the supervision of the Lutheran reformer Andreas Osiander.[17]

By the turn of the century, Danish astronomer Tycho Brahe and the German Johannes Kepler were advancing Copernicus's theories under royal patronage together in Prague. Kepler had studied to become a Lutheran pastor in his native Württemberg until his disagreement with the Eucharistic theology in the *Formula of Concord* kept him from ordination and led him into a career in mathematics.[18] Contemplating the motion of the planets and the work of the Creator, Kepler published his *Harmonices mundi* (The Harmony of the Worlds) in 1619, the book in which he presented the third of his three laws explaining the elliptical orbits of planets around the sun.

Models of cosmic harmony extended to Lutheran hymns and devotional writings. In works extolling the heavenly blessings of music, the pastor Christoph Frick (1577–1640) wrote, "Indeed when a human considers himself, he recognizes a glorious organ with its beautiful concord of all members. For humans were originally in *templo Dei* [the temple of God], like a glorious organ, well-tuned according to the likeness of God so that a lovely concord was heard between the trio of the Holy Trinity and the duets of our first parents."[19]

As noted by music historian Joyce Irwin, this spiritual appreciation of music had long been typical of Lutheran hymnwriters. Yet these Lutherans of the early seventeenth century went a step further: "Not merely was music divinely ordained, but the cosmos as a whole was musically, or harmonically, ordained. Harmony, in other words, became the fundamental element of the cosmos. To pursue harmony in one's voice and soul was to prepare oneself for heavenly existence."[20] Lutheran hymnwriters of the early Baroque era followed the example of composers like Philipp Nicolai, who had responded to plague and war by emphasizing the soul's unity with Christ.

> Nicolai's reflections on eternal life, however, captured the spirit of the age. There followed other writers such as Valerius Herberger, Johann Arndt, Johann Valentin Andreae, and Johann Mattheus Meyfart, who shared both the sense of the vanity of this life and a vivid imagination for the delights of the next. The characteristics noted in Nicolai are in fact traits of the Baroque age in general, whether manifested in literature or music, art or religion. Just as Nicolai described God as appealing to the senses, so the Baroque mentality was drawn to sensuality and illusion as well as to other-worldly spirituality.[21]

Later generations of Lutheran hymnwriters continued to write hymns for congregational and devotional use amid the ravages of war, famine, disease, and death. Paul Gerhardt's prolific poetry included his meditation on Christ's passion, a work titled "O Sacred Head, Now Wounded," which was an adaptation of an older work by Bernard of Clairvaux. Gerhardt found a productive musical match when he became a pastor in Berlin and worked with cantor Johann Crüger. Together they wrote hymns about the believer's intimate relationship with Christ through faith, as in the Christmas song "Once Again My Heart Rejoices" and the Advent hymn "O Lord, How Shall I Meet You," which combines expectation for Christ's coming with personal faith and service to others:

> O Lord, how shall I meet you, how welcome you a-right?
> Your people long to greet you, my hope, my heart's delight!
> Oh, kindle, Lord most holy, your lamp within my breast
> to do in Spirit lowly all that may please you best.[22]

Crüger's collection of hymns, *Praxis pietatis melica* (The Practice of Piety in Song) deeply shaped the German Lutheran musical tradition. Frequently reprinted, it included many of his works with Gerhardt, as well as other foundational Lutheran hymns for which Crüger wrote the music, including "Jesus, Priceless Treasure" (*Jesu, meine Freude*, with lyrics by Johann Franck), "Ah, Holy Jesus" (*Herzliebster Jesu*, with lyrics by Johann Heermann), and "Now Thank We All Our God" (*Nun Danket Alle Gott*, with lyrics by Martin Rinkhart).

Hymns like these have enriched the worship, culture, and spirituality of Lutherans across the centuries. They also complemented a budding Lutheran Baroque architecture, as exemplified in the Dresden *Frauenkirche* (Our Lady's Church) of the early eighteenth century. Far from representing a dogmatic or rigid Lutheran culture, such works show that people turned to the arts and sciences to reflect on faith, understand their world, and look for hope in challenging circumstances. Gaining inspiration from both the early-modern study of the cosmos and the horrors of war around them, composers connected liberating faith and the theology of the cross with the art forms and thought worlds of their time.

1636: Tranovský's Words and Music in Czech

The pastor, teacher, and musician Juraj Tranovský (1592–1637)[23] made rich and lasting contributions to the theology and hymnody of Czech, Polish, and Slovak Lutheran churches.[24] Born in Silesia (now southwestern Poland) and given a Lutheran Orthodox education at the University of Wittenberg, Tranovský became a teacher in Prague in 1611 and a pastor in the nearby region of Moravia around 1616. While living there, he completed a translation of the *Augsburg Confession* into Czech in 1620 and established himself as a well-regarded teacher and pastor in the area.

Tranovský's work around Prague, however, coincided with the violent early years of the Thirty Years' War. He may have been briefly imprisoned; at one point, about half of his congregation—including at least two of his children—died of the plague.[25] He fled Bohemia and went into exile in his native Silesia. Later in the 1620s, Tranovský was hired as a court theologian for a Protestant nobleman in what is now Slovakia. While at Orava Castle, he put together a book of 150 hymns for congregational and devotional use. Many of these were his own compositions or adaptations. According to one music scholar, these pieces "have a somewhat archaic dignity and strength because the voices move together in uniform rhythm."[26]

In an even greater contribution to church music, Tranovský published his *Cithara Sanctorum* in 1636 while serving as pastor and superintendent in the Slovakian town of Liptovský Mikuláš. This hymnal contained over four hundred songs in Czech, including seventeen hymns by Luther and over seventy songs from the Bohemian Brethren (or Hussite) church.[27] Tranovský himself provided about one hundred original texts, sometimes borrowing melodies from existing chorales or local Czech tunes.[28] With songs for the liturgy, the church year, the catechism, and seasons of life, this hymnal has provided the foundation for centuries of worship in Czech and Slovak Lutheranism.

Tranovský's life provides a glimpse into the pain and determination of people during the Thirty Years' War, when large-scale conflicts greatly harmed people's daily lives. In a career that took him west to Saxony and east to Slovakia, Tranovský capably shared the gospel in a variety of languages and cultures: German, Polish, Czech, and Slovak. He worked effectively among both the nobility and the common people in big cities like Prague and the smaller towns of central Europe. While Tranovský's work was always influential for Czech, Polish, and Slovakian Lutherans, his legacy received renewed international attention in the twentieth century through the translations of the Slovak American pastor and hymnwriter Jaroslav Vajda (1919–2008). The following translation of a Tranovský hymn shows his ability to combine a Lutheran Orthodox faith with the painful realities and deep longings of his time.

> Your heart, O God, is grieved, we know,
> by ev'ry evil, ev'ry woe;
> upon your cross-forsaken Son
> our death is laid, and peace is won.[29]

1637: Gerhard's *Catholic Confession*

By the early 1600s, Lutherans and Catholics had engaged in a century of theological conflict with each other: the Church of Rome had excommunicated Luther without an open hearing, Luther and Melanchthon accused the papacy of representing the antichrist, the Council of Trent condemned Protestant teachings like justification by faith alone, and the process of confessionalization solidified religious divisions along political lines. When Lutherans and Catholics wrote about one another, they usually did so from a distance, focusing on theological differences rather than the shared experiences and concern of a common Christian faith. Kenneth Appold has recently described this process as an "increasingly abstract and doctrinal" approach to the controversies of the Reformation era.[30]

Amid the violence of the Thirty Years' War, Lutheran theologian Johann Gerhard (1582–1637) sought out a more constructive method to resolve doctrinal disputes. Gifts in both spiritual care and theological precision had made this professor at the University of Jena a leading voice of Lutheran Orthodoxy. Addressing the works of **Jesuit** theologian Robert Bellarmine (1542–1621), Gerhard looked for points of commonality between Lutheran and Catholic theology. From 1631 to 1633, he published a series of works in which he turned Bellarmine and other Catholic writers into **evangelical** Lutheran theologians. In the words of Bengt Hägglund:

> This series took for its motto a line from [First] Esdras '*super omnia vincit Veritas*' (the truth triumphs over all, 1 Esd 3:12). Gerhard wanted to demonstrate that even in the most controversial issues at hand, Bellarmine actually supported the evangelical truth. Thus, even those biased against Lutheran theology could find in Bellarmine good arguments for the faith as defended by the Lutherans—the original catholic faith.[31]

These writings became the foundation of Gerhard's *Confessio Catholica*, published in three parts from 1633 to 1637. In this Baroque effort of more than a thousand pages, Gerhard aimed not to demonize Catholicism but to show the shared Christian roots of Catholic and Lutheran theology by studying relatively recent Catholic writings. Translated, the full title of Gerhard's work is *The Catholic Confession, in which the Catholic and Evangelical Doctrine, which is Confessed by the Churches Adhering to the Augsburg Confession, is Confirmed by the Support of Roman Catholic Authors.*

While the book looked for points of shared gospel faith, Gerhard took it for granted that the Lutherans had most correctly interpreted the witness of the New Testament and the Christian tradition. Even so, his method followed some of the more generous efforts of Luther and Melanchthon a hundred years prior. In a 1528 work on baptism, for instance, Luther had written:

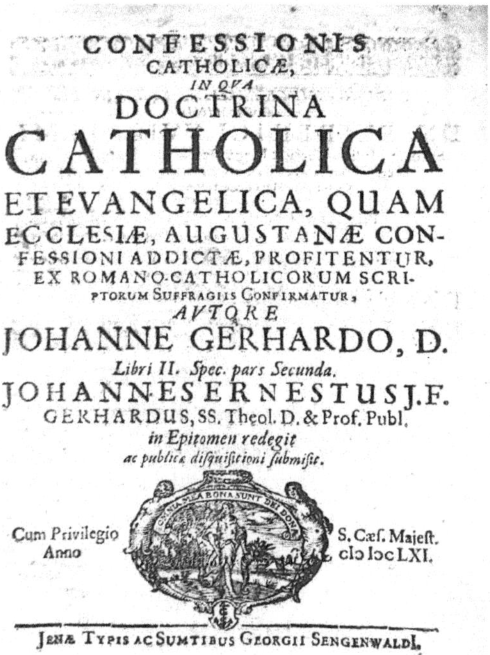

CONFESSIONIS
CATHOLICÆ,
IN QUA
DOCTRINA
CATHOLICA
ET EVANGELICA, QUAM
ECCLESIÆ, AUGUSTANÆ CON-
FESSIONI ADDICTÆ, PROFITENTUR,
EX ROMANO-CATHOLICORUM SCRI-
PTORUM SUFFRAGIIS CONFIRMATUR,
AVTORE
JOHANNE GERHARDO, D.
Libri II. Spec. pars Secunda.
JOHANNES ERNESTUS J.F.
GERHARDUS, SS. Theol. D. & Prof. Publ.
in Epitomen redegit
ac publicæ disquisitioni submisit.

Cum Privilegio S. Cæs. Majest.
Anno clↄ Iↄc LXI.

JENÆ TYPIS AC SUMTIBUS GEORGII SENGENWALDI.

2.3 Title page to *Confessio Catholica* by Johann Gerhard. Photo by Martin Lohrmann, used with permission.

> We on our part confess that there is much that is Christian and good under the papacy; indeed everything that is Christian and good is to be found there and has come to us from this source. For instance we confess that in the papal church there are the true holy Scriptures, true baptism, the true sacrament of the altar, the true keys to the forgiveness of sins, the true office of the ministry, the true catechism in the form of the Lord's Prayer, the Ten Commandments, and the articles of the creed . . . I contend that in the papacy there is true Christianity, even the right kind of Christianity and many great and devoted saints.[32]

In this piece, Luther differentiated between theological and interpersonal controversies. Although the Roman hierarchy had condemned his evangelical preaching, Luther could recognize and value the lived faith of countless Christians who remained in the Roman Catholic Church. Known for his willingness to keep dialogue open,

Melanchthon's sharp denunciation of the papacy in his 1537 *Treatise on the Power and Primacy of the Pope* had similarly focused on the church's primary mission to preach the gospel, a mission that can just as well be lost by Lutheran leaders past and present as by the papal corruptions of the 1500s. As Timothy Wengert has said of Melanchthon's *Treatise*,

> This ferocious usurpation of power in this world happened not just to Roman popes but to all kinds of self-appointed keepers of the public good and morals. . . . When pastors keep their congregants' consciences bound to the pastors' own moral opinions; when congregations demand that pastors and bishops be little more than hired hands and censure them for pointing out the political ramifications of Christian faith; when pastors, bishops, or entire churches claim to be anything more than faithful Christians fulfilling their vocations in the world: then the same kind of tyranny and confusion of faith and Christ's reign with political success threaten the church.[33]

The tendency to move from faith in God and love of neighbor to self-centeredness is equal opportunity. It can exist in Protestant quests for doctrinal purity that fail to see Christ in the neighbor as well as in any other church system or program that puts its own righteousness above anything else.

Although Gerhard's approach provided one possible model for renewed dialogue, it did not catch on in the way its author intended. "Gerhard's aim was clearly a fruitful dialogue instead of a unilateral polemic. But the spirit of his age was not amenable to his efforts."[34] Rather than inspire new forums for dialogue by building upon the work of people like Gerhard, the Peace of Westphalia ended the Thirty Years' War by reinforcing the lines between the churches. With the exception of a budding religious tolerance in the Netherlands, religious difference would continue to mean political and social difference across Europe.

Issues of unity and diversity, however, continued to drive later disputes among Lutherans. For instance, a 1645 debate between Wittenberg theologian Abraham Calov and professor George Calixtus of Helmstedt revolved around how Lutherans might engage others in mutual conversation. Calixtus accused Calov of stressing theological differences at the expense of shared Christian faith, while the Lutheran Orthodox Calov believed that Calixtus's more generous view of Christian unity unhelpfully minimized substantial differences between the traditions. Not until the ecumenical movement of the twentieth century and the Second Vatican Council of the 1960s would Protestants and Catholics build the kind of institutional connections that writers like Gerhard and Calixtus had sought in the early 1600s.

1648: Early Lutheran Attitudes toward Jews

Persecution of Jewish people occurred regularly throughout the Middles Ages and continued into the modern era, including the terrible ***Shoah***, or Holocaust, in which millions of European Jews were killed by the fascist regime of Nazi Germany and its collaborators in the twentieth century. As a minority population, Jews in Europe had long been subject to violence and scapegoating because of their differences from the dominant cultures of Christendom around them. "Starting in the late Roman empire and continuing under Christian rule in the early Middle Ages, many ancient Jewish privileges were suspended, proselytizing was prohibited, rabbinical jurisdiction was curtailed or abolished, sexual relations with Christians were forbidden, and most legal protections were removed."[35] Among many other persecutions over the centuries, European Jews were targeted by the riotous armies of the First Crusade in 1096, expelled from England in 1290, blamed for the spread of the plague in the 1300s, and subjected to the ruthless Spanish Inquisition by King Ferdinand and Queen Isabella in the late 1400s. Many of the same stereotypes used by anti-Semites today have their origins in the long and ugly history of anti-Jewish violence of the European Middle Ages.[36]

Martin Luther inherited these prejudices and—in a perversion of his own teachings about radical grace and divine love—built strong anti-Jewish themes into his theology, excluding Jews from God's salvation and identifying them as threats to Christian faith and communities. Luther's extremely harsh writings against the Jews are sinful contributions to history and theology. In the

1543 tract *On the Jews and Their Lies*, for instance, Luther recommended forcing Jews out of their homes and businesses, destroying their synagogues, and confiscating their sacred writings. His advice began: "First, to set fire to their synagogues or schools and to bury and cover with dirt whatever will not burn, so that no man will ever again see a stone or cinder of them. This is to be done in honor of our Lord and of Christendom, so that God might see that we are Christians, and do not condone or knowingly tolerate such public lying, cursing, and blaspheming of his Son and of his Christians."[37]

With such words, Luther failed to see that his attacks on the Jews recreated the religious self-righteousness and spiritual supremacy that his Reformation had in many ways sought to undo. He declared that some were more righteous or worthy than others based on something other than God's truly free mercy and love. As Kirsi Stjerna has written, "Luther's notorious and explicitly anti-Jewish writings late from his life make it indisputably clear what his conviction had been all along about Judaism as a religion: Judaism was dead and there was no hope for Jews as Jews."[38] While many contemporary Lutherans have repudiated Luther's condemnation of the Jews,[39] more subtle anti-Jewish themes in Luther's biblical interpretation and Lutheran theology remain. Among other responses, theologian Craig Nessan has found correctives to Luther's anti-Jewish thinking in the witness of Dietrich Bonhoeffer, whose experience with African American Christianity in the United States and support of Jews in Nazi Germany taught him to reorient Christian life around seeing Christ in the other, especially the oppressed and victims of state violence.[40]

Most of Luther's contemporaries either agreed with his assessment or only marginally dissented. Justus Jonas, who translated *On the Jews and Their Lies* into Latin, seems to have believed that Jews and Christians had both a common past and future with God.[41] More forcefully, Andreas Osiander of Nuremberg rejected Luther's anti-Jewish views on several occasions. Among Reformed Protestants, the Swiss reformer Heinrich Bullinger called Luther's ideas "filthy" and pastors in Zurich "described it as swinish and shitty."[42] Politically, Luther's writings resulted in harsher policies against Jews in places like Anhalt and Electoral Saxony. In Berlin, however, court preacher Johann Agricola defended the Jews and promoted a more tolerant policy pursued by the rulers of Brandenburg.[43] Regardless of past or present dissent from these hateful views, Luther's words about Jews have left their mark.

Just over a hundred years after Luther's harshest writings against the Jews, Lutherans in the town of Minden wrote to the University of Wittenberg's theological faculty in 1648. Wanting to impose then-typical Christian regulations upon local Jews—such as forced attendance at church services and restrictions on Jewish business practices—the city leaders looked to Wittenberg for moral and practical support; they also referred to Luther's *On the Jews and Their Lies* as evidence for their position.[44] Studying the request from Minden and the published response from the Wittenberg theologians, Kenneth Appold noted that the Wittenbergers did not entirely ignore Luther's violent words. They cited its brutal advice before themselves emphasizing general points about evangelization and civic peace to recommend a slightly more moderate policy. In that way, the theologians neither totally denied nor supported Luther's worst ideas, rather "They bury it in silence."[45]

Appold's study examines a larger historical thesis, which claims that Luther's most infamous writings against the Jews were not directly put into practice until being reclaimed by anti-Semites in the twentieth century.[46] He found that people in the 1600s knew Luther's harshest works against the Jews, even if they did not follow his suggestions. Nevertheless, silence about hatred and persecution was not then and is not now a sufficient response to such inhumane thoughts and actions. Indeed, the anti-Jewish ideas that Luther held never went away but remained implicitly and explicitly in the pages of his theology—and Christian teaching in general—to suggest that Christians can live with two-tiered senses of grace, mercy, and love. To paraphrase George Orwell's *Animal Farm*, it is as if in Christian faith "All people are equally sinners, but some sinners are more equal than others."[47] Such a theology of "us and them" does not match the depth of God's mercy as revealed through the cross of Christ.

Without negating the centrality of faith as personal trust in God, on one hand, or putting oneself in the place of judgment on the other, Christians can see others in light of the same self-giving grace and love that God has given them. On questions of faith and salvation, they might join St. Paul, who concluded a complex reflection on the place of the Jews in God's salvation by writing, "O the depth of the riches and wisdom and knowledge of God! How unsearchable are his judgments and how inscrutable his ways! . . . For from him and through him and to him are all things. To him be the glory forever. Amen" (Rom 11:33–36). Confronted with deep mysteries about life with God in this world and in a life to come, Christians might recall that there is no mystery about the sinfulness of prejudice, discrimination, and hatred, no mystery about the goodness of loving our neighbors as ourselves (Matt 7:12), and no mystery that God truly cares for creation with a wondrously deep love. Lutherans can continue to cherish the God they know in Jesus Christ while also practicing the hospitality, generosity, and compassion that Christ himself showed to the diverse groups and individuals he met on his Way. As we will see in the histories of colonialism and genocide, these issues of interreligious hospitality and compassion (or the lack thereof) have been and remain matters of life and death.

1675: Spener's *Pia Desideria* and the Birth of Pietism

Lutherans have cherished a personal faith that combines head, heart, and hands ever since Luther started his *95 Theses* with a "love and zeal for truth and the desire to bring it to light."[48] Luther described faith as a real union with Christ and encouraged people to apply the sacramental promises of forgiveness, life, and salvation to themselves.[49] Melanchthon similarly spoke of "personal faith" to connect the objective saving work of Christ with the intimate salvation given to real flesh-and-blood individuals through faith.[50] Later generations of Lutherans continued to combine doctrinal convictions and spiritual application, as seen in the hymns of Philip Nicolai, the devotional writings of Johann Gerhard, and the classic of Lutheran spirituality, *True Christianity* by Johann Arndt.

Because Arndt's writings remained influential for generations, the publisher of a 1675 edition of Arndt's *Postils* (notes and commentaries for preaching) requested a new preface for that work from the Lutheran superintendent of Frankfurt am Main, Philipp Jakob Spener (1635–1705). Spener's preface itself became so popular that

PIA DESIDERIA:
Oder
Hertzliches
Verlangen/
Nach Gottgefälliger Besserung
der wahren Evangelischen Kirchen/
sampt einigen dahin einfältig abzweckenden
Christlichen Vorschlägen/
Philipp Jacob Speners/D.
Predigers und Senioris zu Franck-
furt am Mayn;
Sampt angehengten
Zweyer Christlichen Theologorum
darüber gestellten/und zu mehrer auff-
erbauung höchst-dienlichen
Bedencken.

Franckfurt am Mayn/
In Verlegung Johann David Zunners.
Druckts Johann Dieterich Friedgen.
M DC LXXVI.

2.4 Title page from Philipp Spener's *Pia Desideria*, 1676. Wikimedia Commons.

it was republished separately under the title *Pia Desideria or Heartfelt Desire for a God-pleasing Reform of the true Evangelical Church, Together with Several Simple Christian Proposals Looking Toward that End*.[51] With its critique of the institutional church of his day and clear suggestions for reform, Spener's work launched a movement known as **Pietism**.

Spener's practical suggestions for reforming Christian life included support for small-group Bible studies that would take place in people's houses rather than a church.[52] At the request of local church members in Frankfurt, Spener himself had started such *collegia pietatis*: pious gatherings or **conventicles**. Although initially pleased with these groups, Spener experienced a drawback to these private devotional meetings, as rival conventicles started to pop up in Frankfurt, disrupting local church life.[53] This negative potential for conventicles to become churches-within-churches and for personal religious ideas to develop apart from the supervision of a pastor became a common critique of Lutheran Orthodoxy against Pietism. After leaving Frankfurt in 1686, Spener did not advocate the foundation of conventicles; nevertheless, such small-group gatherings became a hallmark of Pietist practice.[54]

Spener also received criticism for Pietism's excessive moralizing, for emphasizing private spirituality rather than communal faith, and for supporting the kind of unsupervised religious gatherings that quickly proved troublesome. Even so, many of the ideas in *Pia Desideria* found wide acceptance and application. As Timothy Maschke has written, "In almost all contexts, the work was perceived as being a legitimate proposal for reform."[55] In his own time, Spener was highly regarded by many fellow pastors and theologians. After serving as superintendent in Frankfurt, he became a court preacher to the Elector of Saxony in Dresden and later an influential adviser to the Brandenburg nobility while working as a pastor in Berlin's St. Nicholas Church.[56]

Within decades, Pietism grew from a local reform movement into an international expression of Christian faith and mission. This happened largely through the efforts of August Hermann Francke (1663–1727), whom Spener had met in Saxony. After pressure about his Pietist views forced him out of jobs in Leipzig and Erfurt, Francke became a pastor in Glaucha, a poor suburb of Halle.[57] He was also a teacher at the University of Halle, which had recently been established by the Elector of Brandenburg. Pietism's concern for social and moral reform resonated with the struggling people of Glaucha. Seeing the tremendous need around him, Francke used a modest donation to start a ministry for poor street children. Within a relatively short time, this ministry expanded into an orphanage, school, library, hospital, and farms.[58] The Halle orphanage became an inspirational model for education, pastoral care, and practical assistance for those in need.

Many of the international movements that will be discussed later in this book had their origins in Francke's Pietist institutions in Halle. The Danish nobility who wanted pastors to accompany their colonial ventures in India turned to Halle for support in the early 1700s. The globally influential—and frequently

2.5 Portrait of August Hermann Francke, founder of pietist movement at Halle, Germany (artist unknown). Wikimedia Commons.

controversial—Count Nicholas Ludwig von Zinzendorf was educated in Halle; Spener had been his baptismal sponsor. Early connections between Halle and the London-based Society for Promoting Christian Knowledge (SPCK, founded in 1698) led to the sending of Henry Muhlenberg as a missionary to colonial Pennsylvania and the founding of the first Lutheran church body in North America. Over the centuries, later streams of Pietism would just as profoundly continue to impact local communities and inspire mission around the world.

Despite the debates that sometimes arose from it, the history of global Lutheranism that follows is unimaginable without the Pietism of Spener's *Pia Desideria* and its "Heartfelt Desire for the God-pleasing Reform of the true Evangelical Church."

1678: The Opera Controversy Erupts in Hamburg

Conflict has never been a stranger to Lutherans. From the Reformation onward, Lutherans have both embraced conflict as a clarifying tool and, at other times, worked hard to minimize the personal, social, and spiritual damage that conflict can cause. Some disputed topics—such as the relationship between church and state or how Lutherans ought to relate to other Christians—have appeared repeatedly across the centuries; other conflicts, however, prove less compelling over time. The "opera wars" that took place in Hamburg beginning in 1678 give a good example of a controversy that may not seem provocative now, even though it disrupted the lives of many in its day.

In the late 1600s, Hamburg was the second-largest German-speaking city after Vienna. It was an independent city governed by two councils: one patrician group of leading families and another body more representative of labor guilds and merchants. The clergy in Hamburg were overseen not by a superintendent but by a **ministerium** that used simple majority votes to make decisions and relied upon the city council to enforce its decrees.[59] Adding international complexity to this unique political scene, the nearby kingdom of Denmark had recently pursued aggressive policies in the area and did not give up its longstanding claims to Hamburg until 1685.

Hamburg's opera, the first in Germany, was built in 1678 by local business leaders and surrounding nobility, most of whom were also Lutheran church members. According to the historian and musicologist W. Gordon Marigold, the only initial religious opposition to the opera came in the form of a "one-man crusade" led by pastor Anton Reiser, who had earlier been banished from his position in Bratislava, Slovakia, due to immoderate religious zeal. Although he did not gain much of a following in Hamburg, he left behind a provocatively titled book called *Theatromania* as his witness against the theater and opera, which he viewed as evil forces in society.[60] The vast majority of Lutheran Hamburg did not share his worries.

Controversy about the new opera house started more intensely in 1686. The opera had closed due to the strained political situation with Denmark and local tensions that included the public execution of two citizens for treason.[61] At this time, three Hamburg pastors influenced by Spener's Pietism began to preach against the reopening of the opera for moral reasons. The most influential of the Pietist pastors was Johannes Winckler; the loudest of them was Johann Horb, a brother-in-law to Spener. The leader of the Lutheran Orthodox party—a group that comprised the majority of clergy, city council members, and the working class—was Dr. Johann Friedrich Mayer. Concerned with the separatism that often accompanied Pietism, Mayer considered Spener to be "the patron saint of religious fanatics."[62] Both sides appealed to outside theologians, almost all of whom recommended moderation and emphasized the Lutheran teaching of adiaphora (tolerance in matters not essential to saving faith); this group of cautious advisers included Spener himself.[63]

Although the religious issues surrounding the theater and Pietism were relatively simple, controversy escalated because of interpersonal attacks and problems of governance. A pattern emerged: a Pietist minister would raise a moral concern, be publicly denounced in pulpits and in print by leaders like Dr. Mayer, the ministerium would support Dr. Mayer but have no real enforcement powers, and the cycle would continue. Hundreds of polemical pamphlets were printed in Hamburg at the time. The crisis reached its peak when the ministerium required a loyalty oath against religious fanaticism, which the Pietists could not support because it was directed against them and because of Jesus's words against taking oaths (Matt 5:33–37).[64]

Pastor Horb was eventually removed from his position, but the process by which this happened exposed further vulnerabilities within the Hamburg city government and the ministerium. A power vacuum developed, leading to the normalization of verbal threats and physical force as tools for control in the city. In particular, members of Dr. Mayer's parish "forced illegal council elections, terrorized the [council], and insisted on supposed rights that had, in fact, never existed."[65] This situation continued even after Mayer took a new job as superintendent and professor in Greifswald in 1701. Peace and order did not return to the city until the Holy Roman Empire intervened decisively in 1712.

In the Hamburg opera controversy, specific theological issues about theater and morality played relatively small roles. The partisan conflict between Lutheran Orthodoxy and Pietism was more significant, but even then, fights revolved more around personal attacks and decision-making processes than theological differences. In terms of popular opinion, most of Hamburg's leaders, clergy, and working class remained solidly committed to the Lutheran Orthodox perspective throughout these decades; unlike other areas, Pietism in Hamburg was identified more with elite outsiders than with grassroots spiritual renewal. Nevertheless, internal uncertainty about policy and enforcement, external worries about religious separatism and foreign influence, and intemperate words and actions combined to create a highly divisive atmosphere.

Hamburg survived its opera wars and remained an important center of German culture and trade. It was home to leading eighteenth-century artists like the musicians Georg Philipp Telemann and Carl Philipp Emanuel Bach and the writer Gottfried Emanuel Lessing, even as Lutheran Orthodoxy remained the dominant theological culture. The opera controversy, however, provides a good example of how relatively minor points have the potential to erupt into more damaging conflicts. In the case of Hamburg's opera wars, these conflicts dominated political and religious life in a large city for an entire generation.

1696: Luther's Catechism Published in Algonquian

The first Lutherans to come to the Americas were Danish explorers looking for a Northwest Passage to Asia. Sailing west from Greenland, they got stuck in Hudson Bay and tried to survive the winter near present-day Churchill, Manitoba. Among the crew was a pastor named Rasmus Jensen who conducted religious services, including a service of Holy Communion on Christmas Day, 1619. The winter grew increasingly harsh, and Pastor Jensen died shortly after the new year. Only three men survived and made it back to Denmark.[66] Other more lasting settlements were established in the following decades, with the arrival of Dutch Lutherans in New Amsterdam and Danes in the Virgin Islands.

In 1638 Sweden founded a colony in North America near the mouth of the Delaware River, an area including the present-day states of Delaware, Pennsylvania, and New Jersey. Unlike other **colonial** projects in the Americas, New Sweden mostly sought peaceful relationships with the native peoples, never practiced slavery, and was organized around trade rather than absolute control of the land and its resources. Although still holding **Eurocentric** cultural assumptions and values, Swedish and Finnish settlers developed some good relationships with the local Lenape (or Delaware) Indians. As related by historian Kim-Eric Williams, a Huron Indian passing through the region in 1647 was shocked to come across Swedish men casually talking and laughing with Lenape women.[67]

Pastor Johan Campanius arrived at New Sweden in 1643. He was the second Swedish Lutheran pastor to serve the colony. He came just in time to bury his predecessor, Reorus Torkillus, the first Lutheran pastor called to serve in North America.[68] In addition to his work with the settlers, Campanius came to know the Lenape well enough to talk about religion in their language and to begin a translation of Luther's *Small Catechism*. Swedish Lutherans had previously translated the catechism into the Sámi language of indigenous Nordic people, Russian, and a Cyrillic version of Finnish.[69]

The Swedish practice of sending pastors for only a few years at a time meant that Campanius returned to Sweden in 1648 instead of staying longer and deepening his connections with the Lenape. Even so, that year he completed his translation of the *Small Catechism* in the Algonquian dialect of the region. A manuscript version of the translation might have been used by the pastors who followed. The chance to build on Campanius's work, however, faded when New Sweden was invaded by the Dutch in 1655 and then came under English control a decade later.

Despite the regime change, Swedes and Finns were allowed to stay in the area and were sometimes joined by new immigrants. In the 1690s, the Church of Sweden restarted its mission work in the Delaware Valley and Campanius's translation of the catechism was finally put into print. Fifty years after its original composition, it became "the first book published in an Algonquin language and shows an attitude that valued the Native Americans as equal members of the Church."[70] Already by this time, however, conflict and disease had killed many Lenape or forced them to find homes elsewhere. Opportunities for respectful sharing of the gospel between the Swedish community and the Lenape had largely passed. One of the pastors who went to the Delaware Valley in 1697 could later say:

> When someone speaks to them [the Lenape] that they should become Christians, they answer, "If the Christians lived better than we live because of their religion, we would become Christians. But we are not able to discern that. For we see and hear them drink, fight, commit adultery, murder, steal, lie, defraud, etc. We have never known such things. Thus we would rather remain as we are."[71]

Although short-lived and often marred by the assumptions and actions of the Swedes themselves, the interaction between Campanius and the Lenape people of the Delaware Valley provides an alternative early example to the unjust treatment of indigenous and enslaved people that so often came with European colonization.

August 1, 1714: A Lutheran King of England

Although it might seem strange, this history of global Lutheranism now takes a trip to London and developments in the Church of England, as political and religious events in England in the early 1700s would have major impacts on the spread of Lutheranism around the world for centuries to come. While the English Reformation represents a fascinating chapter in church history in its own right, it will be briefly described here to help explain its importance for global Lutheranism.

As with Lutheranism in places like Saxony, Denmark, and Sweden, the establishment of a single Protestant church in England in the 1500s came about through a combination of popular desire for reform and the support of the secular government, in this case the English monarchy. Unlike the churches of the Lutheran Reformation that eventually organized themselves around the common faith taught in the *Augsburg Confession*, the English Reformation addressed questions of church unity by focusing on worship and church structure. The English church had strong historical foundations for this path, as liturgy and apostolic succession—the ordination of bishops going back to the apostles—had shaped the early church in the first centuries after Christ.[72] The Protestant church in England did produce confessional statements of faith like the *39 Articles* (1571), which in many places is very similar to the *Augsburg Confession*. Even so, a common worship service, the apostolic office of bishop, and the role of the monarchy played larger roles in the Church of England than confessional statements of faith.

The strong connection of the Church of England to the monarchy began when parliament declared King Henry VIII (1491–1547) to be the head of the church in England in 1534. Henry's Reformation legacy is very complicated: on one hand, he made many Protestant changes like breaking communion with the Church of Rome, approving the publication of an English Bible, and confiscating church properties; on the other hand, even after starting his reforms, Henry executed prominent Protestants like Robert Barnes and supported Catholic teachings like clerical celibacy and transubstantiation. While his personal religious views remain open to speculation, one thing was certain: the monarch was the head of the Church of England.

This top-down Reformation did not keep the people of England from pursuing a variety of religious convictions. Many nobles and commoners wanted to stay in the Church of Rome. Some Protestants, unhappy with the king's reluctance to make more dramatic reforms, could not reconcile themselves to the Church of England and identified more strongly with the Presbyterian form of church government practiced in John Calvin's Geneva or in the Church of Scotland. Still other English Protestants like early Baptists, Congregationalists, and Quakers risked imprisonment and persecution to embrace more radical aspects of the Reformation, including a rejection of church hierarchies, an emphasis on personal spirituality, and a clear separation between church and state.

After the back-and-forth reigns of Edward VI (a Protestant) and Mary Tudor (a Roman Catholic), Henry's daughter Queen Elizabeth I ruled from 1558 to 1603. She brought stability to the Church of England by pursuing a middle way (*via media*) that emphasized unity through worship and openness on theological points like the real presence of Christ in Holy Communion. Nevertheless, by the early 1600s, English Protestantism still included many differing parties: High Church Anglicans who embraced the established church and traditional forms of worship, Presbyterians who wanted to see an established church organized along the Reformed model, dissenters who objected to having an established church, and Puritans—both within and outside the Church of England—who wanted to rid the church of pre-Reformation elements like robes, statues, and medieval worship styles.

Increasing conflict between a Catholic-leaning monarchy and a Puritan-leaning parliament led to a civil war in the mid-1600s. For a time, the victorious parliament supported a Presbyterian-style Church of England, but dissent among Puritans themselves kept this from taking root. Dissatisfaction with parliament eventually brought about a restoration of the monarchy and the strong reestablishment of High Church Anglicanism. The failures of strict religious conformity, however, led to the 1689 Act of Toleration, which affirmed the Church of England as the lone established church but allowed dissenting groups like Quakers, Baptists, Congregationalists, Presbyterians, and (later) Methodists the right to meet and worship privately.

How does this history of the Church of England impact global Lutheranism? First, by the end of the 1600s, the English parliament insisted that its monarchs be Protestant. For this reason, when England's Queen Anne died on August 1, 1714, Duke George of Hanover—the closest Protestant relative to the queen—became King George I, launching the Hanoverian dynasty in England that lasted until 1901. The new king spoke little English and had been ruler of an officially Lutheran land, which caused some consternation among the Anglicans of whom George was now the spiritual head.[73]

Because they oversaw both the Church of England and Lutheran churches in Hanover, these Hanoverian rulers kept Lutheran court preachers with them in London. One of these theologians, Friedrich Ziegenhagen, proved influential in sending Henry Muhlenberg (himself a Hanoverian subject) as a missionary to colonial Pennsylvania. Ziegenhagen provided Muhlenberg with some basic training in English, English-language worship materials, and valuable

2.6 Portrait of King George I of Great Britain in the costume of the Order of the Garter. By the studio of Georg Kneller, ca. 1716 or later. Wikimedia Commons.

institutional support.[74] Lutheranism in the 1700s and beyond, therefore, included a very significant path through London.

A second important point connecting English religious history with the history of global Lutheranism has to do with religious diversity. The 1689 Act of Toleration calmed 150 years of religious fragmentation in England by legalizing Protestant dissent. This religious tolerance became especially prominent in England's American colonies, where members of diverse religious communities—including Lutherans—lived side-by-side as neighbors in secular society. Unlike the homogeneity of established Lutheran churches in Scandinavia and Germany, Lutheran immigrants would learn to practice their faith amid an abundance of other religious options and views, a diversity largely stemming from the complex history of the English Reformation.

Questions

1. As with many other major conflicts, the Thirty Years War grew from smaller causes. What were some of those sources? What role did faith in Jesus Christ play in them?
2. Can you think of other similarly devastating movements that started small but spread fast? What kinds of action might prevent violence between nations?
3. Christians, especially those with roots in the Christendom model of medieval Europe, have long wrestled with how to treat people who are not Christian. This has been especially true of the relationship between Christians and Jews. If the Christian gospel does not ultimately require the subjugation of non-Christian peoples, then what other past or present approaches to religious and cultural diversity might Lutherans consider?
4. The emphasis on small-group devotional meetings (conventicles) helped make Pietism both inspiring and controversial. What are the advantages and disadvantages to private religious gatherings?
5. How did people in the 1600s put their faith into practice? What would you have done in situations like those discussed in this chapter?
6. Hundreds of years later, the Hamburg "opera wars" might seem like a strange controversy. But does it remind you of social or religious conflicts you've encountered in your life?
7. Campanius translated Luther's *Small Catechism* into the language of the Lenape. What does translating the gospel mean to you?

CHAPTER THREE

1717–1817

Introduction to Lutheranism in Its Third Century

Lutherans participated in the vast movements of people and ideas in the 1700s, sometimes eagerly and sometimes reluctantly. Colonial ventures by Denmark, Sweden, and the Netherlands had already brought Lutheranism to North America, the Caribbean, and India before the Reformation bicentennial. In the following years, German refugees fleeing war and persecution would further spread Lutheranism across Europe and North America. More than simply a regional or ethnic variety of Protestantism, Lutheran ways of sharing the gospel, promoting education, and living out the faith in service to neighbors were transplanted into new contexts around the world.

Pietism inspired the early mission work of both Lutherans and **Moravians**, spiritual descendants of Jan Hus and the Bohemian Brethren, whose vision of the church and evangelism sometimes clashed with Lutherans. Within Lutheran lands, grassroots spiritual movements shaped by Pietism continued to come into conflict with the perspectives and practices of Lutheran Orthodoxy. In other settings, however, Pietism and Orthodoxy brought complementary traits that supported vibrant church life. This internal harmony is especially visible in the career of Henry Muhlenberg, who was trained, sent, and supported by the Pietist institutions in

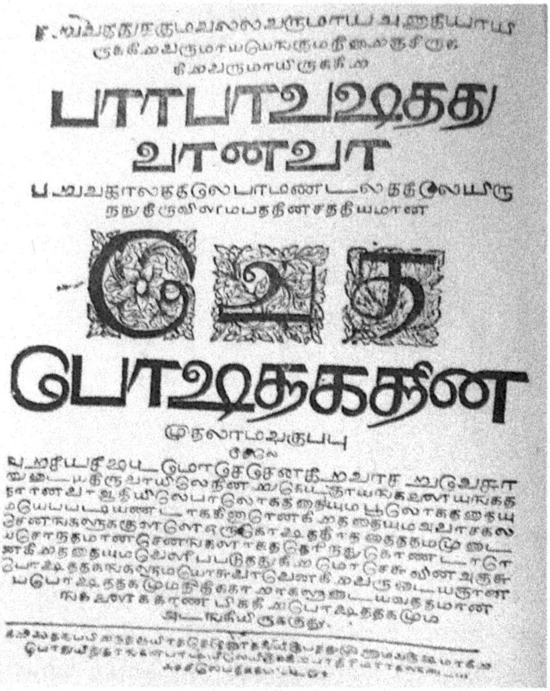

3.1 First page of a Tamil Bible (New Testament) printed in Tranquebar by Bartholomäus Ziegenbalg. Wikimedia Commons.

Halle, even as he loved the confessional theology passed on through Lutheran Orthodoxy.

As introduced in the previous section, this chapter reveals a history not often told, in which Lutherans did not disdain or avoid global evangelism efforts but rather were key participants in early European missions. A particularly stirring witness was made by Ziegenbalg and Plütschau, missionaries from Halle to southeastern India in the early 1700s who learned the Tamil language, respected local customs, and fostered education and literacy.

At the same time, we must recognize that these ventures brought with them the devastating experiences and effects of colonization. As missiologist David Bosch wrote about the Spanish and Portuguese missionary efforts of the early-modern era:

> The new word, "mission," is historically linked indissolubly with the colonial era and with the idea of a magisterial commissioning. The term presupposes an established church

> in Europe which dispatched delegates to convert overseas peoples and was as such an attendant phenomenon of European expansion. . . . The "missionary" was irrevocably tied to an institution in Europe, from which he or she derived the mandate and power to confer salvation on those who accept certain tenets of the faith.[1]

Indeed, this was a period in which many white Lutherans adapted to or even embraced colonialism and slavery in ways that compromised or undermined their gospel message. Lutheran colonists in the Caribbean, for instance, practiced slavery and pursued the interests of a plantation economy, uncritically viewing these arrangements as part of God's order. In the Ebenezer community in colonial Georgia, white Lutherans shifted away from an originally faith-based antislavery position to becoming slaveowners when they started to view slavery as essential to their own economic survival, heeding neither the spiritual nor humanitarian effects of this system on themselves or those in bondage. Still others, like Pastor Berkenmeyer in New York, enthusiastically practiced slave ownership without reservation. While black and biracial people were baptized in Lutheran churches in the Americas, and sometimes became active church members in this period, racial discrimination more often prevented their greater leadership and congregational involvement.[2]

In an era of **Enlightenment**, Lutherans continued to engage various intellectual and artistic movements. The musical culture that had become an early feature of the Lutheran Reformation continued to flourish in the work of composers like Dietrich Buxtehude, Johann Sebastian Bach, and Georg Philipp Telemann. Lutheran centers of learning contributed to the intellectual fermentation of the period, as seen in the philosophy of Gottfried Wilhelm Leibniz and Immanuel Kant, and in the literary works of Gotthold Ephraim Lessing. As a sign of generational cultures of education, it is worth noting that Leibniz's godfather was a Lutheran Orthodox theologian, while Kant and Lessing were both children of Lutheran ministers. The **rationalism** of the Enlightenment era challenged Orthodox and Pietist believers alike to defend their faith, even as it pushed theology, biblical studies, and social theory in fascinating new directions.

On the political level, these years saw the rise of modern democratic movements that dared to undo centuries of aristocratic rule in Europe. Such views challenged the longstanding theological assumption that God had established and maintained existing political structures, including monarchies and aristocracies. The power of aristocracy as a social norm is the reason why the United States' Declaration of Independence begins with an awareness that an explanation is owed to God and human authorities for such a dramatic course of action: "When in the Course of human events it becomes necessary for one people to dissolve the political bands which have connected them with another and to assume among the powers of the earth, the separate and equal station to which the Laws of Nature and of Nature's God entitle them, a decent respect to the opinions of mankind requires that they should declare the causes which impel them to the separation."[3]

Not avoiding involvement in political matters, Lutherans in Europe and North America wrestled with how to balance respect for authority with new forms of governance and new visions of freedom. In the 1700s and beyond, Lutherans found themselves having to reconceive the relationships between faith and reason, freedom and bondage, the individual and the community.

May 1723: J. S. Bach Hired as Cantor in Leipzig

Johann Sebastian Bach (1685–1750) was born into a fourth generation of church musicians, immersed from a young age into myriad aspects of music-making: instrument building and repair, performing, directing, teaching, composing, and earning an income.[4] Able to excel in church and secular settings, the family's religious heritage included the witness of great-great-grandfather Veit Bach, a baker who fled Hungary in the sixteenth century because of his Lutheran beliefs.[5] As musicians and church cantors, family members often received good educations in the liberal arts, found employment in various cities, and worked closely with diverse segments of society, including nobility, city councils, clergy, craftsmen, musicians, educators, parishioners, and students.

As early as the 1520s, Lutheran worship encouraged well-trained instrumentalists, singers, and composers to enrich the sharing of the gospel. Describing the relationship between the goodness of the gospel and the gift of music, Luther wrote in one of his last tracts:

3.2 Statue of Johann Sebastian Bach in Leipzig. Photo by Martin Lohrmann. Used by permission.

> The Book of Psalms is a sweet and delightful song because it sings and proclaims [*predigt*, preaches] the Messiah even when a person does not sing the notes but merely recites and pronounces the words. And yet the music, or the notes, which are a wonderful creation and gift of God, help materially in this, especially when the people sing along and reverently participate.[6]

Trained as a cantor to share this preaching of Christ through music, Bach both learned and taught the theology of Lutheran Orthodoxy. Compositions like his *Magnificat* and *St. Matthew's Passion* demonstrate his ability to match musical form, lyrical expression, and spiritual depth. In this, he built upon the rigorous work of previous generations of musicians including Heinrich Schütz, Dietrich Buxtehude, and family friend Johann Pachelbel.

Bach was already an accomplished composer, director, and court musician when he was hired as cantor of the St. Thomas

Church in Leipzig in 1723. In addition to musical expertise, Bach's employment included a requirement to help provide Orthodox Lutheran religious instruction in the parish school. To this end, he was examined and approved by the Leipzig superintendent and by a theology professor who had not approved a different candidate the previous year due to theological deficiencies.[7] The library of books that Bach collected during his lifetime testifies to his religious convictions: "He had many volumes of sermons, Bible commentaries, studies of the Council of Trent, the Augsburg Confession, the Lord's Supper, and Baptism, as well as devotional writings. He owned two different collected editions of Luther's works, an additional volume of his Psalm commentaries, two editions of the *Hauspostille* [Luther's sermon commentaries], and a copy of the *Tischreden* [Table Talk]."[8] Bach also frequently arranged early Lutheran hymns—including works by Luther, Philipp Nicolai, and Paul Gerhardt—as individual works or for inclusion in his larger compositions.

In the worship services of the time, musical and choral pieces often introduced the reading of the gospel and followed the sermon. Blending Christian poetry with Baroque musical styles, cantatas had become a common feature of Lutheran worship in the seventeenth century. In Leipzig, Bach sought to compose cantatas for each Sunday and festival of the church year, except for the penitential seasons of Advent and Lent. Each cantata was about twenty minutes long. At his most prolific, Bach wrote an average of one cantata per week from the summer of 1724 to the spring of 1725; he eventually composed four or five years' worth of cantatas, over two hundred separate works.[9]

Bach was admired in his own time, both in Germany and across Europe. In addition to his work as a church composer, he was often commissioned to write and perform music for the nobility. His famous *Brandenburg Concertos* were dedicated to Margrave Christian Ludwig of Brandenburg-Schwedt. Later in life, Bach also met King Frederick the Great (Frederick II) of Prussia, for whom he improvised a new composition on the spot, which was later expanded and published as *Musical Offering*.[10] Already shortly after his death, he was compared to the English scientist Isaac Newton. As biographer Christoph Wolff wrote:

> After Bach, music was no longer the same. A paradigm shift had taken place and gradually took hold, comparable to what happened in philosophy (which included mathematics and physics) as a result of Newton's work . . . it appears utterly appropriate to see Bach's musical advances in the light of Newton's philosophical achievements. The two men reached pinnacles of a very different kind, but they lived, thought, and worked in the same intellectual climate of scientific discovery and empirical testing of fundamental principles.[11]

As with other important thinkers and works of art, lifetimes can be spent exploring Bach's rich musical and theological legacy. Unlike other profound pieces of theology and philosophy, however, modern audiences can enjoy Bach's work by practicing an instrument, singing in worship, going to a concert, or simply pressing "Play."

1726: Popular Piety and Power Politics in Sweden

Some governments of Lutheran Europe—for instance, Brandenburg-Prussia and the kingdom of Denmark—gave early institutional support to the Pietist movement led by Philipp Jakob Spener and August Hermann Francke. Other territories like Hamburg and Saxony proved quite hostile to the movement. The kingdom of Sweden became another officially unfriendly place for Pietists with the passage of the **Conventicles Act** of 1726, which made unauthorized devotional meetings illegal. Given this level of hostility from the established church, a study of early Swedish Pietism helps explore issues of popular spirituality, political power, and ongoing church reform.

Despite pressure from both church and state officials, Pietist gatherings were taking place in Sweden's cities in the early 1700s, largely due to the efforts of laypeople who were committed to small-group prayer and Bible study. While more radically anti-institutional Pietist communities later developed in Sweden and elsewhere, many of these early Swedish Pietists remained dedicated to their local parishes, even if they criticized the official church's perceived lack of spiritual rigor.[12] One Pietist leader in Stockholm was an accountant named Elias Wolker, who kept in correspondence with Pastor Francke in Halle. Wolker was typical of the "churchly" Pietists in Stockholm who "were primarily lower government officials and merchants."[13] Rather than sever ties between church and state, Pietists like Wolker followed Spener's lead and sought spiritual renewal within existing institutional structures.

Martin Luther's role in spiritual reform also proved controversial for Swedes of the time. To support its decrees and methods, church officials could invoke Luther's support of state-regulated communities of faith. Pietists, however, could just as easily point to Luther's critiques of out-of-touch religious leaders who merely went through the motions of Christian faith. When challenged about his lack of ordination, for instance, Wolker viewed his nonordained status as a spiritual gift in contrast to the dryness of the pastors around him. Wolker also encouraged his daughter and other women to speak and lead in the conventicles, because he believed that the Holy Spirit puts no limits on quality biblical reflection.[14]

This grassroots push for spiritual reform received further support when Swedish prisoners of war returned from Siberia. What were Swedish Pietists doing in Siberia? At the height of its power, the kingdom of Sweden had fought a coalition of states including Russia, Denmark, and Saxony for regional dominance. A turning point in this Great Northern War was the 1709 Battle of Poltava (a city in present-day Ukraine), where the forces of Czar Peter the Great defeated the Swedish army, sent King Charles XII into exile, and imprisoned many soldiers. Thousands of Swedish and Finnish soldiers became prisoners of war in Tobolsk, Siberia. In the prison camps they gathered in Pietist-influenced worshipping communities and had access to writings by Arndt, Spener, and Francke.[15] Returning to Sweden a decade later and enjoying widespread civic support, many of these soldiers continued to advocate for church reform along the model of the Halle Pietism that had sustained them in captivity.

Unfortunately for these lay leaders, the Conventicles Act of 1726 suppressed this moderate blending of Pietism and the institutional church. Rather than concede a little and take small steps toward internal reform, the institutional church—supported by the state—pursued a policy of strict anti-Pietist Lutheran Orthodoxy. Increasingly restrictive censorship laws were passed, especially in opposition to the rising influence of Moravians in the 1730s. Forced further underground, Swedish Pietism took a more radical turn after this, although "churchly" Pietist exceptions like Pastor Henric Schartau continued to give voice to the more moderate position.[16]

As Ann Öhrberg has shown, instead of minimizing dissent and building popular support for the state-sponsored Lutheran Orthodox Church of Sweden, these attempts to control people's spirituality had the opposite effect of creating a more determined and resourceful resistance.[17] In contrast, some Lutheran Orthodox communities had addressed the spiritual concerns of the people through good preaching or the arts. For example, Dr. Mayer—the champion of Lutheran Orthodoxy during the opera controversy—had been Hamburg's most popular preacher and served a working-class parish. Orthodox support of musicians like Telemann and artistic endeavors like the theater gave people in Hamburg outlets for creativity. Similarly, in the Lutheran Orthodox city of Leipzig, church and civic leaders sought out and supported the musical ministry and artistic contributions of J. S. Bach. The contrasting example of early Swedish Pietism shows that when the dominant church did not provide meaningful opportunities to deepen faith and spirituality, people looked for it elsewhere, even at the risk of political, religious, or social marginalization.

December 1733: Ordination of First Indian Lutheran Pastor

Tradition holds that the apostle Thomas brought the Christian faith to India. Documentary and archival evidence indeed reveals the presence of Christians in India already in the first centuries of the church.[18] Without the political need to agree with the Council of Chalcedon called by the Roman Empire in the fifth century, Christians in India identified with either the Church of the East—a Syrian and Persian church—or the Syriac Orthodox Church. These eastern Christians agreed with the churches of the Roman Empire regarding the Trinity but maintained different interpretations of the relationship between the human and the divine natures in Christ.

Hundreds of years later, the Venetian explorer Marco Polo described visiting the shrine of St. Thomas the Apostle in his travels through India during the later 1200s and shared stories of the local Christians there.[19] The arrival of Portuguese colonists in the 1500s, however, badly damaged those ancient communities and their records, including a "widespread destruction of Syriac [Indian Christian] writings ordered by the Roman Catholic Synod of Diamper in 1599."[20] Despite this destruction from Western Christians who viewed them as heretics, Indian Christianity has continued to exist as a respected minority presence in southern Asia.

Lutheranism first arrived in India with the establishment of the Danish East India Company in Tranquebar (now Tharangambari in southeastern India) in the early 1700s. Although the first pastors were only supposed to lead worship among the Danish colonists, two young men from the Pietist institutions in Halle named Bartholomäus Ziegenbalg and Heinrich Plütschau were ordained in Copenhagen and sent to share the gospel with the local people. Beginning in 1707, they became acquainted with the surrounding culture, preached, established churches and schools, and produced Tamil translations of the New Testament, Luther's catechisms, and Spener's catechism. This was "the first organized, state-sponsored Lutheran/Protestant cross-cultural mission" in the world, which later inspired the work of other missionaries.[21]

In many ways remarkable for their willingness to learn local customs and worldviews, early Lutheran missionaries also perpetuated the Eurocentric views and behaviors of the colonizers. Europeans consistently treated other people, religions, customs, and worldviews as "less than." For instance, two early local converts to the Tranquebar mission named Aaron and Diago served as **catechists**. Looking to expand the church in areas where Europeans were not permitted, the missionaries ordained Aaron as a pastor in December 1733. Despite the successful preaching of Aaron and others, the salaries and living conditions of European pastors were consistently higher than those of their Indian colleagues.[22] Colonial church officials kept Europeans in positions of power and suppressed indigenous leadership. For his part, however, Ziegenbalg was so committed to social justice for the local people "that he even got himself thrown into prison for four months by vexing Danish colonial officials with his vociferous defense of a Tamil woman who was being unjustly treated."[23] He is also remembered positively for bringing the printing press to that part of India.

3.3 Bartholomäus Ziegenbalg monument in Tranquebar, Tamil Nadu, South India. Photo by Michael Gäbler.

Themes of translation, education, and evangelism in cross-cultural contexts continued to appear as Lutheranism and other branches of European Christianity spread around the world. The examples of Ziegenbalg, Plütschau, and Aaron reveal the strengths, limits, and failures that could happen when European Lutherans—frequently in connection with colonizing powers—attempted to share the gospel in new contexts. Lutheran missions made their most positive impacts when they respected local cultures, worldviews, and needs; however, evangelizing efforts could become tremendously damaging when they imposed prejudice, used violence, and failed to respect the God-given worth of all people. Even Ziegenbalg's strong personal commitment to social justice was not enough to overturn or challenge the powerful forces of colonization and prejudice.

Over three hundred years after that first Protestant missionary venture, there are more than three million Lutherans in India. In many cases, Lutheran Christianity has offered an alternative to the caste system in India, especially among the Dalit class and other marginalized peoples.[24] As with other Lutherans across Asia, Indian Lutherans offer strong gifts in education, public health, and interfaith dialogue.

Because Christianity is a minority religion in almost all of Asia, J. Paul Rajashekar has suggested that "Lutherans in Asia and elsewhere need to rethink the adequacy and relevance of inherited Lutheran theology on issues of religious plurality today. Christian experiences of living in the midst of other faiths in Asia have a lot to contribute in the development of a theology of religions that is faithful to Christian convictions and, at the same time, respectful of other faiths."[25] Giving critical attention to what it means to "inherit" European theologies, Indian Lutherans have brought unique insights to the experience of belonging to a minority religious group in majority non-Christian settings. This offers an important corrective to the situation of many church communities in Europe and North America, where Christians have often taken cultural dominance for granted, not reflecting on the impact that their religious views might have on the lives of others.

March 12, 1734: Lutheran Refugees from Salzburg Arrive in Georgia

Lutherans and Catholics had lived together in the area around Salzburg, Austria, since the early Reformation. However, one Reformation Day—October 31, 1731—a Catholic prince archbishop decided he no longer wanted Protestants in his lands. His cruel and unrealistic command that Protestants leave within eight days violated the terms of the Peace of Westphalia and launched an international refugee crisis. Eventually yielding to pressure to give the refugees a little extra time, the prince archbishop did not force the Salzburg Lutherans to leave until the following year, at which time approximately twenty thousand people went into exile.

Several Protestant lands worked together to resettle the refugees. Historian Wolfgang Splitter has shown that Jewish communities in Germany generously supported the resettlement of these refugees, as well.[26] The majority of the Salzburgers were welcomed into East Prussia; others settled in the Netherlands, adding to the minority Lutheran population there. Through the cooperation of the Pietist institutions in Halle and the London-based Society for Promoting Christian Knowledge, another group of Salzburgers was given the chance to emigrate to the new English colony of Georgia. The first refugees arrived in March 1734. Over time, they came to settle an area about twenty-five miles northwest of Savannah.[27] They named their community Ebenezer, a Hebrew name meaning "stone of help" (1 Sam 7:12).

Led by two pastors, Johann Martin Boltzius and Israel Christian Gronau, the community encountered many new challenges, most notably the institution of slavery in the American colonies. Initially chartered as a non-slaveholding colony, Georgia legalized slavery in 1751 due to the perceived need to compete economically with neighboring South Carolina. The Salzburgers had arrived in Georgia very much opposed to slavery for moral reasons. Even so, they expressed prejudice against enslaved Africans early after their arrival.[28] Some community members started to leave Ebenezer in order to own slaves in South Carolina. With increasing external pressure to allow slavery, Pastor Boltzius and the community also came to accept and practice slave ownership.

3.4 Statue of Johann Boltzius in Ebenezer, Georgia. Wikivisually.

As Jeff Johnson described in *Black Christians: The Untold Lutheran Story*, the Salzburgers developed a harmful and ineffective model for engaging the black people around them. Their initial moral objection to slavery was already undermined by a paternalistic attitude about enslaved Africans and their presumedly inferior culture. Even when white Lutherans started to baptize enslaved Africans in the colony, these racist assumptions kept the

Salzburg community from getting to know the people, their needs, or their culture deeply, and resulted instead in trying to turn new converts into German Lutherans, confusing the gospel of Christ with a single cultural expression.

To the detriment of their own flourishing, these prejudices prevented the Ebenezer colony from developing a strong evangelical identity or network. Although Ebenezer remained an important center of North American Lutheranism during the 1700s, pastoral conflicts after Boltzius's death in 1765 and increasing communal fragmentation came to a head around the time of the American Revolution. By the end of the century, little remained of the settlement.[29]

The experience of the Ebenezer community shows both strengths and weaknesses of Lutheran migration. The story of Lutheran refugees connected the experience of the Salzburgers with other victims of religious intolerance around the world; it included inspiring acts of international and interfaith relief efforts. This can be a powerful example of standing with the oppressed and sharing humanitarian aid. More negatively, the new members of the Ebenezer colony quickly succumbed to social forces that betrayed their early antislavery morals, especially under the perceived threat of falling behind economically. Similarly, European Christian prejudice kept the Salzburgers from seeing enslaved Africans as fully human and prevented them from extending the gospel of Jesus Christ effectively.[30] As seen previously in the examples of New Sweden and Tranquebar, India, other models for evangelization were indeed possible. Such mixed legacies as those of the Ebenezer settlement are very much worth learning from and wrestling with.

1739: Zinzendorf Visits the West Indies

Count Nicholas Ludwig von Zinzendorf (1700–1760) is a wildcard in Lutheran history, sometimes admired and sometimes condemned, both in his own time and over the centuries. The constant presence of controversy around him is perhaps not surprising for someone who had Philipp Jakob Spener as his godfather. Educated in Halle and Wittenberg, the young nobleman embraced Pietism and had a strong sense of Christian unity and spirituality. Ordained in the

Lutheran church, he was eventually expelled from the ministry by the Saxon government for religious nonconformity. His passion for evangelism and church unity in North America at once provided positive models for gospel witness with non-European communities and hastened the development of separate denominational identities among American Protestants.[31]

In his early twenties, Zinzendorf used his wealth to protect a persecuted Moravian community by allowing them to settle at his estate in Herrnhut, near today's German-Czech border. The Moravians had their roots in the reform movement started by Jan Hus a century before Martin Luther's *95 Theses*. Not covered by the protections of the Peace of Westphalia, the Moravians were under the same kind of political pressure as the Salzburg Lutherans described above. With his zeal for Christian unity and a sharing the Moravians' commitment to personal piety, Zinzendorf welcomed this refugee community and later encouraged their emigration to North America.

Zinzendorf's interest in sharing the gospel among indigenous and enslaved peoples came alive when he attended the coronation of Danish king Christian VI in 1731. By this time, Denmark had asserted itself as a colonial power over Norway, Iceland, and Greenland and had established the Danish East India Company in South Asia and the Danish West India and Guinea Company in the Caribbean. At the coronation, Zinzendorf met baptized Inuits from Greenland and a baptized enslaved African named Anton Ulrich from the island of St. Thomas. Rather than viewing Christian baptism and chattel slavery as a theological, spiritual, and humanitarian contradiction, "the possession of a baptized slave was a unique status symbol for the aristocracy."[32] Mission work among the Inuits in

3.5 Portrait of Nicholas Ludwig von Zinzendorf. Wikimedia Commons.

Greenland had recently started through the independent efforts of Lutheran pastor Hans Poulsen Egede and his wife Gertrud Rask, who learned the local language and lived among the people.[33]

In 1666, the Danes had established one of the first Lutheran churches in the Americas on St. Thomas in the Virgin Islands. After decades of segregation, the first recorded baptism of an enslaved African by Lutherans in the Danish West Indies occurred in 1712. Anton Ulrich was among these early people to be baptized on St. Thomas. According to Jeff Johnson:

> Anton was very much concerned about the spiritual poverty that existed in the Danish West Indies among the slaves. During the festivities that accompanied the coronation, Anton met and talked with Count Nicolai Louis von Zinzendorf . . . [who] was so impressed with Anton's story that he took Anton to Germany to repeat it for the Moravians. As a result of Anton's efforts, the Moravians launched their first foreign mission. It was in the Danish West Indies in 1732.[34]

Having already begun to support evangelization efforts in India, the Pietist-friendly Danish monarchy of the time also lent its support to Zinzendorf and his Moravian friends going to the Caribbean.

Although Lutheran churches had already existed in the Danish West Indies for decades, they only served the white colonists. The baptism of enslaved people, which was slow to occur, was eventually justified through the condescending lens of saving lost souls rather than an affirmation of spiritual and interpersonal equality. Church services and Bible readings only occurred in Danish and not in the Dutch Creole spoken by most of the local population. As seen in the Ebenezer colony in Georgia, evangelization in such a setting meant not only conversion to faith in Christ but to European culture, as well.

The Moravians sent to the Caribbean by Zinzendorf, however, came with a different approach. Rather than imposing European languages and customs, they went out to the people and ministered in Dutch Creole. As Johnson put it, "Almost from the very beginning, the Moravians had considerable success in winning slaves for the Moravian Church. By contrast, you could count the converts to Lutheranism on two hands."[35] It took the Lutherans decades to put similar evangelical methods into practice. Once they did, however, their efforts bore great fruit. Lutheran churches in the Virgin Islands thrived. A century later, black Lutherans in the Virgin Islands planted congregations for Caribbean émigrés in New York City and supported the careers of Sister Emma Francis of Transfiguration Lutheran in the Bronx and Pastor Daniel Wiseman of Redeemer Lutheran in Washington, DC.[36]

In contrast to the model of converting Afro-Caribbean people into European Lutheran Christians, this model of sharing the gospel by valuing local languages and customs later helped Lutheran churches take root in the former Dutch colonies of Suriname and Guyana on the northern coast of South America. In each of these cases, Lutheran churches that originally existed to support the white colonists started to grow when they became open to the customs and leadership of the local nonwhite population. Such cooperative strategies had long been supported by Zinzendorf, who "instructed missionaries to respect other cultures and preach in the language of the people rather than forcing European languages and culture on them."[37]

After his banishment from Saxony, Zinzendorf himself visited the Moravian missions in the Caribbean (1739) and in Pennsylvania (1741–43), where he hoped to unite German Protestants in Pennsylvania into a single church. This plan ran into difficulty almost immediately, as it neglected the attachment many people continued to have for their unique confessional and spiritual heritages. The arrival of Henry Muhlenberg—sent by church authorities in Halle and London in response to requests from Lutherans around Philadelphia—eventually halted Zinzendorf's plan, as we will discuss below.

In his lifetime, Zinzendorf gained both numerous supporters and energetic opposition. His support for an **accompaniment** model of evangelization remains a powerful positive example, along with his commitment to Christian unity. His strong personality and unique views of Christian faith and life, however, both inspired and repelled, leaving a fascinating legacy of cooperation and conflict.

August 1748: Ministerium of Pennsylvania Founded

With training from the Pietist institutions in Halle, Henry Muhlenberg (1711–1787) hoped to serve as a missionary in India. Instead, he became the answer to a request from the other side of the world. Three congregations in colonial Pennsylvania had written to Halle, asking church leaders to send them a pastor. Agreeing to this call, Muhlenberg spent time with court chaplain Frederick Ziegenhagen in London before visiting Lutheran communities in Ebenezer, Georgia, and Charleston, South Carolina. Taking another boat north, Muhlenberg arrived in Philadelphia on November 25, 1742. Over the next forty-five years, he would help the Lutheran church take root, grow, and spread in North America.

Whether as refugees or colonists, Lutherans came to the mid-Atlantic region of what is now the United States already in the mid-1600s. Descendants of the Swedes and Finns who had settled in New Sweden remained in the Delaware Valley, even after the Swedish colony had been ceded to the Dutch and then the English. Dutch Lutherans had arrived in and around New Amsterdam before it became New York in those same decades. German Lutherans came to the Hudson River Valley in the early 1700s; they were refugees fleeing war and poverty in their homeland of the Palatinate along the Rhine River. So many Palatine Germans sought refuge in London in those years that the English government resettled thousands of them to New York. Large numbers of these refugees later followed the Susquehanna River into Pennsylvania. Another influx of Lutherans arrived when the Quaker founder of Pennsylvania, William Penn, invited first Mennonites and then Germans of all religious background to migrate to his new colony.

The three Lutheran congregations that Muhlenberg would serve for the rest of his life included one church in Philadelphia and two in the countryside towns of New Hanover and Trappe (also called Providence). These congregations were founded by German Lutheran laypeople who wanted to live out their faith in the way it had been handed on to them. While they could easily meet for prayer, hymn-singing, Christian education, and devotions without a pastor, they had a hard time finding trained pastors to provide greater organization and sacramental ministry. A German

Lutheran named Justus Falckner had been ordained by Swedish Lutherans near Philadelphia in 1703; he served congregations around the Hudson River until he died twenty years later.[38] Pastor William Berkenmeyer—a native of Lüneburg, Germany—was then called to the Dutch congregations in New York and New Jersey, but his authoritarian style of leadership got in the way of effective attempts to bring Lutherans together.[39] A further challenge faced by Berkenmeyer and others was the prevalence of itinerant preachers who claimed to be pastors in order to make money by preaching and administering sacraments but who actually had no training for ministry. Such imposters could be hard to remove once they had established themselves in a community.

Muhlenberg encountered this problem as soon as he arrived in Philadelphia in late 1742. A man named Valentin Kraft had recently presented himself to the three congregations as the answer to their call, although he had no papers to prove it. Just before Muhlenberg's arrival, Kraft claimed the authority to organize the churches and ordain new candidates for ministry. He had also been working with Count Zinzendorf, who was then in Pennsylvania assisting the Moravian Brethren and attempting to unite Protestants in North America. When confronted with Zinzendorf and Kraft's claims for leadership, Muhlenberg showed the congregations his letter of call from Pastor Ziegenhagen in London, his diploma from the University of Göttingen, and his certificate of ordination from Leipzig.[40] At a dramatic meeting with Count Zinzendorf at the end of the year, Muhlenberg asserted himself as the only person with the legal right and proper qualifications to answer the call of the congregations.[41] In cooperation with the church **deacons**, the nearby Swedish Lutherans, and the mayor of Philadelphia, Muhlenberg eventually succeeded in claiming his call and working with the local congregations.

This early experience informed Muhlenberg's leadership in several ways. First, Muhlenberg valued the public accountability for ministry described in article 14 of the *Augsburg Confession*: "Concerning church order they teach that no one should teach publicly in the church or administer the sacraments unless properly called."[42] More than a bureaucratic hoop or hierarchical control mechanism, a proper call provides church leaders and congregations with mutual

3.6 Statue of Peter Muhlenberg (see pp. 121–22). Photo by Martin Lohrmann. Used with permission.

accountability to the gospel and the community. Muhlenberg's conflict with Zinzendorf revolved around this call to preach and teach the gospel in ways that were publicly accountable to the wider church and local congregations.

Next, Muhlenberg valued effective congregational policies. Already in his first months in Pennsylvania (as well as several times later), Muhlenberg watched church conflicts turn into civil lawsuits. Frequently involved in these heated arguments and debates, he learned the importance of developing functional processes, keeping good receipts and records, and providing transparent leadership. Not afraid to consult with civic authorities to keep the peace, Muhlenberg knew that clear policies help keep a church focused on Christ and sharing the gospel, amid the many competing interests that can overtake the life of a congregation.

Muhlenberg further recognized that church life in Pennsylvania was drastically different than in Europe, where religious policies were made and enforced by the local government. Surrounded by people with diverse beliefs—including the freedom not to belong to a church—membership in a congregation in America was entirely voluntary. What it meant to be Lutheran was also open to interpretation. No longer attached to state church orders but grafted into William Penn's "noble experiment" of religious tolerance in Pennsylvania, Lutherans learned to live with neighbors who held different or no religious commitments. This diversity invited Lutherans to share positive reasons why their faith mattered to them and why congregations should want to continue to live into the gospel witness of a specific tradition like the one set forth in the *Augsburg Confession*.

3.7 Old Trappe Church, where Muhlenberg preached. Wikimedia Commons.

Bringing these concerns together, Muhlenberg led efforts to establish the Ministerium of Pennsylvania, the first Lutheran church body in the Americas. After previous discussions between Muhlenberg, Berkenmeyer, and Swedish pastors to create a single church structure faltered, Muhlenberg and two other pastors from Halle met in Germantown (now in northwest Philadelphia) in August 1748, where they examined and ordained a candidate for ministry. With twenty-four laypersons representing ten congregations, the new Ministerium then adopted a common worship service, dedicated a church building in Germantown, and agreed to meet again the next year in Lancaster, Pennsylvania.[43]

Because Lutheran liturgies varied across Germany, the Ministerium's original liturgy drew from a variety of sources, including the English service used by Pastor Ziegenhagen in London. In its early decades, the Ministerium examined and approved candidates for ministry, developed church constitutions, resolved disputes between congregations and pastors, and expanded to include churches in New York, New Jersey, Maryland, Virginia, and Ohio. Eventually, the impracticality of meeting across such wide distances led to the formation of new church bodies in those places.

As the "Mother **Synod**," the Ministerium of Pennsylvania held a central role in efforts to connect Lutherans across the United States. Such connections grew increasingly tenuous in the 1800s, as Lutherans not only reckoned with geographical distance but also with differences in theology, language, worship, and what it meant for new generations of immigrants and refugees to become American. In 1820, several statewide synods of early American Lutherans joined in a loose federation known as the General Synod, which partially met its founders' goals of Lutheran unity even as it struggled to bridge all the regional, cultural, and theological distances that could arise between Lutherans of the time. Indeed, the same kinds of questions about context, culture, and theology that arose in the 1700s and 1800s continue to provide challenges and opportunities for Lutherans in North America into the present day.

As early as a 1745 report to his mentors—Ziegenhagen in London and Gottfried Hermann Francke in Halle—Muhlenberg's motto for ministry was *ecclesia plantanda*: planting the church.[44] As a missionary to Pennsylvania, Muhlenberg did not view Lutheranism as a matter of ethnic or cultural identity. Rather than a personal chaplain sent to Germans alone, Muhlenberg saw himself as a Christian preacher of the gospel called to serve diverse communities as needed. He, his colleagues, and Lutheran parishioners were surrounded by fellow immigrants who were Mennonite, Reformed, and Catholic. They nurtured positive relationships with groups including Anglicans, Presbyterians, Quakers, and the Swedish Lutherans. Muhlenberg himself was in correspondence with influential colonial leaders like Benjamin Franklin and enjoyed the friendship of preachers of the "First Great Awakening" like George Whitefield and Gilbert Tenant, who occasionally preached in the German Lutheran church in Philadelphia.

The missionary zeal of the Ministerium, however, had its limits. In the 1600s and 1700s, Lutheran pastors like Falckner and Muhlenberg occasionally baptized free and enslaved Africans and described them as church members. Racial prejudice, though, kept German or Swedish Lutherans from greater efforts to include non-Europeans and from challenging the institution of slavery in colonial America. Like the Ebenezer colony in Georgia, they largely accepted assumptions about European superiority and existing social systems. Because Germans were encouraged to settle what was then the western frontier of Pennsylvania, their interactions with Native American peoples were mostly defined not by the gospel of universal love and mercy in Jesus Christ but by the conflicts of colonialism.

Such realities became part of how the Ministerium of Pennsylvania would do its church planting. As a motto, *ecclesia plantanda* balanced an appreciation for Lutheran roots with an awareness that the church would grow differently in new soil. However, white Lutherans in North America were not aware of how much the soil would shape the church: adapting to new languages and laws is one thing; accepting a world in which conquest and enslavement of non-European peoples were normal and acceptable is another. White Lutherans in the United States put down roots in racist soil in ways that have deeply shaped their proclamation of Christ's gospel.

Amid such complexities, Muhlenberg and the Ministerium wrestled with questions of how to adapt to the new North American context. They sought to work well with other Christians while retaining specific Lutheran teachings like justification by faith alone. They respected congregational autonomy while nurturing participation in and appreciation for membership in larger church bodies like synods. And they built new institutions for the sake of effective parish ministries, social services, and evangelical outreach. Able to preach in German, Dutch, and English, Muhlenberg modeled a willingness to build bridges and connect communities. Further, by emphasizing a ministerium—an assembly of pastoral and congregational leaders—rather than his own personal authority, Muhlenberg helped plant a church that could outlive him and thrive in a new context.

December 1784: Kant Publishes Essay on "What Is Enlightenment?"

In an essay on the question "What is Enlightenment?," Prussian philosopher Immanuel Kant (1724–1804) expressed the goals of the Enlightenment movement with the words *sapere aude*: dare to know.[45] Dedicated to education, freedom, and reason, the Enlightenment dramatically reshaped politics, art, science, and religion on both sides of the North Atlantic. Inspiring to some, these calls for liberation also met with criticism and skepticism from leaders of church and state who held different visions of religious truth and social order.

In many ways, Enlightenment themes of personal and social freedom had direct roots in the Reformation and Martin Luther's "love and zeal for the truth." In France, for instance, Reformation-era divisions between French Protestants (called Huguenots) and Roman Catholics had led to years of riots, massacres, and assassinations. In the St. Bartholomew's Day massacre of 1572, thousands of Protestants were murdered in Paris. In 1598, the Edict of Nantes gave Protestants some new legal protections and rights, although these were often at risk, especially during the Thirty Years' War. Later in the century, the Huguenots were sent into exile with the 1685 Edict of Fontainebleau; hundreds of thousands of French Protestants took refuge in other lands, including England, Prussia, and North America.

The combination of absolute monarchy and strict Roman Catholicism in France led thinkers like Voltaire (1694–1778) to envy the policies of religious tolerance that had developed in England and the Netherlands in the seventeenth century. In his *Letters concerning the English Nation* (1733), Voltaire wrote, "If one religion only were allowed in England, the government would very possibly become arbitrary; if there were but two, the people would cut one another's throats; but as there are such a multitude, they all live happy and in peace."[46] Protestant models of religious liberty and scientific inquiry inspired French philosophers to pursue similar goals.

Whether Protestant or Catholic, church officials were often distrustful of the Enlightenment willingness to question authority and traditional Christian teachings, sometimes with good reason. An example of the novel religious views held by Enlightenment thinkers appears in the work of American statesman Thomas Jefferson, who modified the New Testament to match his rationalist ideals: he "twice prepared private abridgments of the Gospels for his own use, cutting out those stories and sayings he held to be unseemly."[47] Believing that religion best served rational morals and public order, Jefferson preferred a New Testament without miracles, resurrections, or other acts of divine intervention.

More publicly than Jefferson's personal emendations to the Bible, Kant's *Religion within the Limits of Reason Alone* (first published in 1793) challenged typical defenses of religion. He asserted that religion is not necessary for morality, is often coercively attached to secular authority and law enforcement, and—as a branch of knowledge—needs to be accountable to rational methods and common standards for establishing truth. He held that well-grounded Bible study, for example, must include evidence-based study of original languages and historical contexts.[48] Kant also distinguished between true, ideal religion and the Lutheran, Reformed, and Catholic churches that had arisen from specific historical situations.[49] Because Kant reasoned that true religion should be neither coercive nor limited to one historical context, he challenged the rights of churches to claim that they possessed unique insights into divine truth.

These critiques led both to new constructive developments in theology and to strong reactions against rationalist approaches to religion. The Enlightenment's emphasis on proper method, for instance, contributed to increasingly detailed study of biblical texts, archeology, and ancient cultures—hallmarks of modern **liberal theology**, which holds both philosophical and religious commitments to liberation. Today's fields of comparative religion, biblical studies, and human rights owe much to Enlightenment concerns for social ethics, attention to cultural differences, and accountable use of theological methods. At the same time, the Enlightenment raised often unhelpful distinctions between head and heart, truth and faith, objective truth and subjective belief. These distinctions have sometimes led people to think that they need to pick a side—science or religion, reason or faith, tradition or innovation, the community or the individual—rather than integrate these important parts of human life more cohesively.

In contrast to such dualisms, thinkers like Johann Georg Hamann (1730–1788) proposed alternatives to the strict rationalism of the time. Hamann recognized that human reason is deeply mysterious, which means that reason itself belongs to deep questions of what it means to live and think as complex beings.[50] This willingness to engage divine and human realities through faith led Hamann to a renewed appreciation of foundational sources of meaning and reflection like the Bible and Luther's *Small Catechism*. He valued these traditional texts not as alternatives to reason but as a way to give reason a place within God's mysterious and wondrous creation.[51]

In the following century, Hamann's nuanced approach to faith and reason was shared by the Danish philosopher Søren Kierkegaard (1813–1855), who explored the tensions and ambiguities that exist within even the most rational inquiries. In his conclusion to a work on Christ as the prototype of Christian life—as a Lord to be followed rather than merely observed from a distance, Kierkegaard challenged both the religious and rationalist self-satisfaction of his time.

> No, the *prototype* must be advanced in order at least to procure some respect for Christianity, to make somewhat distinguishable what it means to be a Christian, to get Christianity moved out of the realm of scientific scholarship and doubt and nonsense (objective) and into the realm of the subjective, where it belongs just as surely as the Savior of the world, our Lord Jesus Christ, did not bring any doctrine into the world and never delivered lectures, but as the *prototype* required *imitation*, yet by his *reconciliation* expels, if possible, all anxiety from a person's soul.[52]

Aware of the benefits of scientific and ethical rigor, thinkers like Hamann and Kierkegaard emphasized the centrality of the mysterious, personal, and faith-filled sides of life, providing an important corrective to the "pure reason" that often accompanied Enlightenment ideals.

With the benefit of hindsight, we can also see that while the Enlightenment encouraged positive developments in democratic governance and scientific investigation, it left some clearly harmful legacies. By assuming that their methods alone were true and rational, Enlightenment thinkers created exactly what they hoped to overcome: new subjective categories of truth and goodness that could be used to divide and enslave. Enlightenment ideals about progress and reason, for instance, were invoked to justify slavery, scientific racism, and the inferiority of non-European peoples.[53] More than a regional preference or cultural variation, Eurocentrism was rationalized into an ideology of white supremacy that used the full weight of European colonialism to impose itself around the world. Scientific observation was similarly used by many to justify a view of the natural world and human life as commodities to be bought, sold, traded, used, and thrown away. Nevertheless, as flawed and misused as many of these ideas have been, Enlightenment notions of human rights, the responsible use of reason, and attention to the workings of the natural world remain worthy goals for global citizens of the twenty-first century.

3.8 Søren Kierkegaard, sketched by his cousin, ca. 1840. Wikimedia Commons.

April 1, 1789: First Speaker of the US House of Representatives

Henry and Anna Maria (Mary) Muhlenberg's children provide good early examples of how Lutherans participated in American public life, especially as seen in the election of their son Frederick Muhlenberg as the first Speaker of the United States House of Representatives in 1789.[54] Both parents set strong examples for public engagement. Mary was the granddaughter and daughter of German Palatine refugees who fled war and disease to settle in New York and later Pennsylvania. Mary's father, Conrad Weiser

Jr., became a prominent leader among Pennsylvania Germans and held key roles in colonial Pennsylvania, serving for many years as Pennsylvania's emissary to the Six Nations of the Iroquois Confederacy.[55] Through her father's influence, Mary was trilingual: she could speak English, German, and a dialect of the local indigenous people. She also inherited land that she kept separate from her joint accounts with Henry, which was an essential financial asset after Henry died in 1787.[56] As people strongly defined by recent experiences of immigration, Henry and Mary Muhlenberg became important community figures.

It was not always clear to the Muhlenberg parents that their children might value public service in the same way. In letters to his patrons in London and Halle, Henry asked in 1759 if his two oldest boys, Johann Peter and Friedrich August (commonly known as Peter and Frederick, respectively) might study in Halle. Candidly expressing his thoughts on parenting, education, and morality in colonial Pennsylvania, Muhlenberg worried that this setting was having a negative effect on their character:

> Once more, I need to submit, most humbly, a request concerning my children, and to ask you for your fatherly advice and response. My eldest boy, Johann Peter, is now in his thirteenth year. He has a lively temperament and the potential to become either a harmful or a useful member of human society, depending on his education. The second, Friedrich August, is in his tenth year. He is calm, steady and sincere. The English academies and schools here teach too little about practical Christianity. In fact, they do not even teach respectable discipline. I do not have the means to have them raised by other people. I am rarely at home and cannot raise them myself, nor can their mother. It is likely that they will grow wild, to their own detriment and as an offense to my office . . .
>
> I do not care whether they become farmers or craftsmen, just as long as they are raised in accordance with the purpose of Creation and salvation and will be saved as Christians. I would consider it a special act of mercy if they would be allowed to stay in the blessed orphanage [in Halle] or remain under a Christian regimen for just a few years, so

3.9 Frederick Muhlenberg was elected the first Speaker of the United States House of Representatives. Wikimedia Commons.

> that they could be grounded and confirmed in true Christianity and then apprenticed to honest craftsmen . . . I would rather save my poor mite than spend it on food, if only my two children could enjoy care for their temporal and eternal well-being for a while there.[57]

In 1763, Peter, Frederick, and younger brother Gotthilf Heinrich (Henry) left Philadelphia to study in Europe. As feared, Peter followed his wilder side: he abandoned his apprenticeship to become a soldier and returned to America some time later with a British regiment; Frederick and Henry studied in Halle, but returned in 1770 without having made much of an impression on their European patrons.[58]

Despite these inauspicious beginnings, all three brothers soon became capable pastors. Frederick and Henry were ordained by the Ministerium of Pennsylvania, while Peter went to London to receive an Anglican ordination in order to serve an English-speaking Lutheran congregation in Woodstock, Virginia. Two of their sisters, Margaret (Peggy) and Eve, married other Lutheran pastors,

Johann Christopher Kunze and Christopher Schulze, respectively. Another sister, Maria Catherine, married a sheriff; youngest sister Maria Salome (Sally) married Matthias Richards, a businessman and judge. Heavily involved in the life of public ministry, the Muhlenberg family members continued to take a variety of leadership roles in their communities.

Such public service moved beyond church work when the American Revolutionary War broke out in 1775. Peter enlisted in early 1776. He became a brigadier general in the Continental Army and fought in the Battle of Valley Forge—not far from his parents' home—and later the decisive Battle of Yorktown. Frederick was also called into public service after being nominated and elected to the Continental Congress in 1779.[59]

From this point onward, the two oldest Muhlenbergs left ministry and worked in state and national politics. At the opening meeting of Congress that took place under the new constitution in 1789, Frederick Muhlenberg was elected the nation's first Speaker of the House of Representatives. Peter also served in that first Congress as a representative from Pennsylvania. Brother Henry continued in the ministry, serving Holy Trinity Lutheran Church in Lancaster, Pennsylvania, while becoming an accomplished botanist and the first president of Franklin College (now Franklin and Marshall College).[60]

Due to gender norms of the time, we do not know much about the gifts that the Muhlenberg sisters might have had for public service, but—as mentioned above—each one's husband held leadership roles in church and society. Peggy's husband, Pastor Kunze, went on to work as a professor at the University of Pennsylvania in Philadelphia and Columbia College in New York City.[61] Christopher and Eve (Muhlenberg) Schulze's son John served two terms as the governor of Pennsylvania in the 1820s.[62]

Although we are only able to guess at the impacts the sisters had on their communities, the Muhlenbergs nevertheless provide many examples of how religious faith and social engagement worked together to serve the common good. This notable family included the first Speaker of the House and a Revolutionary War general. But beyond such public figures lay the even more important legacy of people of faith honoring God by serving their communities in everyday life. This included the women in the family, whose work and witness certainly affected people far beyond the scant public record that we have today. In short, the Muhlenberg family presents a unique glimpse of the strong legacy of public leadership that Lutherans have shown in the past and can continue to provide.

1799: Schleiermacher's *On Religion: Speeches to Its Cultured Despisers*

Although not a Lutheran, Friedrich Schleiermacher (1768–1834) must be counted among the influential shapers of modern Lutheranism. Born into a family of German Reformed pastors, Schleiermacher combined diverse traits of his place and time. He shared his parents' love of Moravian Pietism, pursued the Enlightenment thinking of Immanuel Kant, and took part in the budding romantic movement inspired by the German writer Johann Wolfgang von Goethe. From Pietism, Schleiermacher developed an appreciation for religious feeling, spiritual transcendence, and Christian unity. Although critical of the Enlightenment's dispassionate quest for objective truth, Schleiermacher nevertheless believed that it was entirely reasonable to explore and describe religious mysteries. This embrace of reason and mystery would later push his simultaneously rational and romantic programs to promote Christian unity and theological education, especially as experienced in the increasingly powerful kingdom of Brandenburg-Prussia.

These diverse impulses came together in Schleiermacher's first great work, *On Religion: Speeches to Its Cultured Despisers*, published in 1799. As the title indicates, Schleiermacher was addressing a new modern audience: people for whom traditional forms of religion seemed old-fashioned or irrelevant but who still desired the kind of spiritual knowledge and experience that philosophy alone could not provide. The adjective "cultured" in the title also reveals a widening gap between the religious experiences of different social classes in the early years of the Industrial Revolution.

The book certainly reached its intended "cultured" audience, as Schleiermacher soon became the Reformed chaplain for the royal court in Berlin. In the ruling family, the centuries-long split between Lutheran and Reformed Protestants carried political and personal dimensions. The political challenge revolved around the fact that the rulers of Brandenburg-Prussia had long been Reformed, even though most of the population was Lutheran. On the personal side of this religious situation, King Friedrich Wilhelm III was happily married to Louise of Mecklenburg, who was a committed Lutheran. According to the laws and customs of the time, this meant that the king and queen could not take Holy Communion together.[63] Having already proposed in 1808 that the Lutheran and Reformed churches in Prussia should come together, Schleiermacher would prove instrumental in the merger that became known as the Prussian Union, which indeed began with a joint communion service held in the royal court. More will be said about this in the next chapter.

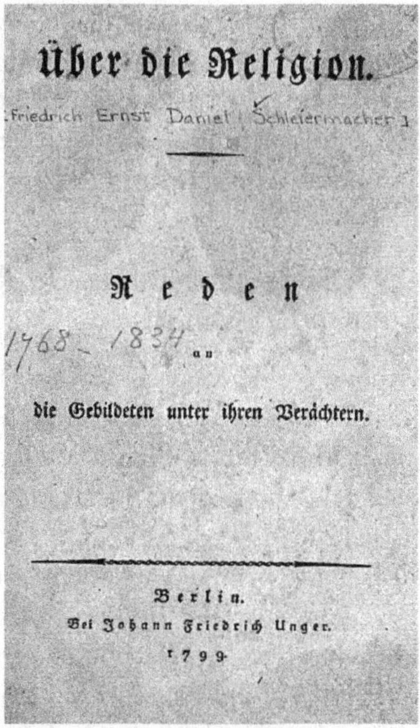

3.10 The cover of the first edition of *On Religion* by Friedrich Schleiermacher. Wikimedia Commons.

In addition to gaining the support of the Prussian king, Schleiermacher's proposals brought him to the attention of Wilhelm von Humboldt, who had been put in charge of organizing a new university in Berlin (now known as Humboldt University). In his design of the school's theology program, Schleiermacher wanted to base theology and ministry on sound rational and practical principles. He thereby created the distinctions between subjects like biblical studies, systematic theology, church history, and practical theology that have remained typical of theological education ever since.[64] Within the decade, Schleiermacher's model transformed religious education not only in European universities but also in the American theological schools of Harvard, Yale, and Princeton.[65]

Schleiermacher's influence on theological education was immediate and profound. Separating disciplines like biblical studies, theology, history, and pastoral care allowed for immense depth and growth in each field. This nineteenth-century attention to specific fields of study pushed subjects like archeology, linguistics, anthropology, and church history to new levels of investigation of primary sources and theoretical analysis. For these reasons, Schleiermacher is often associated with the rise of modern **liberal theology** that seeks to integrate faith and reason.

On the other hand, Schleiermacher's rational approach to theological study brought some new challenges to the church. Clergy became religious specialists, making them more likely than before to be disconnected from the lives and experiences of their parishioners. Also, studying the Bible "scientifically" accelerated debates between **modernism** and **fundamentalism** that have divided many religious communities ever since. Should the books of the Bible be read as a collection of ancient stories, whose meaning depends on original context? Or should the Bible be received as divine revelation whose truths exist beyond human scrutiny or rational inquiry? While many people of good faith have continued to seek mediating positions, the use of modern scientific methods in biblical studies launched controversies that remain pressing for global Christianity.

Although intended to overcome the confessional differences that arose in early-modern Europe, detailed historical research of controversial periods like the Reformation came to be used not only to understand or transcend past divisions but to intensify them. More careful study of thinkers like Luther, Calvin, or texts from the Council of Trent could be used either to enrich mutual understanding across denominations or to entrench existing Christian divisions. Perhaps most telling of all, the creation of a discipline called "practical theology" artificially separated Christian thought from practice, as thinkers like Kierkegaard were quick to point out.[66]

With such lasting influences over theology, education, and church organization, Schleiermacher left a challenging and mixed legacy. This should not be surprising, since his own life combined many complex traits: he was a rationalist and a romantic, an idealist and a pragmatist. Beloved by many as one of the most popular preachers and writers of his time, Schleiermacher also had access to the most powerful people, as he advised royalty and launched influential reforms of higher education. He was a Reformed pastor with a Pietist background who united two major Protestant traditions, thereby creating a third: namely, the Union churches of the nineteenth century and beyond. Through such a life and legacy, Schleiermacher impacted Lutheran church life like few others.

Early 1800s: Women's Leadership in the Hauge Movement

As a young man working on his father's farm in southeastern Norway, Hans Nielson Hauge (1771–1824) had a vision in which the Lord told him, "You shall confess My name before the people; exhort them to repent and seek Me while I may be found and call upon Me while I am near; and touch their hearts that they may turn from darkness to light."[67] Hauge interpreted this as a call to witness to Christ far and wide.

The problem, of course, was that Norway (then ruled by Denmark) already had an official Lutheran church and numerous ordained preachers. Instead of being warmly welcomed, Hauge's calls for renewal were frequently perceived as public disturbances, attacks on the clergy, and religious fanaticism. In his travels, he was often brought before the local police for violating Denmark's 1741 law against conventicles, those private religious meetings inspired by Spener's Pietist reforms. Hauge was also regularly charged with vagrancy, which meant simply being somewhere other than his home.

When faced with such accusations, Hauge would reply that he was merely living out the faith of the Bible as taught by Luther's *Small Catechism*, which in its explanation to the commandment about honoring the Sabbath, says, "We are to fear and love God, so that we do not despise preaching or God's word, but instead keep that word holy and gladly hear and learn it."[68] Here was a Lutheran gladly hearing, learning, and sharing God's word. Other influences on Hauge's faith similarly fit well with a traditional Lutheran upbringing: regular worship attendance, confirmation instruction as a teen, reading the Bible at home, a love of Lutheran hymns, and familiarity with Lutheran devotional resources like the catechism of Danish bishop Erik Pontoppidan and the devotional writings of Johann Arndt.

In many ways typical of Lutheran spiritual life, Hauge's efforts to share his faith were exceptional in his eagerness to work outside established channels of church authority and social norms. His ministry truly challenged many aspects of the status quo in the church and across socioeconomic lines. For his efforts, Hauge endured three beatings and several brushes with the law, before being imprisoned from 1804 to 1813. For most of those years, he was held without charges and without a sentence. When his trial finally came in 1812, Hauge felt that his good name was upheld, as rumors that he may have embezzled funds from his supporters came to naught. Over the next year, he served out the rest of a prison term imposed for violating the Conventicles Act and for unlicensed preaching.[69] Always an enterprising individual, Hauge went on to manage a successful farm and other profitable financial ventures, including a publishing business. Indeed, much of Hauge's success—and troubles—stemmed from his deep concern for the economic well-being of Norwegian peasants. As Mark Granquist has noted, Hauge "sponsored many pragmatic activities among the peasantry for their own economic advancement. And although Hauge himself was not politically active, the Haugean movement symbolized a new wave of Norwegian nationalism and of the self-determination of the Norwegian peasantry."[70]

Women's leadership and preaching played important, if also controversial, early roles in Hauge's movement. According to scholar Inger Furseth, "Hauge was convinced that if a woman had the gift to speak, she should use it."[71] Aware of New Testament prohibitions against women speaking to the assembly, Hauge interpreted such words as referring to public disruptions; he contrasted those verses with the promise of Pentecost that the Holy Spirit would come to both men and women (Joel 3 and Acts 2).[72]

Hauge publicly recognized and honored the leadership of women. In an 1817 collection of autobiographies that Hauge gathered from members of the movement, seven of the eighteen entries were by women.[73] One such early leader was Sara Oust, who worked as an itinerant lay preacher in the early 1800s. Furseth tells the following story about Oust's faith and courage in the face of physical and verbal assault:

> Sara was not afraid to speak against the clerical authorities. Once she visited a Haugean couple in Tynset, where she held devotions. The local clergyman, Andreas Fuglsang Dircks (1763–1828) heard of the meeting and came storming in the door. Facing this woman who acted in ways women were not allowed, he tore a book out of Sara's hand, threw it into the fireplace and slapped her face, while he yelled at her. Sara remained quiet. Dircks calmed down and got ready to leave. Suddenly, he stopped and asked her: "You probably think I have done you wrong and acted poorly against you?" "Oh, no," Sara answered, "it won't hurt me because I believe that everything the Lord lets happen to me will serve me well; but it seems to me that the Dean has acted poorly against himself." At this response, Dircks began to cry, turned around and left.[74]

In addition to being a stirring example of faith and courage, this story reveals the structural power frequently employed against women who challenged the authorities: they endured verbal attacks, physical aggression, attempts to revise the story about men's bad behavior, and legal barriers to public leadership.

During Hauge's lifetime, women provided leadership by preaching, organizing devotional meetings (the often-illegal conventicles), inviting new people and family members into the movement, and providing financial support. As the movement became more established, however, "later changes reducing the role of women were related to the need for further mobilization and legitimacy from the state-church clergy."[75] As will be discussed in the discussion of women's ordination (chapter 5), this fits a common pattern of Christian accommodation to cultural expectations and structures when it comes to gender roles. Even so, Hauge's movement provided an effective way for Lutheran women to hold public leadership and to impact the wider society of the time.

Throughout his career, Hauge supported a Christianity that was for all people. He traveled extensively across Denmark and Norway. He visited Sámi and Finnish people in the far north, preached in Norway's remotest villages, and established Pietist religious communities in the cities. A testimonial by Bishop Brun about Hauge's general harmlessness expressed the disdain that many in leadership held for him; it also gives a taste of the social prejudices experienced in a colonial Norwegian church ruled from Denmark. In a written statement composed for Hauge's trial, Bishop Brun noted: "Nearly all of Hauge's followers are miserable weaklings, the least influential part of the commonwealth, and therefore could never become dangerous to the state."[76] Unlike many church and political officials, Hauge saw the holiness, worthiness, and capabilities of the common people around him.

Questions

1. What were some examples of Lutherans sharing the gospel in culturally and personally meaningful ways in these years? What ways of sharing the gospel might be inspiring in your community today? What ways of sharing the gospel might be keeping you or others from hearing or experiencing the gospel effectively?
2. As European Lutherans encountered an increasingly diverse world in the eighteenth century, what did being Lutheran mean to them? What did it mean to someone like Zinzendorf, or to someone like Muhlenberg? What does it mean to you to claim a religious identity while also respecting the views of others?
3. What are some of the ways that the colonialism of the 1700s has impacted your life and the communities you belong to now?
4. In the Age of Enlightenment, people wrestled with the relationships between faith and reason. Others, like Hamann and (later) Kierkegaard, valued both critical thinking and a sense of mystery that sees the limits of reason. How do you balance reason and mystery?
5. Did you know that the first Speaker of the US House of Representatives had previously served as a Lutheran pastor? Did you know that his brother was a Revolutionary War general? How might these stories inform your views of how and why Lutherans get involved in politics?
6. Thinkers such as Kant and Schleiermacher pushed Christians to view the Bible as something that could be beneficially

studied using the tools of reason. From the Reformation to the present, most Lutherans have appreciated the importance of using reason in various ways to understand and learn from the Bible. What does it mean to you that the Bible can be read with the lenses of both faith and reason?

7. Hauge brought the spiritual and social concerns of Pietism to Norwegian peasants. To do that, he had to work outside of the existing church structures, resulting in a lengthy imprisonment. What do you think about working for church renewal both within and outside of established church structures?

CHAPTER FOUR

1817–1917

Introduction to Lutheranism in Its Fourth Century

The 1800s were a time of many contradictions: industrial and scientific progress created new crises of poverty, pollution, and disease; enlightened, democratic movements often came with warfare, slavery, and oppression; new intellectual fields of thought inspired romantic or fundamentalist reactions.

The political scene of nineteenth-century Europe was defined by the Napoleonic Wars of the early 1800s, which ended with the Congress of Vienna in 1814. Instead of supporting modern democratic principles, this gathering of European leaders sought a "balance of power" by strengthening monarchies like Prussia, Austria-Hungary, and Russia. This high-level attempt to suppress democratic reform led to a fragile and frequently broken peace, while popular demands for economic and political rights only continued to increase. This "balance of power" between competing European empires also created the complicated web of alliances and rivalries that erupted into the violence of World War I in 1914.

Amid the dramatic rises of both imperial power and popular reform, the year 1848 stands out for its numerous uprisings, which included a revolution in Hungary and the end of serfdom in Austria, the start of the Second Republic in France, a new constitution in

Denmark, demonstrations in Germany and Poland, and the publication of *The Communist Manifesto* in London by Karl Marx and Friedrich Engels. Later in the 1800s, the modern nations of Germany and Italy were created not by democratic agreement but by the diplomatic and military conquests of a single regional power—the kingdoms of Prussia and Sardinia, respectively—over their neighbors. In nineteenth-century Europe, the old and still strong power of the aristocracy often came into violent conflict with the confident and organized efforts of the general population to have more of a say in the policies that determined their lives.

At the same time, European nations and the United States of America expanded their efforts to colonize other parts of the world. The British Empire ruled colonies across Africa, the Middle East, India, China, Southeast Asia, the South Pacific, Canada, and the Caribbean. France had colonies in northern and western Africa, Madagascar, and Southeast Asia; Belgium colonized the Congo region of West Africa; and Germany had colonies in southwestern and eastern Africa. After the Spanish-American War of 1898, the United States gained the territories of Cuba, Puerto Rico, the Philippines, and Guam; the Panama Canal Zone became a US territory through military involvement in a local uprising against Colombia in the early 1900s.

Defined as "the exploitation of a people by another nation for the purposes of gain," **colonialism** combined economic injustice, enslavement, and race-based discrimination as it devastated many communities around the world.[1] Lives and cultures were lost and destroyed through these heavily one-sided interactions. At the same time, colonialism also changed the people who came to conquer. The words of historian Justo González about Spanish and Portuguese colonialism in the Americas also apply to the worldwide colonial projects of the nineteenth century: "The impact of the Iberian enterprise in the Western Hemisphere was so momentous—and so tragic—that it tends to eclipse the parallel impact of the Western Hemisphere on Europe and the events taking place there."[2] Such impacts on European Christians included every aspect of life. Socially, colonialism changed the colonizers' diets and lifestyles, as Europeans encountered new foods like corn, potatoes, tomatoes, and chocolate, and new drugs like opium and tobacco. Politically, colonialism highlighted the vast inequalities and inhumane situations that arose from plantation economies and slavery, even if white people often responded by supporting, ignoring, or minimizing those conditions. Religiously, Europeans came into closer contact with global religions and had to confront their own histories of Christian division in overseas mission fields. Among the most lasting changes to global Christianity would be the rise of indigenous churches that would reframe the Christian gospel in ways that make sense for local contexts and communities.

Many contemporary aspects of global Lutheranism have direct roots in the nineteenth century. This includes positive legacies like contextual gospel preaching and negative impacts like the spread and implementation of racist and colonialist structures. For these reasons, the history described in this chapter can often be challenging and painful. The power of Luther's first Reformation thesis on lifelong repentance provides a good way to approach these stories: being honest about sin, confessing wrongs, and turning to God in humility, faith, and love are essential to the health of our relationships with God and one another.

October 31, 1817: The Prussian Union Begins

As the three-hundredth anniversary of the Reformation approached, King Friedrich Wilhelm III of Brandenburg-Prussia declared that he would be holding a joint communion service in which both his Lutheran and Reformed court chaplains would take part. With the intention of uniting his subjects into a single Protestant church, he explained,

4.1 King Friedrich Wilhelm III. Wikimedia Commons.

> Such a truly religious union of the two churches, separated only by external differences, is in conformity with the major purpose of Christianity; it suits the spirit of Protestantism, it promotes an ecclesiastical sense, it is salutary for domestic piety; and it is the source of many useful improvements in churches and schools that have often been obstructed by the differentiation between the confessions.[3]

Several factors contributed to the king's optimism. First, King Friedrich Wilhelm admired the rational approach to religion advocated by thinkers like Kant and Schleiermacher. He shared the Enlightenment's view that Protestant divisions stemmed from the misunderstandings of the past or the accidents of history more than essential religious differences. Second, the nobility of Brandenburg-Prussia had embraced Reformed Protestantism already in the early 1600s. At that time, the opposition to that conversion which arose from both pastors and the common people—including public riots—led to a unique situation: in a time of *cuius regio, eius religio* (whose region, their religion), the Reformed faith of the nobility did not match that of their Lutheran subjects.[4] This made Brandenburg-Prussia more primed for intra-Protestant cooperation than other places. Finally, in the wake of the Napoleonic Wars, Prussia was becoming a European superpower. By the early 1800s it controlled lands that had been legally established as Lutheran, Catholic, and Reformed territories for centuries. From an administrative point of view, a reorganization of Protestantism in Prussia was now both possible and desirable.[5]

4.2 Pastor Claus Harms. Wikimedia Commons.

Despite its apparent advantages, the king's top-down decree brought strong negative reactions. One famous response came from Pastor Claus Harms of Kiel. For that same three-hundredth anniversary, Harms published Luther's original *95 Theses* and added ninety-five new points of his own. His first thesis started where Luther's did, then went on to identify an overemphasis on human reason as the trouble afflicting the church of the day: "When our Lord Jesus Christ said 'Repent!,' he willed that people be shaped by his teaching; but he did not shape his teaching to fit people, as one now frequently does in this divergent Zeitgeist [spirt of the times]."[6] Harms continued his attack on rationalism by writing in thesis 32: "The so-called 'rational religion' comes either from reason or religion, or it is bereft of both."[7] Finally, summarizing the conviction that Lutheranism contained all the best of both Protestantism and Roman Catholicism, Harms concluded:

> 92. The Evangelical Catholic (the author means the Roman Catholic) Church is a glorious church. It knows and grows itself especially in the sacraments.
> 93. The Evangelical Reformed Church is a glorious church. It knows and grows itself especially in the Word of God.
> 94. More glorious than both is the Evangelical Lutheran Church. It knows and grows itself in both the sacraments and the Word of God.
> 95. The other two are growing into this, though without human assistance. But the way of the godless will perish, as David says (Ps. 1:6).[8]

This conclusion about Lutheran superiority stands in stark contrast to King Friedrich Wilhelm's proposed union. Where the king emphasized unity and a common Christian faith, Harms emphasized confessional difference and the unique strengths of the Lutheran tradition. These two divergent views expressed in 1817 shaped the debates to come.

In the following decades, the Prussian Union gradually gained legal status, along with a good measure of popular support. For a time, the Evangelical Church in Royal Prussian Lands was the single largest Protestant church in the world. Nevertheless, dissatisfaction with the Prussian Union also inspired many Christians to revisit their Reformation roots, which strengthened rather than weakened denominational identities. Among Reformed Protestants, scholars Heinrich Heppe and Philip Schaff began to revisit the writings of John Calvin and reclaim the Reformed confessional tradition for themselves. Lutherans, too, began to go back to their own sources, as scholars assembled new editions of Reformation writings, notably the Weimar Edition of Luther's Works (published in more than one hundred volumes between 1883 and 1993) and the *Corpus Reformatorum*, a collection of writings by sixteenth-century theologians that began with twenty-eight volumes of Melanchthon's works (published between 1834 and 1860).

Globally, the conflicts surrounding the Prussian Union made many lasting impacts on Lutheranism. First, the Prussian Union created a new form of established religion in Germany: Protestant churches might now be Reformed, Lutheran, or Union. Instead of reducing difference, the union increased religious diversity. Second, people who emigrated from German lands in the nineteenth century often identified more strongly with the older traditions than previous generations had. In some cases, Lutherans even departed from their homelands for the express purpose of leaving the Prussian Union behind. This was true, for instance, of the first Lutherans to emigrate to South Australia and of the founders of the Buffalo Synod and the Missouri Synod in the United States. Third, although it left a complicated and even divisive legacy, the Prussian Union created positive institutional models for ecumenical cooperation by focusing on what unites Christians rather than what divides them.

1832: Ordination of Jehu Jones

African Americans were among the earliest members of Lutheran churches in North America, including the Dutch Lutheran congregations in New Amsterdam and the Hudson River Valley in the 1660s. One of the first people baptized and admitted to membership by Pastor Jacob Fabricius when he came to New Amsterdam in 1669 was "a black male who took the name Emmanuel. Emmanuel is said to have had a Caucasian wife and two children."[9] Similarly, Pastor Justus Falckner listed a free black couple, Aree van Guinea and his wife Jora, as members of the New York City congregation. Aree and Jora later moved to New Jersey, where Aree donated the land for the first Lutheran church building in the Raritan Valley.[10] Henry

4.3 Plaque commemorating Jehu Jones, the first African American pastor ordained in the United States. Photo by Claire Burkat, used by permission.

Muhlenberg and other German and Swedish pastors also occasionally recorded the baptisms of free and enslaved people of African descent, some of whom were also listed as church members.[11]

Racism—the combination of racial prejudice and social power—frequently kept Lutherans of European descent from embracing the leadership of black people. An example of the convoluted approach to evangelism among African Americans is the one developed by Lutherans in Charleston, South Carolina. Under Pastor John Bachman, a native New Yorker who served at St. John's Lutheran Church in Charleston from 1818 to 1869, Lutheran churches launched ministries among free and enslaved black people. Although a single congregation on paper, St. John's effectively became two churches: one white and one black. By the 1840s, there were about 200 black worshippers and 150 black students in St. John's Sunday school.[12]

In the early 1830s, the African American members of St. John's decided to support missionary work in Liberia, which was then a private colonial settlement in West Africa for freed slaves run by the American Colonization Society.[13] To this end, the church members raised money and supported three candidates for ministry: Daniel Payne, Jehu Jones Jr., and Boston J. Drayton. Although he never joined the Lutheran church, Payne's contact with Pastor Bachman led him to study at the Lutheran seminary in Gettysburg, Pennsylvania. Payne went on to serve as a bishop in the African Methodist Episcopal Church and to found Wilberforce University in Ohio.[14]

Unlike Daniel Payne, Jehu Jones Jr. was a son of the congregation and a dedicated Lutheran. His father had bought his own freedom in 1798 and was a leader in the congregation and the Charleston community.[15] Because state law did not allow black men to be ordained for ministry in South Carolina, Jehu Jones Jr. traveled to New York City to meet church officials and receive ordination. He was ordained there on October 24, 1832 at St. Matthew's Lutheran Church. Upon returning to Charleston, however, he was arrested for violating another state law, which said that free blacks who left South Carolina and returned could be enslaved.[16] This turn of events radically altered Jones's life and ministry.

Instead of going to Liberia, Jones immediately had to flee north. Already in his forties, he was now an exile from his home and far removed from the plans that he and the congregation had made. After discussing his situation with pastors in New York and Pennsylvania, Jones decided to start an African American Lutheran congregation in Philadelphia. He visited families, held worship services, and bought a church property using mostly his own money. In this way, and with little assistance from white leaders, he and his parishioners started St. Paul's Evangelical Lutheran Church. Despite an energetic ministry, fundraising tours, and the support of colleagues like Pastor Bachman, the lack of consistent institutional support and the loan he personally owed on the church building created a strain. The congregation lost the building in 1839, though it seems that Pastor Jones continued to lead African American Lutheran ministries in and around Philadelphia through the 1840s.

The life and witness of Rev. Jehu Jones Jr. shows many of the effects of racism in North American Lutheranism. In the South, leaders like Pastor Bachman supported sharing the gospel with African Americans, but their simultaneous defense of slavery and white supremacy undermined their gospel witness and effectiveness. A racist law preventing a free black man from returning to Charleston kept Jones from making his intended trip to Liberia. Learning from this episode, Bachman himself later ordained Boston J. Drayton in 1845. Drayton then went to Liberia, where he worked first as a missionary and later as a political official and judge.[17]

In the North, Pastor Jones's ministry suffered from a persistent lack of institutional support and broken promises. Jones later recalled a conversation with Pastor Mayer of Philadelphia, who wondered why Jones would want to remain Lutheran: Why not join the Methodists, Baptists, or Presbyterians? In the words of biographers Karl E. Johnson Jr. and Joseph A. Romeo, Jones responded that he "was not to be deterred; he was Lutheran, he countered, and could be nothing but Lutheran. His nine children had been baptized at the Lutheran church in Charleston, and he and his wife had been members of the church for many years. Mayer must have realized that Jones would not be put off, and the two finally came to an understanding."[18]

Rev. Jones's experience of obstacles about who is Lutheran and what Lutheran leadership looks like was not unique. As seen in the witness of Pietists like Hans Nielsen Hauge and Sara Oust, Lutherans in previous centuries had also fought over questions of leadership, inclusion, and social justice. In the setting of American slavery, however, these already-challenging issues bore the additional weight of racist ideas and dehumanizing social structures, which Pastor Jones personally worked under and fought against. His life and work show both a legacy of hardship due to intolerance and the possibilities that can arise through people of courageous faith.

October 1836: Deaconess Community Founded in Kaiserswerth

The Industrial Revolution that began in the later 1700s brought radical change to European and North American social life. People left rural homes and lifestyles to work in factories, which transformed both city and countryside populations. Low wages, poor housing, industrial pollution, disease, and the absence of labor laws created harsh living conditions for many. To address these desperate social conditions, many Christian ministries and groups arose, including the international Sunday school movement, associations for young men and women like the YMCA and YWCA, and group homes for men, women, and children living without shelter.

Seeing the tremendous need around them, Pastor Theodor Fliedner and his wife Frederike organized new social services for their poor, recently industrialized community of Kaiserswerth, Germany. Having already started to address local challenges concerning health care and prison rehabilitation, Fliedner visited the reforming prison ministries of the English Quaker Elizabeth Fry in London and of Mennonite deaconesses in Amsterdam. Wanting to provide both social ministries and leadership training, Pastor Fliedner started a deaconess house in Kaiserswerth in October 1836, establishing a female diaconate among Lutherans for the first time. Frederike Fliedner ran the deaconess house until her death in 1842; Theodor's second wife Karolina Bertheau then filled that role after they married the following year.[19]

4.4 Florence Nightingale, ca. 1860.
Wikimedia Commons.

Like the Francke institutions in Halle, the Kaiserswerth deaconess center came to include schools, medical centers, and an orphanage.[20] It also started to make an international impact. Florence Nightingale—the English social reformer and founder of modern nursing—visited the hospitals and schools in Kaiserswerth in 1850. She later published a glowing description of her experience in a tract titled *The Institution of Kaiserswerth on the Rhine, for the Practical Training of Deaconesses, under the Direction of the Rev. Pastor Fliedner, Embracing the Support and Care of a Hospital, Infant and Industrial Schools, and a Female Penitentiary.*[21]

Another international visitor was Rev. William Passavant (1821–1894) of Pittsburgh, Pennsylvania. Already interested in social ministry, Passavant traveled to Europe in 1846. Along with prominent American Lutherans Samuel S. Schmucker and Benjamin Kurtz, he represented the General Synod at the first meeting of the World Evangelical Alliance, which was held in London that year. After attending the assembly, Passavant toured historical sites and significant institutions in Europe, including the deaconess house in Kaiserswerth. Upon his return to Pennsylvania, he started to plan a similar institution in Pittsburgh, where a deaconess house opened in 1849 under the leadership of four Kaiserswerth women. This became the first of several Lutheran deaconess houses and hospitals in the United States, which in turn inspired the founding of many other Lutheran hospitals, orphanages, schools, and senior homes.

In Germany, the Kaiserswerth model also inspired Pastor Wilhelm Loehe to start a deaconess house in Neuendettelsau, Bavaria. Already active in foreign missions, Loehe organized a deaconess community to serve local social needs like rural poverty, elder care, care for people with disabilities, an orphanage, and safehouses for former prostitutes. Amalie Rehm oversaw the community and led the women in Neuendettelsau for nearly three decades.

Both the Kaiserswerth and Neuendettelsau houses supported and developed women's gifts in order to address pressing social needs. Although still limited by traditional expectations about women's roles in society, this new office of deaconess provided women with leadership opportunities that had not previously been available. The deaconess houses trained young women for nursing, social work, teaching, and spiritual care. Unlike Catholic nuns, these Lutheran deaconesses did not make perpetual vows, but they did live in relatively strict intentional communities. For the first several decades of this Lutheran deaconess movement, only single women could take part; they had to leave their deaconess career behind if they chose to marry. Loneliness could certainly become a challenge, especially to those women who left their homeland to work overseas.

In one such example, Deaconess Rosette Wibel left Neuendettelsau to work with Loehe's missionary colleagues on the American prairie in Iowa. She and another deaconess traveled together before separating to serve in different places, leaving Rosette very lonely. In an 1857 letter to Amalie Rehm, she described living by herself in a rented house near the church and wrote, "I also cook for myself, but it doesn't taste right to eat so alone and I am always overjoyed when I have a guest."[22] Social isolation and precarious finances were certainly factors that led the deaconesses in Iowa—including Ms. Wibel—to get married within a couple of years.

The deaconess movement also spread to Scandinavia. Elizabeth Fedde (1850–1921) was a Norwegian deaconess who responded to a request from Anna Børs—the wife of the Norwegian consul general—and others that she serve among Norwegian sailors and immigrants in New York City.[23] Arriving in 1883, she started a deaconess house and a hospital in Brooklyn, which quickly grew in size and impact. Connecting medical care with gospel witness, she told her fellow deaconesses, "You sisters are the Bible the patients read."[24] Keeping a written correspondence with pastors like William Passavant, Fedde eventually left Brooklyn to establish another deaconess house in Minneapolis. She returned to Norway in 1895, having founded several Lutheran social ministries in the United States that still exist today.

4.5 Elizabeth Fedde, ca. 1880. Wikimedia Commons.

Lutheran deaconesses have served in mission fields around the world, often with little direct oversight from male church leaders. As the Fliedners intended, these women have used their training in medicine, spiritual care, and education to minister among underserved communities. In a time when women had few opportunities for public leadership, the female diaconate offered many women a chance to receive quality educations that they could put into practice in diverse ways. While many more opportunities for women to provide public leadership exist now than before (a fact due in good part to the effective witness of the deaconesses themselves), deaconess communities continue to promote Lutheran understandings of diaconal ministry and enrich the church's witness through word and service.

1842: Lutheran Missionaries Arrive in Namibia

Africa has been an important home of Christianity since the beginning of the church: Mary and Joseph took refuge in Egypt to escape King Herod's wrath (Matthew 2), Jews from Egypt and Libya were among those gathered in Jerusalem to celebrate Pentecost when the Holy Spirit filled the apostles (Acts 2), and an Ethiopian eunuch studied the Bible with Philip the deacon and was baptized by him before continuing "on his way rejoicing" (Acts 8). Although impossible to verify, many early church traditions describe apostles like Simon the Zealot and St. Mark as having been evangelists to African lands.

In the centuries that followed, many Africans became influential church leaders. The city of Alexandria, long famous as an educational center, remained a significant source of Christian learning in the early centuries of the church, raising up such thinkers as Clement of Alexandria and Origen. Athanasius, the great defender of Trinitarian theology in the fourth century, was a black African who served as bishop of Alexandria when he was not in exile for his bold theology.[25] Early roots of Christian monasticism also grew in Africa among desert fathers and mothers like St. Anthony of the Desert, St. Moses the Black, and Amma Syncletica.

In Latin-speaking North Africa, church leaders like Tertullian, Cyprian, and Augustine of Hippo left indelible marks on Western Christianity. Augustine himself seems to have been a person of mixed ethnic heritage, with a Roman father and a Berber mother, St. Monica.[26] Although the spread of Islam across North Africa—which began in the seventh century—challenged many of these communities, Christianity continued to thrive in places like Egypt and Ethiopia, which had become one of the first Christian nations in the world when its royal family converted in the fourth century.

Modern European colonization in Africa began in the late 1400s with the arrival of the Portuguese, who began the transatlantic slave trade and established colonies in western Africa, Angola, the Cape of Good Hope, and Mozambique. Other nations like Spain, Britain, France, the Netherlands, the United States, Belgium, and Germany also joined in the colonization of African lands and the enslavement of African people.

European Christianity arrived in Africa as the occupying powers brought church officials to serve the colonists. In many cases, decades or even centuries passed before colonial white churches attempted to share the gospel with local people. Evangelization then often included Eurocentric views about cultural and religious superiority that further suppressed the full humanity of Africans. As in other parts of the world, the connection with the dehumanizing forces of colonialism meant that the spread of European Christianity in Africa carried with it the sins of racism, slavery, genocide, theft, and greed.

In addition to the establishment of churches in Africa through state-sponsored colonization, European and North American missionary societies became especially active in the 1800s. Unlike the political and economic motives of colonialism, the mission societies emphasized the salvation of souls, education, and health care. Even so, these missionary ventures often included racist cultural assumptions, intentionally or not. According to Namibian Lutheran scholar and bishop Shekutaamba Nambala, missionaries brought many good things, including their honest intentions. And yet, he wrote,

> The most unfortunate thing about even the best missionaries is that most of them never took the pains to relinquish their European conceptions of all Africans as godless and savage. They failed to see that the people of Africa were religious and had a sincere reverence of worship. Neither was civilization introduced by the European missionaries or colonists. Africa had its own civilization before they came. . . . The Europeans felt free to treat the Africans in any way they pleased simply because "Africans were not Christians."[27]

The first German missionaries to Namibia in southeastern Africa arrived in 1805, but those initial efforts did not last. In 1842, however, the Rhineland Missionary Society began work that took root. Lutheran missionaries from Finland came to the area in 1869. They worked separately from the Germans, mostly among the Ovambo people.

In Namibia, the German missionaries of the later 1800s prepared the way for a devastating colonization of the area. At first supportive of increased political and military presence from Germany, some missionaries eventually saw that the local people's disdain for occupation hindered the spread of the gospel. Nevertheless, mass baptisms started to accompany military victories over tribes like the Herero and Nama. This further blurred the lines between colonization and Christianity, especially since these military victories were sometimes achieved through genocidal tactics, which reduced "the Herero nation from 80,000 to 20,000, and the Nama nation from 20,000 to 9,700."[28] These German atrocities in Namibia are among the first occurrences of modern genocide. In the years that followed, the German Lutheran churches were slow to integrate, with one Lutheran denomination remaining an exclusively white church through the 1980s. In contrast, the Finnish mission work in Ovamboland supported more indigenous leadership and cultural integration, with the first Ovambo pastor ordained in 1925.[29]

4.6 Doll, dressed in the traditional clothes of the Herero people of Namibia, from the Namibia Archives of Wartburg Theological Seminary.
Photo by Martin Lohrmann, used with permission.

While Namibia's population now has one of the highest percentages of Lutherans in the world, its journey to political and religious independence was long and painful. After German colonization, Namibia became part of South Africa and its apartheid regime, a system of government built upon racism. With roots in a Pietist tradition that taught noninvolvement in political issues, many Lutheran churches that stemmed from the Finnish missionaries did not actively challenge apartheid. For their part, the German missionaries had tended to stress obedience to the political authorities, especially because their churches existed with the blessing of the colonial and apartheid governments.[30] As will be described more in the next chapter, Namibian Lutherans started to organize effective challenges to apartheid in the 1960s and '70s.

4.7 History of the Lutheran Church in Namibia by Shekutaamba Nambala (Lutheran Quarterly Books).

April 26, 1847: Founding of the Missouri Synod

Dissatisfied with the increasing influence of the Prussian Union on church life in Saxony, a group of Lutherans in the Dresden area sought greater religious freedom in the United States. They were led by Pastor Martin Stephan, a charismatic leader who built up a group of loyal followers opposed to rationalism and eager to practice a purer form of Lutheranism. A controversial figure in Dresden, Stephan was twice suspended for disturbing the peace and for immoral conduct; Stephan's own parish eventually brought charges of sexual misconduct against him.[31] To Stephan and his followers, however, these troubles signified the unjust persecution of a corrupt state church, from which the best hope for freedom was emigration. In November 1838, over six hundred Saxons left for New Orleans; the group then traveled up the Mississippi River to the state of Missouri. Within a few months, though, the settlers received credible reports that Stephan had been mismanaging the group funds and had sexual relationships with several women.[32]

With Stephan then cast out of the community, an existential crisis arose for these earnest Saxon Lutherans. If their leader had been a fraud, what kind of church could they be? Young pastor C. F. W. Walther (1811–1887) determined that because the church exists in the faithful proclamation of the gospel and in the evangelical use of the sacraments (as defined in *Augsburg Confession*, article 7),[33] the Saxon immigrants could consider themselves a proper Christian church and organize themselves accordingly. Stephan's abuse of his leadership position led Walther and his colleagues to develop church structures that emphasized congregational authority, so that proper pastoral calls take place when assemblies of baptized believers invest their ministers with responsibility to preach and teach the gospel. With origins in both the quest for spiritual purity in Saxony and the early experience of pastoral misconduct, questions of right doctrine and proper authority would remain key issues for this growing community. Mission work to German immigrants and a focus on local education became early strengths of the Saxons in Missouri.

Around this same time, Pastor Friedrich Wyneken—then a frontier preacher supported by the Ministerium of Pennsylvania—sent a widely published letter to European Lutherans requesting pastoral care for the many Germans then arriving in the American Midwest. His call was answered by Wilhelm Loehe of Neuendettelsau, who eventually formed partnerships with Walther, Wyneken, and their colleagues.[34] These collaborations led to the founding of a seminary in Fort Wayne, Indiana, the establishment of towns for German immigrants around Frankenmuth, Michigan, and a new German Lutheran **synod** in the Midwest, commonly called the Missouri Synod. Founded at a meeting in Chicago in 1847, the Missouri Synod started with twelve pastors—several of whom had been sent by Loehe—and sixteen congregations as charter members; Walther was elected the first president and Wyneken served as the second.[35] The church steadily grew, with baptized membership of about 728,000 by the year 1900.

Of course, the Missouri Synod was not the only group of committed Lutherans in the Midwest. Pastor J. A. A. Grabau had led a group of Lutherans out of Prussia in 1839; they settled around the Great Lakes and formed the Buffalo Synod in 1845.[36] Despite

4.8 Replica of first log cabin seminary in Missouri; Concordia Seminary, St. Louis. Photo by Martin Lohrmann.

a shared disdain for the Prussian Union and liberal theology, Grabau's belief that ordained pastors held an authority apart from the congregation conflicted with the Missouri Synod's views and experiences of the office of ministry. The two groups remained antagonists for decades.

After receiving a personal visit from Walther and Wyneken in Neuendettelsau, Pastor Loehe expressed a mediating position between Buffalo and Missouri concerning church authority. He believed that the differing views should not be divisive, based on the traditional Lutheran teaching about adiaphora. Even so, continued disagreement on this point led pastors who supported Loehe to be excommunicated from the Missouri Synod in 1853; they founded the Iowa Synod the following year.[37] Similar doctrinal debates and personality clashes continued to keep the Missouri Synod from working more closely with other American Lutherans. Over time, an association of midwestern German and Norwegian immigrant churches—including the Wisconsin Evangelical Lutheran Synod—came together as the Synodical Conference in the later 1800s, providing shared opportunities for theological dialogue and evangelical mission among these groups.

With its emphasis on education, the Missouri Synod became a leader in the parochial school movement of the 1800s, often establishing schools as part of their congregations. Members of the Missouri Synod also participated in the deaconess movement, international missionary work, women's organizations, and youth societies, usually by creating their own versions of these popular movements. As part of the Synodical Conference, the Missouri Synod nurtured vibrant—albeit still largely segregated—ministries among African Americans when black Lutherans in North Carolina and Alabama reached out for institutional support.[38]

In the twentieth century, the Missouri Synod worked with other American Lutherans in war relief efforts, refugee resettlement, chaplaincy, and social services. Globally, the Missouri Synod belongs to the **International Lutheran Council**. With membership of about two million people in the US and two Canadian provinces, the Lutheran Church—Missouri Synod (LCMS) is the second-largest Lutheran denomination in North America. Its members value their commitments to doctrine, education, and mission. Consistent with its origin as a dissent movement, the LCMS plays a leading role among Lutherans around the world who share its interpretation of the Lutheran confessional tradition.

1861–1865: Civil War, Slavery, and Abolition

While Baptists, Methodists, and Presbyterians in the United States experienced denominational splits over slavery before the American Civil War, Lutherans in the General Synod—the direct heirs of the Muhlenberg tradition—long avoided such division by addressing slavery as a political issue rather than as a theological one that would require direct church action or doctrinal stands.[39] For this reason, an institutional split between white Lutherans in the North and South did not occur until after the war began, despite many heated exchanges beforehand. The views of black Lutherans were not widely included in the church's public discussions of slavery, either in the North or the South.

As seen earlier in this book, black Lutherans in the North sometimes experienced welcome into baptism and church membership. Even then, discrimination and lack of institutional support were common. This contradictory experience of welcome and rejection had long been typical in the northern United States: Pastor William Berkenmeyer, for instance, had personally owned slaves and wrote the distinction between the spiritual freedom of baptism and the physical bondage of slavery into a 1735 church constitution.[40] As the economics of slavery shifted and northern states abolished slavery, most white Lutherans in the North remained indifferent to the plight of enslaved peoples, having largely accepted the cultural assumptions and theological rationale of white supremacy.[41] This included many prominent Lutherans agreeing with the notion that because slavery had existed in biblical times, modern chattel slavery should not be condemned as an evil in itself.

Samuel S. Schmucker—a professor at Gettysburg Seminary and longtime leader of the General Synod—modeled the moderate abolitionism of many northern Lutherans. In 1825, Schmucker married Mary Catherine Steenbergen, who belonged to a slaveholding family in Virginia where the new couple lived. The marriage brought two slaves into the household. Because Virginia law at the time made it illegal to set slaves free, Schmucker gave his "servants" their freedom when he and his family moved to Pennsylvania the following year.[42] Increasingly identifying with the abolition cause, Schmucker made his home in Gettysburg a stop on the Underground Railroad, wrote publicly against slavery, and advocated for laws that supported Pennsylvania's African American population. At the same time, Schmucker did not identify wholeheartedly with abolitionism, because he preferred a slower end to slavery and believed that groups like the Anti-Slavery Society were too radical.[43]

As mediating political solutions about how to address slavery disappeared on the national level, northern leaders in the General Synod grew bolder in their denunciations of slavery. In 1837, a small group of ministers and congregations in upstate New York formed the Franckean Synod with abolition at the core of its preaching and witness. In a *Lutheran Herald* article of 1839, they wrote,

> We, the ministers and delegates of the Franckean Evangelic Lutheran Synod, do repudiate the whole system of American slavery, as equally opposed to civil and religious liberty; as endangering the rights and liberties of the free wherever it is tolerated; as a disgrace to the government where it exists; as supporting and encouraging the most corrupt and depraved state of morals; as an offence to God; and as provoking his just indignation.[44]

At first a fringe perspective, such sentiments spread over the decades. The Pittsburgh Synod, in which William Passavant was a leading voice, stretched the fragile relationship between northern and southern Lutherans in the General Synod by aligning itself publicly against slavery in the 1850s. In 1857, a group of Pittsburgh Synod pastors found great agreement among northern Lutherans when they wrote, "We hold that slavery, as it exists in this country, wars not only against the principles of the word of God, but against some of its express and plain declarations, and is therefore sinful."[45]

4.9 Scenes from the Battlefield at Gettysburg, PA. Schmucker Hall, or the "Old Dorm," sits off in the distance on the morning of July 1, 1863. A. R. Wentz Library Archives, Gettysburg Seminary.

Pastor Bachman of St. John's Lutheran Church in Charleston, South Carolina, defended the faith and practices of congregations in the South, reminding northern Lutherans of their shared racial prejudices: "In our Northern States and Canada, [black people] are everywhere regarded as an Inferior race, and . . . are not admitted as equals by many of the laws of custom in any State. They are not invited to their tables, and a union with their daughters would be regarded as a degradation."[46] This diagnosis of the prejudices and supremacist views of white Lutherans in the North was largely accurate. As he did in many of his writings, Bachman appealed to biblical examples of slavery and maintained that the institution of slavery was of mutual benefit to masters and slaves. Bachman supported South Carolina's secession from the United States, believing that the North had succumbed to abolitionist fanaticism.

An 1862 General Synod pronouncement condemning the Confederacy and supporting the Union war effort led most of the southern synods to form a separate church body. Lamenting the war, denouncing northern abolitionism, and defending the secession of southern states, they wrote,

> It is under such circumstances, and for these reasons, we renounce them [northern Lutherans] as brethren; and it becomes us this day to make our separation from them final and complete. In taking so grave and decisive a step, we call God to witness that we are influenced neither by malice nor revenge, but by the teachings of His own Word, which require that we withdraw ourselves "from every brother that walketh disorderly," and from "men of corrupt minds and destitute of the truth," while at the same time we believe that the peace and prosperity of our Southern Church will be thereby promoted.[47]

Bachman then put forward a motion that southern Lutherans form a new General Synod of the Evangelical Lutheran Church in the Confederate States of America. It passed unanimously.

While many political and economic factors led to the American Civil War, slavery indeed formed the heart of the issue, including debates over states' rights. Aware that the lack of westward expansion of slavery would likely mean its eventual demise, southern states seceded from the Union to protect the institution of slavery. In his first inaugural address on March 4, 1861, President Abraham Lincoln made his case that one party does not have the right to nullify a contract without the consent of another, with the Constitution of the United States being the contract in question; far from being a committed abolitionist at that point, Lincoln nevertheless considered it his duty to enforce the Constitution and maintain the Union.

Responding to Lincoln's speech, Alexander Stephens, the vice president of the Confederate States of America, reaffirmed slavery and white supremacy as being the "cornerstone" of the Confederacy, which "rested upon the great truth that the negro is not equal to the white man; that slavery subordination to the superior race is his natural and normal condition. This, our new government, is the first, in the history of the world, based upon this great physical, philosophical, and moral truth."[48] As seen in the "scientific racism" of the Enlightenment and colonialism discussed earlier, Stephens's words about the "physical, philosophical, and moral truth" of white supremacy show how far racism had come to pervade not just the southern states but the entire worldviews and customs of Europeans and white Americans.

The war that followed took the lives of over half a million American soldiers and ravaged countless communities. In the North, the Battle of Gettysburg (July 1863) turned the Lutheran college and seminary there first into a battlefield and then into an infirmary. Dr. Schmucker's home was ransacked during the war; he had fled beforehand because he was told that the Confederates would be targeting him as a prominent abolitionist.[49] Henry Eyster Jacobs, who later became a distinguished historian and theologian at the Lutheran seminary in Philadelphia, was a Gettysburg native who served the wounded as a chaplain and nurse; he was among the crowd gathered for President Lincoln's reading of the Gettysburg Address later that year.

The strategy of total war pursued by Union General Philip Sheridan in the Shenandoah Valley and by General William Tecumseh Sherman across Georgia and the Carolinas left much of the South in ruins. Having fled Charleston, Pastor Bachman was beaten by Union soldiers in the countryside. As an early biographer put it, "The close of the war found him a mere wreck of his former self"; he had lost much of his estate and never fully recovered from his injuries.[50] Bachman's experience matched that of many other white people in the South, for whom the war's destruction reinforced anger about the North and the abolition of slavery instead of inspiring national reflection on the inequalities that caused the war.

After the war, the Lutheran communities that Henry Muhlenberg had helped bring together over a century earlier were divided into three main groups: the General Synod, led by Schmucker in Gettysburg; the General Synod South (later called the United Synod of the South) with a seminary in Columbia, South Carolina; and the General Council, a northern church body that was formed in 1866. The impetus for founding the General Council came from the Ministerium of Pennsylvania, whose leaders had grown dissatisfied with Schmucker's method of bringing Lutherans into the Protestant mainstream by weakening Lutheran confessional commitments. Although fascinating to consider, it remains unknown how much the issues of slavery, abolitionism, the Civil War, and the Battle of Gettysburg played in the Ministerium of Pennsylvania's 1864 decision to suspend their membership in the General Synod. These three church bodies remained separated for decades. Cooperation on a new hymnal started to bring them closer together again in the 1880s. The preparation of another hymnal in the 1910s and joint planning for the four-hundredth anniversary of the Reformation paved the way for these churches to reunite. They formed the United Lutheran Church in America in New York City in 1918, over fifty years after the end of the Civil War.

Just as it did not end racial prejudice in the nation, the Civil War did not end discrimination in American Lutheran churches. In the antebellum South, many congregations had been integrated under a master-slave model. Despite this system's inherent racial inequality, this had led to significant black participation in Lutheran churches. "By 1860, slaves and 'free persons of color' constituted almost one-quarter of the South Carolina Synod's entire membership."[51] After the war, however, white Lutheran leaders in the South "formally requested black members to form separate congregations and a separate black ecclesiastical organization, effectively putting many black people out of the Lutheran Church."[52] This led to a decline of black Lutheran churches in the South, although such communities never entirely vanished. Over time, a group of concerned black Lutheran ministers in North Carolina formed the Alpha Synod; they worked with the Missouri Synod and the Synodical Conference for institutional support.

In the North, the "myth of the Unbridgeable Chasm" suggested to white Lutherans that "the religious tradition of black people is so different from that of Euro-American Lutherans that blacks simply won't respond to the Lutheran Church."[53] The continuing arrival of new Lutheran immigrants from Europe in the later 1800s and early 1900s helped make that myth persuasive to many. However, that model erred by wrongly identifying Lutheranism with certain European ethnicities and cultures rather than with the gospel of Jesus Christ. It failed to apply either evangelical freedom or the Lutheran confessional tradition to the demonic and dehumanizing experiences of slavery and racism in meaningful ways. This faulty model of an "Unbridgeable Chasm" also gave white people in the North a theological reason to ignore discriminatory laws and segregationist policies against African Americans after the Civil War, a legacy that remains to the present day. While many black Lutherans have made deep and lasting contributions to the church, Lutherans in the United States have continued to be among the least racially integrated branches of Christianity in the country.

1866: Mission and Revival in Ethiopia and Madagascar

Two of the largest Lutheran communities in the world today are the Ethiopian Evangelical Church Mekane Yesus and the Malagasy [Madagascar] Lutheran Church. While these churches developed entirely separate from each other, they share some common history and traits. In both lands, Scandinavian Lutherans first arrived in 1866, when Swedish missionaries came to Ethiopia and Norwegians to the island of Madagascar. Unlike mission stations in other parts of the world, these missionaries were not directly tied to political colonization efforts. Instead, they focused from the beginning on preaching the gospel, supporting education, and providing medical care. Both churches grew as they encouraged local leadership, incorporated the spiritual views of the people, and practiced care for body and soul.

Lutheranism in Madagascar has its roots in the Norwegian Missionary Society (NMS), which first sent two missionaries to the central part of the island. By the later 1800s, Norwegian-American Lutherans also began to work with the NMS and expanded the mission to southern Madagascar. This ministry gained new energy among the local people in 1894 when a traditional healer named Rainisoalambo prayed for help and received an answer from the Christian God, telling him, "Cast away all your charms and idols."[54] After this conversion, Rainisoalambo started the ***Fifohazana*** (awakening) movement, emphasizing a ministry of lay preaching and the exorcism of harmful spirits led by *mpiandry* (shepherds). Training as *mpiandry* has remained foundational for ordained and lay leaders in the Malagasy Lutheran Church.[55]

With backgrounds in the spirituality and holistic concerns of Hauge's Pietism, the Norwegian missionaries encouraged this development and supported local leadership. Later spiritual revivals among

4.10 Fourth class at the seminary for pastoral education at Masinandraina, Madagascar, 1893. Wikimedia Commons.

Lutherans in Madagascar were led by a catechist named Rakotozafy Daniel (1919–1947) and Volahavana Germaine (ca. 1920–1998), who was called Nenilava (tall mother). As a young woman, Nenilava had visions of Jesus and showed gifts of healing. The missionaries began to recognize her ministry in 1953, and she considered herself to be "an evangelist within the Lutheran church."[56]

Before the end of French colonial rule in Madagascar, the Malagasy Lutheran Church became independent in 1950 and elected Rakoto Andrianarijaona as its first president. Education and medical care remain strengths of the church. Revivals and an emphasis on the spiritual gifts of all believers continue to keep Malagasy Lutheranism a central part of people's religious and social lives.

As in Madagascar, Scandinavian missionaries first came to Ethiopia in 1866. Forbidden to start Protestant missions among Ethiopian Orthodox Christians, missionaries from Sweden began to work in Eritrea among exiles and former slaves; they also reached out to the Oromo, a large ethnic group in Ethiopia that was often in conflict with the Amhara ruling class. Emphasizing gospel freedom in body and spirit, the missionaries met a young man recently freed from slavery named Onesimus Nesib. Onesimus was baptized in 1872 and began to study at the missionary school. In 1876, the missionaries sent him to Johannelund Seminary in Stockholm, where he lived for the next five years.[57] Upon his return, Nesib became a great preacher and leader for the church in Ethiopia. With the assistance of a young woman at the Mission named Aster Ganno, Nesib translated hymns, devotional works, Luther's *Small Catechism*, and eventually the entire Bible into the Oromo language.[58]

In the following decades, Lutherans continued to organize churches, schools, and hospitals in Ethiopia, especially among people who had not been Christian. In 1959, the Swedish mission and six other missionary groups merged to form the Ethiopian Evangelical Church Mekane Yesus (EECMY; Mekane Yesus means "Place of Jesus"). With about eight million members, it is now the single largest Lutheran church body in the world. Building on its early witness to the needs and cultures of local communities, EECMY focuses on ministry to the whole person, so that preaching the gospel and caring for people's health and living conditions go together.

This **holistic theology** was described and nurtured by EECMY Bishop Gudina Tumsa (1929–1979), who wrote in 1975,

> Western theology has lost the this-worldly dimension of human existence, and holistic theology is an effort to rediscover total human life. Apolitical life is not worthy of existence, uninvolvement is a denial of the goodness of creation and of the reality of incarnation. We are interested not in creating medieval monasteries, in setting up ghettoes (modern monasteries), but in being involved in the complex social life of our people as we find it daily, with full knowledge of our Christian responsibility.[59]

With emphases on serving the whole person, encouraging lay preaching and local spiritual gifts, and providing public witness to Jesus Christ, the EECMY has continued to grow in the face of major obstacles. Bishop Gudina was martyred by the dictatorial regime in 1979. His wife Tsehay Tolessa (d. 2014) was imprisoned and tortured throughout nearly all of the 1980s. In Ethiopia, as elsewhere, faithful Christians have shared the gospel at great personal risk and suffering. Carrying on the witness of bold leaders like Nenilava, Onesimus Nesib, Gudina Tumsa and Tsehay Tolessa, Lutherans in both Ethiopia and Madagascar continue to provide inspiring and effective testimony to God's work in the world.

1885: First Ordination of Batak Ministers in Indonesia

The Republic of Indonesia is the fourth-largest country in the world by population. A nation of islands, it stretches from Sumatra in the Indian Ocean to the western half of New Guinea in the South Pacific. Indonesia is home to diverse ethnic, linguistic, and religious cultures. It has a majority Muslim population, along with significant Hindu, Buddhist, Christian, and indigenous religious groups. In the era of European colonization, the Dutch East India Company controlled much of Indonesia until the company was dissolved in 1799 and the Dutch government took possession. Japanese occupation of Indonesia in World War II ended nearly 350 years of Dutch colonial rule; the end of the war led to Indonesian independence.

With a longtime Dutch Reformed presence in Indonesia, Lutherans came to the island of Sumatra in 1861 through the Rhineland Missionary Society and the arrival the following year of Pastor Ludwig Nommensen (1834–1918). Beginning his work among the Batak people as a young man, Nommensen served in Indonesia for over fifty years. Blending education, catechesis, spiritual care, medical care, and the development of an indigenous church, Nommensen completed a translation of Luther's *Small Catechism* into the Batak language in 1874 and "has justifiably become known as 'the apostle to the Bataks.'"[60] The mission church that started in the 1800s gained its autonomy in 1931 as the Huria Kristen Batak Protestan (HKBP, or Batak Christian Protestant Church).

Nommensen worked to integrate Christian teachings with Batak culture. Although European missionaries led the church in Sumatra for many decades, Batak people also provided leadership and gave the church its voice and character. As Nommensen taught to mission students later in his life, "Some missionaries do everything themselves and so the helpers learn nothing. They should give more guidance, they ought to be more forgers of weapons and sharpen the tools rather than wanting to do everything themselves."[61] Although many of the names and stories of the first Batak converts are unknown, early indigenous church leaders included Bartimaeus Panggabean, Sister Needham, and Johannes Hutapea, who was a church evangelist from his ordination in 1885 until his death in 1896.[62]

After Nommensen's death, Batak leadership continued to increase. A growing independence movement and the outbreak of World War II resulted in the election of the first Batak *ephorus* (bishop), Kasianus Sirait in 1940. He was succeeded two years later by Justin Sihombing (1890–1976), who led the church through the war years, independence, and the political instability that followed.[63] Sihombing was also the primary author of the ***Batak Confession***, a statement of faith that combines the gospel center of the *Augsburg Confession* with the Reformed influence of the Rhineland Missionary Society. Even more significantly, it incorporates the local religious context of the Batak people into its confession of faith. Based on this *Batak Confession*, the HKBP was admitted into the **Lutheran World Federation** in 1952.[64]

With over four million members, the HKBP is among the largest Lutheran churches in the world. Several other Lutheran denominations exist in Indonesia, too, as different groups developed in response to ethnicity, geography, political pressure, and theology. Women have been ordained in the HKBP since the 1980s. The authoritarian regime of General Suharto, who ruled Indonesia from 1967 to 1998, included a military takeover of the church in the 1990s that caused tremendous division.[65] Describing the situation facing Indonesians in 2008, Pastor Binsar Pakhapan of Jakarta Theological Seminary wrote, "Despite the fact that since 1998 a new era has begun, a lot of things remain as they were (i.e., strong military influence, corruption, limited transparency, and a confusing justice system). This is why accessing the past is considered a difficult task in Indonesia."[66]

Even with these major challenges, the Lutheran witness in Indonesia remains a unique testimony to the power of translating the gospel across cultures. As contemporary Indonesian Lutherans Fridz Pardamean Sihombing and Jubil Raplan Hutauruk have written: "Lutherans in the Batak land have not denied or separated Lutheranism from their own ethnic culture and tradition. In fact, they have incorporated what they have received from the West into their own system of *adat*—the wisdom and values of their ancestors."[67]

Later 1800s: Luther and Liturgical Renewal

In addition to being shaped by those around them, Lutherans have also contributed to the development of other branches of Christianity. This became clear in the worship debates and liturgical renewal that took place in the nineteenth-century, as people from a variety of perspectives turned to Luther for insight and support of their views.

As the 1800s began, Protestant interest in historical patterns of worship was at a low point. Enlightenment-era rationalism led many clergy to focus on moral teachings and human progress. Efforts like the Prussian Union to join Lutheran and Reformed churches downplayed historical uniqueness in doctrine and worship. Even so, in his classic study *The Lutheran Liturgy*, Luther Reed found that the personal attention that Prussian king Friedrich Wilhelm III gave to liturgical reform was remarkably thoughtful and constructive for the time.[68] In general, though, the Enlightenment's emphasis on reason largely shifted people's focus away from mysterious aspects of worship like prayer and the sacraments.

Pietism and **revivalism** impacted worship practices in the early 1800s, as well. Compared to the Pietist emphasis on personal faith and feelings, traditional liturgies could seem to lack spirituality, spontaneity, and sincerity. Skeptical of rituals and church structures, Pietist movements frequently included a critique of ordained ministry as a calling set apart for sacramental leadership. Whether motivated by rationalist or Pietist outlooks, therefore, many Lutheran communities of the nineteenth century held worship services without Holy Communion, focusing instead on Bible readings and moralistic sermons. The weekly celebration of Eucharist—the standard pattern of Christian worship from the early church across the centuries, including in the Lutheran Reformation—became rare among Lutherans.[69] In nineteenth-century United States, Lutheran worship was further influenced by the charismatic preaching, emotional songs, and spiritual ecstasy of the tent revivals and camp meetings that were then growing in popularity.

Such developments, however, inspired many Christians across denominational lines to pay closer attention to the worship practices of earlier times, leading to a liturgical renewal movement. In Germany, the return to liturgical roots provoked by the Prussian Union brought new attention to historic Lutheran liturgies, especially the worship of the Reformation era. In the north German region of Mecklenburg, Theodor Kliefoth launched impressive studies on the history of Lutheran worship. Pastor Wilhelm Loehe of Neuendettelsau also studied the worship practices of previous centuries and composed an order of service for Lutheran churches in Bavaria and for missionaries going to North America. Loehe and others examined not only sixteenth-century Lutheran sources but also revisited historical elements of Eastern Orthodox and medieval Catholic worship. Their work was mirrored in England by the influential Oxford Movement, in which leaders like John Keble, John Henry Newman, and Edward Pusey worked to reconnect Anglican worship with its deep traditions.

The liturgical renewal of the nineteenth century was a reaction to both rationalism and revivalism. In contrast to rationalism, this renewed attention to traditional forms of worship focused on divine mystery and embodied religious practices like the sacraments. In that regard, liturgical renewal shared traits with other nineteenth-century romantic or neo-Gothic movements in the arts, literature, and architecture that valued feeling and mystery over the Enlightenment's intellectual ideals of progress and reason. At the same time, groups like the Oxford Movement provided an alternative to Pietist or revivalist movements that often saw tradition and history as obstacles to faith rather than as resources for sharing the ancient faith in lively ways in the present. More than simply a reactionary movement, therefore, liturgical renewal showed a conscious appreciation for the depth and breadth of Christian worship practices across time. Because participants were examining common Christian roots, these church leaders laid important foundations for the **ecumenical movement** of the late nineteenth and early twentieth centuries.

As in other Protestant times of trial, people involved in the liturgical debates of nineteenth-century England looked to Luther to support their position. In the conflicts between high church Anglicans and English Evangelicals, both sides invoked Luther's legacy. As Bethany Kilcrease described it, "the conflict among Victorian Anglicans led them to use historical and contemporary Lutheranism both to legitimate their own practice and also as a rhetorical weapon against opponents."[70]

High church Anglicans influenced by the Oxford Movement appreciated Luther's respect for traditional forms of worship and his relatively conservative approach to church reform. By contrast, with their preference for revivalist and Pietist approaches to the faith, English Evangelicals praised Luther as the first charismatic modern preacher of the gospel. Each side saw itself in how Luther viewed the Roman Catholic Church of his day: the "Ritualists" saw Luther as one who wanted to preserve and reform the many riches of the tradition, while the Evangelicals claimed Luther's example as one who defied hierarchical structures and ritualistic forms of false belief.[71]

The sheer volume of Luther's influence, writings, and reforms has often made it possible for people of many different perspectives to find support for their own views in his work. Whether amid the diverse reforms of the sixteenth century, the liturgical debates of the nineteenth century, or contemporary questions of what worship ought to be and do, Luther's witness has both inspired and challenged. Living before the Enlightenment, Luther valued reason as a God-given tool but not as a source of salvation or freedom in itself. Concerned that faith be a living relationship with God in each human heart, Luther was nevertheless also skeptical of faith becoming purely a matter of individual feeling or subjective experience. He both valued tradition and saw the need for change, based on a consideration for how best to share the gospel and build up people's faith. As seen in the ways English Protestants of the Victorian era and others have turned to him as an authority, Luther's influence in past and present debates about worship around the world continue to provide intriguing food for thought, as contemporary Christians explore what it means to worship a timeless God in timely ways.

1914: Australia, Papua New Guinea, and the First World War

German Lutherans wanting to leave the Prussian Union first arrived in South Australia in 1838. Seeking to practice a purer form of their faith, German Lutherans in Australia were slow to enter the surrounding Anglo-Australian culture. While these close-knit immigrant communities generally thrived in the nineteenth century, they shared the struggles taking place among Lutherans in Germany and North America, with internal divisions arising due to fights over church organization, differing interpretations of the Lutheran confessions, responses to modernism, and questions about the end-times.[72] Also common to the experience of German Lutherans in the United States, Australian Lutherans had to reckon with the anti-German sentiments that came with World War I, which broke out in 1914. In those years, these immigrant communities experienced acts of vandalism against Lutheran churches, the banning of the German language, and the forced closure of church missions.

The first Lutherans in Australia had included mission work with the Aboriginal people as part of their witness. During the 1800s, pastors from the Herrmannsburg and Neuendettelsau mission societies in Germany supported ministry among the Aborigines.[73] Recognizing the devastation that Western colonialism brought upon the indigenous people, missionary Carl Strehlow and his wife

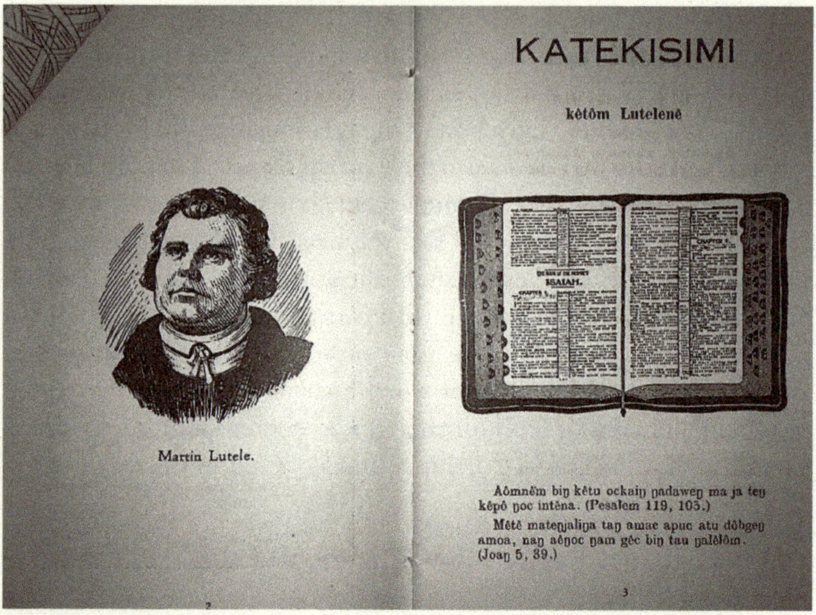

4.11 Luther's *Small Catechism* published by the Australian Lutheran Mission for use in Papua New Guinea. Photo by Martin Lohrmann, used with permission.

Frieda "campaigned for the rights of the Aborigines and defended them against the widespread abuses by farmers and policemen."[74]

When a German colonial presence was started in northeastern New Guinea in 1884, German Lutheran missionaries in Australia quickly tried to get involved. Johann Flierl, who had worked among the Aboriginal people in South Australia, "wanted to save the inhabitants of New Guinea from the fate he experienced among the Aborigines," namely, the destruction of indigenous lives, cultures, and communities for the sake of colonial profit.[75] Through connections with church officials in Germany, Flierl eventually received legal permission to go to the German colony in Papua New Guinea as a missionary.

Flierl's concerns proved well founded. Low views of both the local people and missionaries included the following statements by German colonists: "Hopefully we remain spared of priests and missionaries [who] would spoil everything" and "guns to shoot down the blacks are better than missionaries."[76] These dehumanizing views were not exceptional but belonged to the mainstream of

European colonialism. Even with their more sympathetic perspectives, however, some white missionaries also looked down on local cultures and described the native people as suffering from "stupidity, arrogance, and superstition."[77]

After a slow start, evangelism in New Guinea spread by treating conversion not as an individual experience but as something for the entire community. Missionaries immersed themselves in a village, working and teaching; if there were conversions, groups of newly baptized people would then share the gospel with the next village. As Dean Zweck of Australian Lutheran College has described it, "From the very beginning Lutheranism in New Guinea was a grassroots movement, and that has been one of its enduring strengths."[78] The first local people baptized were two men named Kaboing and Kamunsang in 1899; the first two women were baptized in 1903. New Guineans long served as elders, teachers, and evangelists in local churches, but were not ordained as pastors until 1950.[79] From those early baptisms, the church continued to grow. By the time Pastor Flierl retired in 1930, the Lutheran community in Papua New Guinea numbered about fifty thousand people.[80]

As happened to Lutherans in South Australia, German missionaries in New Guinea encountered serious challenges during World War I. Australia took military possession of the island. Some missionaries took an oath of neutrality and stayed; others who objected to the oath were sent to internment camps. After the war, much of New Guinea came under Australian oversight (the western half of the island remained part of Indonesia). With German missionary societies unable to give support in those years, Lutherans in Australia and the United States provided the financial and human resources that had previously come from Europe.[81] This was an early example of international cooperation among Lutheran churches.

With about thirty thousand baptized members today, the Lutheran Church in Australia—and a partner church in New Zealand—has remained largely connected to its German immigrant roots. It also has significant Indigenous Australian membership and ministries. It participates in both the Lutheran World Federation and the International Lutheran Council.[82]

With a similar origin in nineteenth-century German missions, there are now about a million Lutherans in Papua New Guinea, where the gospel is translated in the Jabim language as *Miti*, meaning "everything which is good and nicely done or spoken" or "the Word of God like fire."[83] The Evangelical Lutheran Church in Papua New Guinea became autonomous in 1956. A local statement of faith was written in 1972, which connects the Lutheran witness of the Reformation era with New Guinean culture and contexts.

Questions

1. What were some of the harmful effects of European and American colonialism on local peoples in the 1800s? In what ways did white Lutherans participate in those harmful actions, knowingly or unknowingly?
2. What were some of the ways Lutherans viewed the relationship between national identity and religious identity in the nineteenth century? What do you think about the relationship between ethnicity, nationality, and religious faith? What are possible strengths and weaknesses of those connections?
3. Most white Lutherans in the United States at the time of the Civil War addressed slavery as a political rather than religious or spiritual issue. What do you think of that approach?
4. How can Lutherans today reckon with historical participation in evils like racism, slavery, cultural supremacy, and genocide?
5. What do you value more in worship: something grounded in tradition, or something that speaks more to a contemporary culture? How have you seen people address these issues, either effectively or poorly?
6. Lutheran churches in places like Ethiopia, Madagascar, Indonesia, and Papua New Guinea thrived when local people became leaders. Why do you think good local leadership matters so much to healthy faith communities? What are some traits of healthy local leaders?
7. Lutherans in Indonesia and Papua New Guinea found it important to write statements of faith that reflected their local cultures. What cultural elements do you think are important to name and claim for your community?

CHAPTER FIVE

1917–2017

Introduction to Lutheranism in Its Fifth Century

Whatever fragile "balance of power" had existed in Europe in previous decades erupted into the destruction of World War I, which began in 1914. Nationalist and fascist reactions in the following decades led to even more violence, as World War II started when Nazi Germany invaded Poland in 1939, launching a global conflict that took the lives of over seventy million people, including millions killed in Nazi concentration camps. The war ended in 1945 with the United States using atomic bombs against Japan, introducing a new weapon of mass destruction and the possibility of "mutually assured destruction." After the war, hostility between capitalist and communist governments led to a "Cold War" between global superpowers and many related armed conflicts around the world.

Amid such large-scale violence, people continued to seek liberation and well-being, both personally and socially. Many nations that had been under colonial rule in Africa and Asia fought for independence. Both in those regions and in South America—where many countries had gained independence in the 1800s—**neocolonial** economic systems frequently continued to serve the wealthy while leaving the majority of people in poverty. Struggles for voting rights, gender equality, and environmental protection reshaped and redefined communities, including communities of faith.

These factors all influenced the ongoing development of Lutheranism as a branch of world Christianity. Lutherans participated in acts of genocide, colonial rule, and racism. They also worked to resettle international refugees and build stable institutions to promote peace, equality, and justice. Such contrasts existing within the same religious tradition raise legitimate questions about what it means to belong to a faith community. Religion can easily be co-opted by powerful and dehumanizing forces. At the same time, religious faith has led to inspiring acts of compassion and freedom. In light of twentieth-century history, these are important realities for Lutherans to ponder as people of faith in a complex and often violent world.

By the later twentieth century, most Lutherans in the world came to support the ordination of women into ministry. This expansion of leadership to women, and later to people in committed same-sex relationships in some parts of the world, generated large amounts of controversy and continues to be an issue that divides Lutherans. While many Lutherans found ways to build connections during the twentieth century and lift up the witness of historically marginalized people, social and religious differences also increased divisions between various Lutheran communities. Complicated issues of culture, power, tradition, biblical interpretation, and human rights have impacted how people understand central matters of faith, gospel freedom, and church life together.

Lutheran leadership at the international level started to reflect a church whose center was no longer the North Atlantic but was increasingly moving to the Global South. Indeed, by the early twenty-first century, nearly half of the world's Lutherans live in Asia, Africa, and South America. In case there was any doubt before, the history of global Lutheranism was clearly no longer a story about northern Europeans and their descendants but rather a story of cross-cultural, international Christian movement. As discussed in this book's introduction, Lutherans today have a greater opportunity than ever to live into their belief that the church "consists of people scattered throughout the entire world who agree on the gospel and have the same Christ, the same Holy Spirit, and the same sacraments, whether or not they have the same human traditions."[1] This dynamic expression of global Lutheranism is true both in places where there are many Lutherans—like Ethiopia, Tanzania, and Namibia—and in places where Lutherans represent a minority religious perspective, for instance in Latin America and Asia.

Even though many of the forces and events of recent world history can seem massive and impersonal, the stories described in this chapter show that the persistent efforts of individuals and local communities often formed the basis for inspiring acts of faith and love. Far from being overwhelmed by the messiness and complexity of modern life, Lutheran theology has continued to point people back to the essentials of trusting God and sharing Christ's good news to nourish people in body and soul.

Early 1900s: Women's Missionary Societies

The women's church societies that started in the nineteenth century grew to be indispensable parts of Lutheran communities, first in Scandinavia and later across Europe and North America. In the United States, where congregations were still learning how to grow and thrive without direct support from the government, women's groups raised much-needed funds for local churches and for national and international projects. These groups also gave women opportunities to lead in ways that their male-dominated churches' structures did not allow. As organizers, supporters, and missionaries, women directly impacted their communities and reshaped the church. This often occurred despite the opposition of male leaders, who suspected that these women's groups might undermine rather than advance the work of the institutional church and its gospel witness.

In the United States, women's missionary societies often started at the local level as groups that would meet for fellowship, share devotions and educational time (frequently led by the pastor), and raise money for mission work. Well-organized national women's networks were eventually founded in most American Lutheran denominations around the turn of the twentieth century: Lena Dahl launched the Women's Missionary Federation of the United Norwegian Lutheran Church, Mary Nelson Wee organized the Mission Dove group among the Norwegian-American Pietists of the Hauge Synod, Danish Lutherans on the West Coast started a society to support missions in Japan, Wilhelmina Young Kuhlmann and Katherine Lehmann led the Women's Missionary Conference of the Joint Synod of Ohio, and Emmy Evald served as president of the Swedish-American Augustana Synod's Woman's Missionary Society.[2]

Whether as deaconesses, independent missionaries, or pastors' wives, women themselves worked around the world as teachers, evangelists, nurses, and doctors.[3] Women in the mission field could often get to know the interior lives of families in ways that men could not. This contributed to the fact that "by the early twentieth century, the number of women engaged in world missions of American Protestant churches was larger than the number of men."[4]

5.1 Elizabeth Facktuo and Helen Frost, excerpted from "Helen C. Frost's Missionary Images of the Inuquiq (Eskimos)" by Julieanna Frost. The ELCA Region 3 Archives. Used by permission.

One such longtime missionary was Doctor Anna Kugler (1856–1930), who received her medical training in the Philadelphia area. She spent a distinguished career providing medical care and Christian instruction in Guntur, India, where a hospital she founded continues to operate. Kugler attended the first Parliament of World Religions in Chicago in 1893 and regularly spoke at gatherings of the Ministerium of Pennsylvania when she was in the United States.[5] Working among both upper-class Brahmins and the so-called "untouchable" Dalit caste in India, Kugler encouraged local leadership and developed strong personal and professional relationships with Indian men and women.[6]

In some cases, female missionary leadership included preaching and sacramental ministry when no men were around to do it. This was true of Helen Frost's work among the Inupiaq people of Alaska. She originally went to Teller, Alaska, to work as an orphanage nurse in 1926. As she recalled in her memoirs,

> So here I was, supposedly only a nurse by profession, but later finding myself preaching, teaching, baptizing, even giving communion privately, when we had no pastor. The day also came when I was given a license to perform marriages. Many times I felt very inadequate, but when there was no one else to do it, I did what had to be done. With God all things are possible if we are in His will.[7]

Working around the borderlands region of Texas, Irene Mellenbruch similarly found herself performing a wide array of social and pastoral services—including leading worship—because she was the only missionary from her American Lutheran church body who spoke Spanish.[8] Productive partnerships like hers with the local people led to lasting bilingual congregations and ministries in South Texas. These examples highlight how vocations as missionaries sent women into work that they might not otherwise have had the chance to perform. Women like Kugler, Frost, and Mellenbruch also showed a strong capacity for **accompanying** local people and their cultures rather than demeaning or displacing them. These efforts fostered positive and enduring cross-cultural experiences of the gospel.

Sexist ideas and policies limiting women's roles in Christian leadership have made female contributions to Lutheran congregational life and evangelization relatively hard to identify, study, and appreciate for much of history. In their own time, organizers like Lena Dahl and Katherine Lehmann often had to fight within their church structures to shape ministries in ways they thought were best. Their examples provide important snapshots into the essential contributions that women have made in the church, from the time of Jesus' ministry to the present. The hard work of so many women gave precious support to churches in their times and paved the way for greater equality in leadership for many in the generations that followed.

1925: Archbishop Söderblom Leads Lutherans into the Ecumenical Movement

Nathan Söderblom (1866–1931) developed a unique set of skills and ideas that helped him build a remarkable career as a pastor, professor, and archbishop. His father had been a stern Lutheran Pietist minister in northern Sweden. Nathan respected his father's intense faith, even as his own convictions led him in different directions. Sharing the friendly personality of his kind mother, Nathan's outgoing nature became as typical of his leadership style as his commitment to a vibrant personal spirituality. With combined gifts of spiritual devotion and warmth for others inherited from his parents, Söderblom showed a similar ability throughout his ministry to bring together people and ideas that might otherwise seem far apart.

5.2 Swedish archbishop Nathan Söderblom. Wikimedia Commons.

As a student at the University of Uppsala, Söderblom embraced the revival movement represented at the time by the American preacher Dwight Moody. He even had a chance to hear Moody speak in person in 1890, when he went to New Haven, Connecticut, as a Swedish representative to an international meeting of the Young Men's Christian Association (YMCA). The nondenominational character of the YMCA and the easy sharing of Christian faith that he experienced there provided a good foundation for Söderblom's later ecumenical work. At the same time, Söderblom found himself drawn to the liberal theology of Berlin professors Adolf von Harnack and Albrecht Ritschl. Building on the legacy of Schleiermacher, these theologians had applied rigorous scientific reasoning to their theological and historical studies. Although such liberal methods were controversial in Sweden, they inspired Söderblom to pursue a doctorate in comparative religion, which he completed in 1901 while serving as a pastor to Scandinavians living in Paris.

Along with his love of both evangelical revival and liberal reforms, Söderblom retained a strong affinity for the living faith he encountered in Martin Luther, especially in writings like *The Freedom of a Christian*. Further combining his unique gifts for bridge-building, Söderblom could feel socially at ease with people of all economic classes, a pastoral mixture drawn from his rural upbringing and cosmopolitan interests. His public support for the 1909 Great Strike in Sweden earned him the longtime trust of the labor movement, even as he continued to nurture the support of wealthy patrons.[9] On this latter point, Söderblom's energetic work as a young professor in Uppsala came to the attention of a woman named Anna Lindblad, who wanted to establish an endowment that would serve the church. She reached out to Söderblom, who used the endowment to start the Olaus Petri Foundation, which has supported international ecumenical awareness and activities to the present day.[10] Throughout his career, Söderblom proved himself to be a good networker and organizer, who cared as much about connecting with grassroots communities as cultivating relationships with leaders of public policy.

Söderblom was elected archbishop of Uppsala and head of the Church of Sweden just as World War I was breaking out in Europe. He opposed the war and advocated for peace (Sweden stayed neutral during the war). Having most recently worked as a professor in Leipzig, Söderblom had many contacts on both sides of the battle and lamented the great destruction and loss of life that the war brought. After the war, he used his position as leader of the Church of Sweden to bring Christians together across borders. Already in 1909, he and colleagues in the Church of England had begun a mutual dialogue based upon the Anglican convictions of the Lambeth Quadrilateral, which defined scripture, creed, sacraments, and the historic office of bishops as foundational for Christian unity. Uniquely among Lutherans, the Church of Sweden had retained the office of bishop in ways that the Anglicans found acceptable, as the traditional bishops in Sweden during the Reformation all became Lutheran, thus retaining the **historic episcopate**. Even so, Söderblom was clear that Lutherans believed that the office of bishop provides important practical oversight for the gospel without itself being a necessity for saving faith.[11] These discussions bore fruit, so that in 1922 the Church of Sweden and Church of England entered into **Eucharistic fellowship** with each other, an important moment in international and interdenominational Christian cooperation.

From Greek roots meaning "one house" or "the whole world," the **ecumenical movement** had developed in the later 1800s from a common desire to address social needs and from the growing awareness that Christian divisions negatively impacted global missionary efforts. Instead of exporting their divisions, many Protestants began to wonder how they might better cooperate for the sake of the gospel. In his role as archbishop, Söderblom turned the Church of Sweden into a leading advocate for international ecumenism. He organized and oversaw the 1925 Universal Christian Conference on Life and Work, which took place in Stockholm and Uppsala. Connecting high-level discussions with daily life in Sweden,

> Many of Stockholm's citizens had opened their homes for the foreign guests; others had contributed to hotel costs. The [Eastern Orthodox] Patriarch of Alexandria was seen fishing for perch from the Djurgården bridge of the royal furrier Lindahl and four of the conference leaders with the [English] Bishop of Peterborough at the helm were guests of Crown Prince Gustaf Adolf at Ulriksdal.[12]

In addition to putting local citizens in contact with representatives of global Christianity, the Stockholm Conference became a watershed moment in ecumenical cooperation and an important step in the later formation of the **World Council of Churches**. In the years that followed, Söderblom continued to participate in international attempts to make peace a central platform of churches, governments, and political parties. These views were adopted at the 1928 meeting of the World Alliance in Prague, the 1929 meeting of the Life and Work committee in Eisenach, and an ecumenical council meeting in Chexbres, Switzerland in 1930.[13]

In November 1930, Söderblom gave a radio address titled "Is the idea of peace an illusion?" In that talk, he addressed the rising forces of totalitarianism, nationalism, and fascism.[14] Far from viewing nonviolence as an impractical ideal compared to the use of military force, the archbishop emphasized the practical value of peace and the inevitable damage that comes from war and nationalism. Shortly after that speech, Söderblom received the Nobel

Peace Prize. Having long suffered various health problems, much of Söderblom's activity in those years came from an awareness that he may not have long to live. He died in 1931 at age sixty-five. By that time, he had become a major voice for international peace and ecumenical dialogue. In the wake of the tremendous suffering of World War II, the seeds of such efforts grew into postwar institutions like the United Nations, the World Council of Churches, and the Lutheran World Federation.

As an aside, it is worth nothing that Nathan Söderblom is not the only Lutheran to have received the Nobel Peace Prize. Other Lutheran recipients have included Albert Schweitzer, Dag Hammarskjöld, Norman Borlaug, and Leymah Gbowee. Schweitzer was already an internationally renowned theologian and organist when he felt called to become a medical missionary in Lambaréné in French Equatorial Africa (now in the country of Gabon). With the support of Söderblom and the Olaus Petri Foundation, Schweitzer visited Sweden in 1920 to give lectures and raise money for the Lambaréné hospitals. Dag Hammarskjöld served as the second secretary-general of the United Nations. From knowing Söderblom personally, he "learned that a society without a religious compass would only drift, that faith and intellectual honesty must be held together, that each and every person must find his or her own path, and that everyone must take responsibility in the world."[15] Years later, the American Lutheran Norman Borlaug received the Nobel Peace Prize for his pioneering work in food science and agricultural development; his research earned him the nickname "the man who saved a billion lives."[16] In 2011, Liberian Lutheran social worker Leymah Gbowee was one of three women to receive the Nobel Peace Prize for organizing a women's peace movement to end Liberia's civil war. Ms. Gbowee continues to advocate for peace and social justice, as described in her autobiography *Mighty Be Our Powers: How Sisterhood, Prayer, and Sex Changed a Nation at War* and in the documentary *Pray the Devil Back to Hell*.[17]

Such lives reveal the power that can come from faithful witness to Christ and love of neighbor. Of course, effective servant leadership does not mean personal perfection or constant success. Instead, as Söderblom's biographer Jonas Jonson wrote of him, "As long as he lived, he met with opposition. After his death he was accounted among the saints, who by his own definition were people who by their lives showed that God lives."[18]

April 9, 1945: Martyrdom of Dietrich Bonhoeffer

The word "fascism" comes from the Latin word *fasces*, which is the name for a bundle of sticks bound together around an axe blade. As an image that combines rural romanticism with imperial might, it served as a symbol of power for the Roman Empire. After World War I, Italian fascists led by Benito Mussolini proudly used this word to describe their nationalist ideas, policies, and methods. In Germany, the far-right National Socialist German Workers' Party (shortened to Nazi) used nationalism, racism, intimidation, and violence to rise to power. Often disguised by a seemingly noble longing for an idealized past, fascism is essentially government by bullying, as it uses all kinds of verbal and physical force—from ridicule and propaganda to imprisonment and brutality—to achieve its goals.

The Nazi regime gained power in Germany through a combination of popular support, political maneuvering, and "wait and see" opposition in both secular society and Christian churches. As discussed in chapter 2, Luther's legacy of hateful anti-Jewish writings were revived in these decades to support the racist ideology and politics of the Nazis. Shortly after Adolf Hitler became chancellor in early 1933, he used the burning of the Reichstag (the German parliament building) to declare a national emergency, suspending the constitution and revoking civil liberties. This gave the Nazis legal cover to arrest minority groups like Jews, Poles, Romani, communists, socialists, and homosexuals as enemies of the people, imprisoning them as early as 1933 in concentration camps like the one in Dachau, Bavaria. These camps later became places for the Nazis to carry out their genocidal policies, killing people they deemed inferior or deviant. Despite some opposition, most Lutherans in Germany either supported the Nazi party or did not take steps to resist the ever-growing tyranny.

In 1934, a group called the **Confessing Church** met to create an alternative to the pro-Nazi "German Christian" church. The Barmen Declaration—written largely by Swiss Reformed theologian Karl Barth—rejected the Nazi takeover of the church.[19] Within a couple of years, however, the movement had split into factions for theological and political reasons. Barth was deported, pastors like Paul Schneider and Martin Niemöller were arrested for preaching against the regime, and no large-scale Protestant opposition to Nazism took hold.[20] Resistance was further undermined in 1938 when pastors were forced to either swear allegiance to Hitler or lose their jobs and then get jailed or drafted; most ministers signed.[21]

Dietrich Bonhoeffer (1906–1945) was among those who resisted fascism, racism, and war. Born into an aristocratic family, Bonhoeffer had been an enthusiastic theology student, completing his first dissertation—*Sanctorum Communio* (Communion of Saints)—at age twenty-one and a second dissertation at age twenty-four. During post-graduate studies at Union Seminary in New York City, Bonhoeffer worshipped with fellow student Albert Fisher at Abyssinian Baptist Church in Harlem, where he encountered African American preaching, theology, and music. At Union he also became friends with a French seminarian named Jean Lasserre, who introduced him to the values and strategies of pacifism.[22] Along with experiences like teaching confirmation students in impoverished areas of Berlin, Bonhoeffer's experiences with the African American community and Christian pacifism deepened his commitment to faith as the living out of a risky trust in the crucified and risen Christ.

In connection with the Confessing Church, Bonhoeffer led an unauthorized seminary in Finkenwalde on the Baltic Sea in the mid-1930s. Reflecting upon this crucial and intimate time, he wrote a little book about Christian community called *Life Together*. In it, Bonhoeffer explored the challenges and blessings that come with following Jesus, both as individuals and as people who always belong to the wider body of Christ in the world. He stressed that Christian love means loving others in light of the selfless love of God and not through our own ideas of holiness or worthiness. This is a love that truly sets people free.

> The freedom of the other goes against Christians' high opinions of themselves, and yet they must recognize it. Christians could rid themselves of this burden by not giving other persons their freedom, thus doing violence to the personhood of others and stamping their own image

> on others. But when Christians allow God to create God's own image in others, they allow others their own freedom. Thereby Christians themselves bear the burden of the freedom enjoyed by these other creatures of God. All that we mean by human nature, individuality, and talent is part of the other person's freedom—as are the other's weaknesses and peculiarities that so sorely try our patience, and everything that produces the plethora of clashes, differences, and arguments between me and the other. Here, bearing the burden of the other means tolerating the reality of the other's creation by God—affirming it, and in bearing with it, breaking through to delight in it.[23]

After the Finkenwalde seminary was shut down by the authorities, Bonhoeffer was forbidden to preach or teach. Through family connections in Berlin, Bonhoeffer received a government job that allowed him to meet with church leaders in England, Sweden, and Switzerland.[24] In this work, he came to assist German officials in a conspiracy to kill Hitler; his role was to deliver messages from the conspirators to foreign diplomats. When the plot was discovered, Bonhoeffer was arrested and jailed at Tegel military prison in Berlin in April 1943. Like the other conspirators, he was transferred to concentration camps as the Nazi regime was collapsing. He was executed on April 9, 1945.

Bonhoeffer's martyrdom testifies to the power of following Christ and loving one's neighbors. As theologian Reggie Williams has written, "For Bonhoeffer, Christians must see society from the perspective of marginalized people since faithful Christianity is calibrated from the perspective of suffering rather than from dominance. This is costly yet crucial to true Christian discipleship."[25] Bonhoeffer's commitment to social justice and Christian discipleship stands as a powerful witness to the church and the world.

At the same time, the courageous faith of Bonhoeffer was lamentably the exception during the horrors of Nazi rule. Lutherans of the time massively failed to confront tyranny, stand up for their neighbors, and follow Christ in word and deed. In the face of fascism, bullying, fearmongering, racism, war, and genocide, Lutheran faith made little public difference. Any social authority the church might have had as a centuries-old spiritual resource was either neutralized

5.3 Flossenbürg concentration camp, Arrestblock-Hof: memorial to members of German resistance executed on April 9, 1945. Wikimedia Commons License 3.0.

or used to advance tyranny. Millions of people around the world died because of the racist ideas, dehumanizing policies, and eager militarism of the period. The same kinds of harmful forces have not vanished from the earth but continue to destroy lands and lives. What, if anything, have Lutherans learned from this history and from the example of people like Dietrich Bonhoeffer?

1947: Founding of the Lutheran World Federation

In the aftermath of World War II, Lutherans around the world came together to provide aid, help resettle refugees, and foster stronger relationships with each other. Building on the foundation of the Lutheran World Convention that had met after World War I, the **Lutheran World Federation** (LWF) came into being at a meeting in Lund, Sweden, in the summer of 1947. Four priorities set the tone for both the LWF's early years and its later directions: rescue for the needy, common initiatives in mission, joint efforts in theology, and a common response to ecumenism.[26] The humanitarian crisis was especially pressing, because in the war's aftermath about ten million Lutherans were refugees forced from their homes.[27]

Early LWF leadership came mostly from Scandinavia and North America, as well as from German theologians who had publicly resisted the Nazification of the church.[28] The first president of the LWF was Anders Nygren, a Swedish successor to the ecumenical legacy of Nathan Söderblom. Sylvester Michelfelder of the American Lutheran Church had become a respected leader in the US government's postwar relief efforts; he led the organization of the Lund meeting and coordinated LWF's budding humanitarian aid programs. Hanns Lilje, Bishop of Hanover, had supported the Barmen Declaration and been imprisoned for his resistance during the war. He was elected LWF's second president at the 1952 assembly.

Another influential leader who served on early executive committees was Eivind Berggrav, bishop of Oslo, who had organized church resistance against the pro-Nazi Quisling regime in Norway and was imprisoned from 1942 until the end of the war. For Berggrav, Luther's legacy had not been one of indifference or obedience in the face of political injustice but rather one that inspired an obligation to resist.[29] As he later recalled, "It was a joy to sling Luther in the face of the Gestapo. His theology was our best weapon in the fight against the Nazis."[30]

In the following decades, LWF assemblies gave increasing attention to issues of gender equity and global representation. The 1957 assembly in Minneapolis included a resolution from the Committee on Women requesting female representation on all commissions, not only on those related to women and children.[31] The 1963 assembly in Helsinki received requests from African and Asian churches that Lutherans more intentionally bridge the gap between Reformation-era theology and the diverse global contexts of the twentieth century.[32] One early step toward that goal was support for Radio Voice of the Gospel, a radio ministry that the LWF had launched earlier that year in Addis Ababa, Ethiopia; at its peak operation in 1972, Radio Voice of the Gospel offered twenty hours of programming a day in twenty different languages.[33]

International politics continually impacted the Lutheran World Federation. Plans to hold the 1970 assembly in Weimar,

East Germany, fell apart due to the strains of the Cold War. As Lutherans around the world continued to gain independence from colonialism after World War II, a new dynamic between the global North and South was developing. To increase the visibility of the church beyond the North Atlantic, Lutherans in Brazil invited LWF to hold the 1970 assembly there instead of Weimar. Concerns about the military dictatorship ruling Brazil at that time, however, led to a third change in venue to Évian, France.[34] This concern over the assembly's setting mirrored the increasing awareness among LWF members about the need to honor the geographical and cultural diversity of a truly global Lutheran community. More about this will be said in the discussion of the 1977 LWF assembly held in Dar es Salaam, Tanzania.

From its modest beginnings in the rubble of World War II, the Lutheran World Federation has grown into a communion of international churches. Members share altar and pulpit fellowship, which means they fully honor each other's ministries and teachings. This is true even though some Lutheran churches around the world do not ordain women and despite continued disagreements about sexual orientation. As Kathryn Johnson has observed, LWF's long-term ability to maintain unity amid these significant differences remains to be seen.[35] After being led mostly by men from North Atlantic countries, leaders of recent decades have included Josiah Kibira of Tanzania, Ishmael Noko of Zimbabwe, Gottfried Brakemeier of Brazil, Munib Younan of Palestine, Martin Junge of Chile, and Panti Filibus Musa of Nigeria, who was elected general secretary at the LWF's twelfth assembly held in Windhoek, Namibia, in 2017. To date, no women have been elected to the offices of president or general secretary; nevertheless, women hold other leadership roles throughout the LWF, which "works toward the full participation of women in the communion's life and pursues this commitment at all levels of LWF."[36]

Germany remains the nation with the most Lutherans. But because German churches that belong to the Lutheran World Federation are organized by region rather than nation, the five largest LWF member churches are in Ethiopia, Tanzania, Sweden, Indonesia, and Denmark.[37]

Of the approximately eighty million Lutherans in the world, about 90 percent belong to churches that are in the Lutheran World

Federation; as of 2016, LWF had 145 member churches in ninety-eight countries.[38] The original emphasis on humanitarian aid, especially care for refugees, continues to serve as a major focus of the LWF's work: "The LWF has been the largest faith-based partner of United Nations High Commissioner for Refugees (UNHCR), in 2015 providing assistance for more than 1.3 million refugees in more than thirty countries."[39]

LWF was also founded to provide Lutheran representation in international ecumenical efforts. To that end, it has shared a building in Geneva with the World Council of Churches since the founding of both groups in the 1940s. The groundbreaking Leuenberg Agreement between Lutheran, Reformed, and Union churches in Europe in 1973 paved the way for further cooperation between Protestants around the world. It included a shared statement about the Lord's Supper that reconciled many of the Eucharistic debates of the Reformation era.[40] Other ecumenical and interfaith dialogues at the LWF level have included the 1999 *Joint Declaration on the Doctrine of Justification* with the Roman Catholic Church, statements renouncing the anti-Jewish writings of Martin Luther and repenting of the Lutheran role in the Holocaust, a 2010 apology to Mennonites for persecution against Anabaptists, and ongoing international dialogue with Orthodox, Baptist, Pentecostal, and Muslim communities.[41]

April 28, 1948: Church of Denmark Begins Ordaining Women

The Bible presents many women as public leaders and ministers: from Miriam, Deborah, and Huldah in the Hebrew scriptures to Prisca, Lydia, Junia, and Mary Magdalene—the apostle to the apostles (John 20:18)—in the New Testament. The examples of Perpetua and Felicity provide rare glimpses into the experiences of female martyrs in the early church.[42] The brief biography of Macrina by her brother Gregory of Nyssa similarly testifies to the powerful leadership women provided in early Christian communities.[43] With these and many other biblical and historical examples, the question is not if women have led Christian communities across the centuries, but rather why we know so little about them.

Scholars examining this topic have noticed that the subordinate status of women in church and society is often closely connected to dominant patterns of male leadership from ancient to modern times. As Barbara MacHaffie has written, "The synagogues were governed by groups of elected elders who were men, reflecting the patriarchal character of first-century Judaism . . . It is likely that the early churches were overcome by inherited customs and prejudices regarding the status of women"; in similar encounters with a Greco-Roman culture suspicious of Christianity, early believers minimized social conflict by adopting "traditional cultural views on appropriate behavior for women and in so doing effectively stifled female leadership in the churches."[44] Around the world and across the centuries, cultural values regarding gender and leadership have often determined women's roles in church communities more than any inherently gospel-centered theology of leadership.

In the 1800s Pietism, the deaconess movement, and missionary societies each offered new opportunities for women to lead in church. The international women's suffrage movement of that time also led to new political and legal rights for women, beginning with the right to vote. Quite apart from the question of female ordination, some professional theologians believed that the secular right of women to vote was itself already an affront to God, nature, and the rule of law. Male American Lutheran theologians, for instance, said that woman's suffrage is "a proposal that stands all natural order on its head" and that female subordination is a "line drawn, not by man's hand, but by God's over which woman may not step without upsetting the order of God."[45] Among the few female writers to join the conversation in print, Mary Devers wrote in a 1904 issue of *Lutheran Quarterly*:

> The question of sex should never come up in any line of service. Whom do we serve? Is not life itself "divine service"? If one is able to perform certain work admirably and well, let him do it in God's name, and let us cheer and hearten him with high praise. There is no woman's cause apart from man's cause. It is our common cause. Therefore, let us not blind and hamper those who are helping to solve the great questions of life. In so doing we would be running counter to him who bestows "every good and perfect gift."[46]

As theologians had themselves made a connection between God's order and social customs, changes in the political rights of women naturally began to impact Lutheran churches.

Protestant groups like Quakers, Methodists, Baptists, and the Salvation Army had welcomed female preachers early in their histories. Among Lutherans, the Dutch were the first to move toward female ordination. Jantine Auguste Haumersen, who had been educated and worked in both the Reformed and Lutheran communities, was ordained to serve a Lutheran congregation in November 1929.[47] By the early 1960s, five women in the Netherlands were ordained Lutheran pastors.[48] Original restrictions against married women serving as pastors were eventually lifted there, as well.

In 1928 a Danish woman named Ruth Vermehren volunteered to provide pastoral care in a women's prison. Although she became a paid chaplain at the prison in 1938, the bishop of Copenhagen denied her request for ordination, saying that her call did not come from a congregation. In 1946, however, valid calls were extended to Vermehren and two other women, Johanne Hermansen Andersen and Edith Brenneche Petersen. Although other bishops were not in favor of female ordination, the "first among equals" relationship of Danish bishops that went back to the Reformation meant that any bishop could ordain them if he chose. Bishop Hans Øllgaard ordained the three women in the Odense Cathedral on April 28, 1948.[49]

In the reverse case of official opportunities existing before a specific request for ordination was made, the Church of Norway had voted to allow the ordination of women already in 1938, but no female pastors were ordained until over twenty years later.[50] In the following years, Lutheran women were ordained into ministry in France, Czechoslovakia, Norway, and Sweden.[51] In the United States, Elizabeth Platz was ordained into the Lutheran Church in America on November 22, 1970 in College Park, Maryland; Barbara Andrews of the American Lutheran Church was ordained in Minnesota one month later.[52] Over the next generation, the ordination of Lutheran women continued to take place around the world, for instance, in Indonesia in the 1980s and in India and Tanzania in 1991.[53]

Over 80 percent of the churches that belong to the Lutheran World Federation now ordain women.[54] Other Lutheran groups—for instance, those belonging to the International Lutheran

Council—distinguish between male and female roles in the church. While this topic continues to be a point of difference and even division among Lutherans, much good has come from the ordination of women, who now work as deacons, pastors, professors, seminary presidents, bishops, and archbishops. While the majority of the world's Christians still do not ordain women, Lutheran support of female leadership is a strong testimony to the liberation, new life, and transformation given by the gospel.

1958: Translating Luther in Latin America

Through a combination of immigration, mission work, and local evangelizing, Lutheran communities slowly grew in Latin America and the Caribbean during the nineteenth century. Lutheranism first came to South American shores when Dutch Lutheran colonists arrived in present-day Suriname and Guyana in the 1740s. Those churches existed exclusively for white settlers until intentional integration efforts began in the later 1800s. Pastor John Mittelholzer, a man of Swiss and Creole heritage, was particularly effective at building a vibrant, racially inclusive Lutheran church in late-nineteenth-century Guyana.

As Dutch and British colonies, Suriname and Guyana did not share the Spanish or Portuguese language and culture that spread in other parts of South and Central America, making them somewhat distinct. Ever since the Reformation, Spanish and Portuguese monarchs had identified strongly with Roman Catholicism, a connection that carried into the colonization of the Americas. In the early 1800s, popular movements swept across South and Central America and led to the formation of many independent countries. With independence, new immigrants—including German Lutherans—came to places like Brazil, Argentina, and Chile.

The Lutheran communities that settled in southern Brazil as early as 1824 kept German as their primary language for over a century. Pressure on ethnic minorities applied by the authoritarian regime after World War II pushed Brazilian Lutherans into closer relationships with the wider population.[55] Repeating a global pattern of church division based on various responses to ecumenism and liberal theology, there are two large Lutheran denominations

5.4 Rev. John R. Mittelholzer, New Amsterdam, British Guiana, ca. 1878. Rev. Mittelhauser, born in the Berbice River district, was initially a Congregational minister trained by the London Mission Society, until taking a position as pastor of Ebenezer Lutheran Church, New Amsterdam. Photo ELCA Archives.

in Brazil, with a combined membership of about one million: the Evangelical Church of the Lutheran Confession in Brazil is the largest South American member of the Lutheran World Federation; the Evangelical Lutheran Church of Brazil relates to the International Lutheran Council.[56]

Despite their differences, these two groups have worked jointly to translate Luther's works into Portuguese as volumes of *Martinho Lutero, Obras Selecianadas* (*Martin Luther, Selected Works*). The first volume, focusing on Luther's early Reformation writings, was published in 1987; as of 2012, twelve volumes had been completed, with four more still to come. The impact of both **liberation theology** and **Pentecostalism** on Lutherans in Brazil influenced the decision to publish two volumes focused on Luther's social and ethical thought.[57]

As with the legacy of Portuguese colonization, the close relationship between the Spanish monarchy and Roman Catholicism meant that works by the arch-Protestant Luther were not translated into Spanish until relatively recently. Similar to the situation in Brazil, Lutherans who had moved to nations like Chile and Argentina as early as the mid-1800s retained their use of the German language and did not become majority Spanish-speaking communities until after World War II. Therefore, the insularity of these German Lutheran communities meant that Lutheran resources continued to be read in German instead of being translated into Spanish. Translations would come from a variety of places and people during the twentieth century.

Instead of immigration, other Spanish-speaking Lutheran communities in the Americas started with mission work from the United States. For instance, in 1899—a year after Puerto Rico became a territory of the United States—a Swedish American seminary student named Gustav Swenson went to the island and started preaching in San Juan, without having any official approval from his church.[58] Swenson's ministry had started at the request of a black Jamaican tailor named John Browne, who knew Lutherans through his time in the Virgin Islands and who offered his shop for the first meetings. Within a few years, local people and missionaries from the United States had expanded the ministry.[59] From that beginning, over thirty congregations in Puerto Rico and the US Virgin Islands now belong to the Caribbean Synod of the Evangelical Lutheran Church in America (ELCA), currently led by Bishop Idalia Negrón Caamaño. Lutherans in the Bahamas belong to congregations of both the ELCA and the Lutheran Church—Missouri Synod.

Even more recently, a Lutheran church consisting of several congregations was founded in 2009 in Haiti, where French and Haitian Creole are the official languages. This new church grew from the efforts of Lutherans in Florida and from Lutheran World Federation offices in Venezuela to provide Haitians with new economic and educational opportunities, especially for women and young people.[60] In this case, social and educational ministries led to a church, instead of the other way around. As Mytch Dorvilier—a participant in those ministries—has written, "Some of us were very intrigued by the 'solas' identified by the Reformation, *sola fide*, *sola gratia*, and *sola scriptura*, that is, by faith alone, by grace alone and scripture alone. There came an urge to continue to know more about these 'solas' that continue to be important for a church that seeks to uphold the gospel insights Luther brought to the church."[61]

Such missionary efforts in Latin America and the Caribbean often included the translation into Spanish of shorter works like Luther's *Small Catechism* but did not involve more comprehensive translation projects. For many years, an 1878 Luther biography by Federico Fliedner provided the best access to Luther's life and works.[62] A son of Theodor Fliedner of Kaiserswerth, Federico had moved to Madrid when Spain legalized Protestantism in 1868 and spent the rest of his career building Spanish Lutheran churches, schools, and social institutions.[63]

In 1958, two Argentine seminaries launched an international project to translate Luther's works into Spanish, *Obras de Martín Lutero* (*Martin Luther's Works*). Published in ten volumes between 1967 and 1985, the *Obras* incorporated scholars from across the Americas. It aimed both to serve Lutheran communities and to contribute to ecumenical dialogue and awareness among Spanish-speaking Christians; the *Book of Concord*, *Libro de Concordia*, received its first full translation into Spanish in 1989.[64]

Today, Lutheran churches in Latin America and the Caribbean face unique challenges and opportunities. In the book *Wittenberg Meets the World*, Missouri Synod theologians Albert García and John Nunes frame the issues facing many Latinx communities in terms of biblical and Reformation values like justification and justice (*iustitia*), mercy, witness (*martyria*), service (*diakonia*), and community (*koinonia*). On the positive side, the openness of many Lutherans to liberation theology, ecumenism, and issues of gender justice have given Lutherans a unique place in the Latin American religious landscape. From participation in the antiwar movements in El Salvador and Nicaragua to a commitment to social welfare in Argentina and Haiti, Lutherans provide important social services and courageous witness to Christ. Lutherans are still numerically small in comparison to Catholics and Pentecostals, so that persistent challenges include the lack of financial and human resources. Even so, these communities continue to find ways to share a Lutheran perspective of the gospel that resonates in Latin American contexts. This reveals the extent to which translation of the gospel is not just a linguistic issue but a cultural one, essential to the health of local and global communities of faith.

1950s and 1960s: The Rise of Independent Churches

In the aftermath of World War II, many nations gained independence and entered a new era of self-determination. Rather than being entirely freed from colonial power, however, these countries had to reckon with both enduring structures of injustice and the international politics of the Cold War, in which the Soviet Union and Western democracies battled each other directly and indirectly. Warfare related to this global struggle broke out in Korea, Vietnam, Afghanistan, Eritrea, Ethiopia, Mozambique, Cuba, Chile, Nicaragua, and El Salvador, among other lands. The political instability generated during the Cold War continues to lie beneath many of the armed conflicts and humanitarian crises of the twenty-first century. Such conflicts are also legacies of the colonial past and participants in the neocolonial present. These complicated situations have been true both in the Americas—where countries like Haiti, Brazil, Argentina, and Mexico had gained independence in the late 1700s or early 1800s—and in many parts of Africa and Asia, where direct colonial rule lasted into the twentieth century.

The Christianity that spread around the world through Western colonialism has been inextricably connected to European and North American racial prejudices and quests for power. The leadership of missionary churches replicated and reinforced Eurocentric values, regardless of the intentions of the missionaries themselves. Amid such pains, the quest for liberation in those settings has led to essential new insights about the gospel of Jesus Christ and brought important transformations to global Lutheranism.

In the fragile and frequently violent settings of the Cold War era, vibrant new nations and independent churches came into being. The United Republic of Tanzania, for instance, was established in 1964 when the former German colony of Tanganyika united with the British colony of Zanzibar. Church independence followed a similar path. Already in the 1930s, seven Lutheran missionary groups from Europe and the United States had merged their ministries in these former colonies. With independence and the unification of Tanganyika and Zanzibar, the Evangelical

Lutheran Church in Tanzania (ELCT) was born in 1963. With over six million members, it is now one of the largest Lutheran churches in the world.[65]

Lutherans in Tanzania serve body, mind, strength, and soul by supporting schools, hospitals, public infrastructure, economic opportunity, and local congregations. The worship life of the church balances the *Augsburg Confession*'s attention to scripture and sacraments with charismatic forms of preaching and singing. Tanzanian Lutherans have founded new churches in Kenya, the Democratic Republic of Congo, Malawi, Mozambique, Zambia, and Rwanda, raising up new generations in Christian freedom and service.[66]

The holistic theology of African churches has deepened the theology of faith and good works expressed by Luther and Melanchthon in the sixteenth century. Global examples of this concern for the whole person can be seen in the ***fifohazana*** movement in Madagascar, the faithful witness of Ethiopian bishop Gudina Tumsa and his wife Tsehay Tolessa, the leadership in politics, education, medicine, and economic mobility provided by Lutherans in Tanzania, participation in the fight against apartheid in South Africa and the surrounding region (described in the next section), and the leadership of Liberian Lutheran women in the peace movement that ended a civil war. With concerns for body, mind, and soul as central to a life of faith, the 2017 assembly of the Lutheran World Federation held in Namibia observed the five-hundredth anniversary of the Reformation under the theme "Liberated by God's Grace," interpreted through theological, humanitarian, and environmental points emphasized by African theologies: Salvation–Not for Sale; Human Beings–Not for Sale; Creation–Not for Sale.[67]

Born amid struggles for physical and spiritual liberation, these spiritual and social commitments have become essential, life-giving expressions of what it means to follow Jesus in today's world. Despite national independence and the end of the Cold War, poverty and violence remain entrenched across the world, often due to the economic interests of wealthy nations and corporations. Rooted in the gospel of Jesus Christ, Lutheran Christians have a strong message of reconciliation and wholeness to share.

In Latin American contexts, the commitment to justification and justice shines in books like Walter Altmann's *Luther and Liberation*,

Vítor Westhelle's *The Scandalous God*, and *Wittenberg Meets the World* by Alberto García and John Nunes. In each of these works, Lutherans from a variety of Latin backgrounds have searchingly examined the Lutheran tradition to connect gospel proclamation with the lived experience of oppressed peoples. Describing contemporary applications of Luther's view of scripture, for instance, Altmann wrote, "What matters is the realm of God manifested in Christ and made reality in our historical situation. The Bible is the means: forward, to our historical reality; back, to the life and activity of Jesus."[68]

Further recognizing that the gospel speaks to not only our human relationships but also our relation to creation and climate change, Westhelle wrote, "Ecological responsibility, thus, is neither a mystical or romantic response to the positive goodness of creation, nor 'conformity to a natural law,' but a doxological act of repentance and renewal out of the depth, out of the void that threatens us from the cracks of a fissured mask."[69] Confronting a sinful view of the planet and its people as resources to be exploited, care for creation provides a central point for getting to know the God we believe in and living out God's love through our lives.

Another example of profound faith and service in Latin America comes from the Nicaragua Lutheran Church of Faith and Hope, a community that started as a church in exile from the civil war and violence in neighboring El Salvador during the 1980s. Bishop Victoria Cortez Rodríguez described her community as:

> A church that advocates for holistic salvation of human beings as the children of God: body and spirit. This is evident in the practice of holistic ministry in which the diaconia of the church is part of the ecclesial ministry. The social projects are understood as a ministry, because they are the fruit of our faith and our commitment to the communities and they are implemented in order to give life.[70]

Through such Latin American perspectives as those voiced by Altmann, Westhelle, and Rodríguez, Reformation legacies of grace and liberation continue to resonate and inspire.

In Asia, the Philippines is the only country with a majority Christian population, yet even there, Protestants—including the

Lutherans who started churches in the Philippines after World War II—are a minority among the predominantly Roman Catholic population. China and Japan, which had not permitted European missionaries for centuries, opened to European missionaries in the nineteenth century. Lutheran men and women coming mostly from the United States and Scandinavia shared the gospel and offered social services like medical care and schools in China in the later 1800s. As was true in other places, these missionary societies were starting to merge and grow into independent churches before World War II. After the war, however, China's communist revolution of 1949 led to the imprisonment or expulsion of missionaries. In exile, many Chinese Christians and missionaries spread the gospel in nearby places like Hong Kong, Malaysia, and Singapore, giving rise to new Lutheran churches in those lands.

Lutheran missions in Japan started in 1892, when American Lutherans from the United Synod of the South arrived; they were followed by Finnish missionaries who came in 1900 and worked primarily in the northern part of Japan.[71] An important milestone came in 1946 with the publication of Kizoh Kitamori's book *Theology of the Pain of God.* Translated into English in 1958, Kitamori addressed topics like the quest for the historical Jesus, the theology of the cross, and Christian living in specifically Japanese ways, not as an "exotic" alternative to Western theology but as "its own unique contribution to the understanding of the gospel."[72] Although a relatively small presence, Japanese Lutheran churches support schools and social service agencies that serve the wider population. As pastor and historian Toshihiro Takamura has written: "The aim of preaching is not to create Christianized Japan or Japanized Christianity; rather, it is to help Christians to live out their already-given identity as Christians, in struggles found in the tangible, concrete context of encountering and serving their neighbors from God."[73]

Western Asia, of course, is the birthplace of Jesus Christ and Christianity. Many branches of the Christian church have practiced their faith alongside Jewish and Muslim neighbors in the Middle East for centuries, including members of Syrian Orthodox, Eastern Orthodox, and Roman Catholic traditions. As retired bishop Munib

Younan has written, "This, my homeland, is where Jesus taught us to feed those who are hungry, welcome those who are strangers, and liberate those who are oppressed."[74]

Lutheranism in Palestine grew from missionary roots that included a nineteenth-century partnership between Anglicans and Prussians who established churches, deaconess institutions, schools, and hospitals across the Holy Land. In 1959, these and other missionary organizations established the Evangelical Lutheran Church in Jordan and the Holy Land. Working for peace, human rights, and interfaith cooperation are major focal points of these communities. The Augusta Victoria Hospital was established by the Lutheran World Federation in 1948 to serve Palestinian refugees in Jerusalem. In a land now separated by a barrier wall, Augusta Victoria Hospital provides essential medical services to people in East Jerusalem and across the West Bank of Israel. Palestinian Lutheran theologians like Munib Younan and Mitri Raheb have enriched the global church through their writings, advocacy, and leadership.

5.5 Rev. Dr. Monica Melanchton of India speaks at the Lutheran World Federation's Twelfth Assembly in Windhoek, Namibia, May 2017. Photo: LWF/Albin Hillert.

Living amid great religious diversity, Lutherans across Asia have powerful testimonies to share about what it means to be Christian in pluralistic settings. Reflecting on the damaging legacy of colonial and neocolonial experiences in Asia, Indian theologian Monica Melanchthon has written, "We come to exist as human beings by grace. Consequently, only through grace can we attain the fullness of our humanity and build a community of equals."[75] Five hundred years after the Reformation, the Lutheran focus on God's radical grace is still a compelling and life-changing message to share around the world. As a religious tradition that values education, effective social structures, and personal faith, Lutherans often hold an important place between extreme forms of fundamentalism and secularism. In such settings, Lutherans can continue to provide powerful examples of ecumenical, interfaith, and humanitarian cooperation, honoring all people as created in the image of God. The faith-filled leadership of these communities has been and will continue to be essential for effective global Lutheran witness.

5.6 Rev. Dr. Mitri Rahab in his office in Bethlehem. Wikimedia Commons.

June 1977: Lutheran World Federation Declares Apartheid a *Status Confessionis*

At the 1977 assembly in Dar es Salaam, Tanzania, the Lutheran World Federation (LWF) declared that resisting the racial politics of apartheid was a matter of *status confessionis*, a situation demanding public confession of faith. With origins in the adiaphoristic controversy, this doctrinal standpoint was expressed in the 1577 *Formula of Concord*, which asserted:

> We believe, teach, and confess that in a time of persecution, when an unequivocal confession of the faith is demanded of us, we dare not yield to the opponents in such indifferent matters [*rebus adiaphoris*]. As the Apostle wrote, "Stand firm in the freedom for which Christ has set us free, and do not submit again to the yoke of slavery" [Gal 5:1] . . . For in such a situation it is no longer indifferent matters that are at stake. The truth of the gospel and Christian freedom are at stake. The confirmation of open idolatry, as well as the protection of the weak in faith from offense, is at stake. In such matters we can make no concessions but must offer an

> unequivocal confession and suffer whatever God sends and permits the enemies of his Word to inflict on us.[76]

Members of the Confessing Church had invoked this principle in their protests against the Nazification of the church in Germany in the 1930s. Only a few decades later, Lutherans came to apply this confessional stand to the apartheid policies governing South Africa, which included Namibia.

Although long the *de facto* policy of South Africa, in 1948 apartheid became the official law of the government led by Afrikaners, white descendants of Dutch colonists. It was based upon white supremacy and strict racial categorization and segregation. As the South African comedian and author Trevor Noah described it in his memoir *Born a Crime*,

> Apartheid was perfect racism. It took centuries to develop . . . As the British Empire fell, the Afrikaner [descendents of Dutch colonists] rose up to claim South Africa as his rightful inheritance. To maintain power in the face of the country's rising and restless black majority, the government realized they needed a newer and more robust set of tools. They set up a formal commission to go out and study institutionalized racism all over the world. They went to Australia. They went to the Netherlands. They went to America. They saw what worked, what didn't. Then they came back and published a report, and the government used that knowledge to build the most advanced system of racial oppression known to man.[77]

Internal resistance to apartheid arose in groups like the African National Congress in South Africa and its Namibian counterpart SWAPO (South West Africa People's Organization). International objections to apartheid also started to grow, with criticism from the United Nations increasing in the 1960s and a global boycott organized against South Africa taking place in the 1980s.

Lutheranism had come to Namibia through missionaries from Germany and Finland; Germans and Scandinavians also started mission work in South Africa in the nineteenth century. As discussed in the fourth chapter, German colonial rule of Namibia had included the genocide and displacement of native people. By the time of apartheid, black Lutherans in Namibia had developed vibrant indigenous churches, even as many white Lutheran churches supported the government and its racist laws.

In the 1960s, black Lutherans in Namibia were active members of SWAPO, publicly calling for an end to apartheid. A 1971 letter to the South African prime minister from Bishop Auala of the Ovambo-Kavango Church and Pastor Gowaseb, a leader in the Evangelical Lutheran Church in South West Africa, concluded: "The Church Boards' urgent wish is that in terms of the declaration of the World Court and in cooperation with the [United Nations], of which South Africa is a member, your government will seek a peaceful solution to the problems of our land and will see to it that human rights be put into operation and that South West Africa may become a self-sufficient and independent state."[78]

Many Christians—including those belonging to the World Council of Churches and the Roman Catholic Church—worked to confront the injustices of apartheid. The issue came directly before the Lutheran World Federation at the 1977 assembly in Dar es Salaam in the resolution to declare apartheid a *status confessionis*, an essential matter of faith requiring a clear principled stand. Especially poignant was that black Lutheran churches in South Africa and Namibia "were committed to unity without regard to race," while the white Lutheran churches "did not welcome black Christians to common worship or to participation in the Sacrament of the Altar."[79] This resolution came after white Lutherans supporting apartheid had already failed to honor a 1970 LWF statement calling for racial inclusion in the sacrament of Holy Communion.

After much discussion, the assembly passed a statement titled "Statement on Southern Africa: Confessional Integrity," which said,

> Under normal circumstances Christians may have different opinions in political questions. However, political and social systems may become so perverted and oppressive that it is consistent with the confession to reject them and to work for changes. We especially appeal to our white member Churches in Southern Africa to recognize that the situation in Southern Africa constitutes a *status confessionis*. This means that, on the basis of faith and in order to manifest the

unity of the Church, Churches would publicly and unequivocally reject the existing apartheid system.[80]

In the following years, the two LWF member churches supporting apartheid did not change their "whites only" policies. These churches—the Evangelical Lutheran Church in Southern Africa and the German Evangelical Lutheran Church in South West Africa (Namibia)—were therefore suspended from membership by a vote of the next LWF assembly, which was held in Hungary in 1984. This action also increased worldwide Lutheran participation in the boycott of South Africa and support for Namibian independence.

Apartheid ended with Namibian independence in 1990 and a series of democratic elections in South Africa in the early 1990s. Lutherans had played a prominent role in SWAPO and continue to provide public and religious leadership in Namibia. With the end of apartheid, the Lutheran World Federation lifted its suspension of the two denominations in 1991, though racial separation remains a reality among Lutherans in South Africa and Namibia.[81] To this end, Professor Elelwani Bethuel Farisani wrote that "the church has a role to play in encouraging coexistence and harmony among different ethnic groups. Thus, it will have to insist that there is nothing wrong with ethnicity, but the problem is the 'polarising and destructive forms of ethnicity,'" specifically, the racist power structures and values of apartheid and white supremacy.[82]

In hindsight, the actions of the Lutheran World Federation were modest, especially considering that it took fourteen years and three LWF assemblies to create and enforce the policy that member churches are not allowed to discriminate at the altar on the basis of race. Both at the time and in retrospect, however, the action of the LWF against apartheid is among the most visible steps that Lutherans have taken together on a global institutional level. It provides a compelling model for future witness to gospel freedom and political accountability.

Autumn 1989: Peaceful Protests in Leipzig

By September 1989, Monday-night prayers for peace at the *Nikolaikirche* (St. Nicholas Church) in Leipzig had become a catalyst for peaceful protests attended by the wider population of East

Germany. Along with other local and international factors, these peaceful protests contributed to the fall of authoritarian regimes in Eastern Europe.

Two world wars and decades of totalitarianism had decimated centuries-old Lutheran communities in Central and Eastern Europe. Before World War I, Eastern Europe was home to ethnically, culturally, and religiously diverse populations, with Jewish, Catholic, Lutheran, Reformed, and Eastern Orthodox communities living together throughout the region. Lutheran churches had long existed in places like Estonia, Latvia, Hungary, Slovakia, Slovenia, Transylvania, and Russia. The religious and social makeup of these lands was radically changed by the wars and dictatorships of the twentieth century.

The end of World War II left Europe divided. The western powers of France, the United Kingdom, and the United States oversaw what became the Federal Republic of Germany (West Germany) and the Soviet Union (USSR) controlled the German Democratic Republic (East Germany). The city of Berlin was divided along

5.7 Markers identifying the site of the former Berlin Wall. Photo by Martin Lohrmann, used with permission.

the same lines, creating West Berlin and East Berlin. Nations like Poland, Czechoslovakia, and Hungary were under Soviet control, while other places like Ukraine and the Baltic states of Estonia, Latvia, and Lithuania became states within the USSR itself. Hostile to a free press, democratic elections, and freedom of religion, the Soviet government was a police state that imprisoned dissenters, forcibly suppressing revolts like the Hungarian Uprising of 1956 and the Prague Spring of 1968. The Berlin Wall was built around West Berlin in 1961 to keep that city from becoming a place for people to escape the Soviet bloc.

Lutheran churches in Eastern Europe in these years existed under severe pressures from communist dictatorships. Leaders like Bishop Lajos Ordass of Hungary were imprisoned.[83] Pastors and church members routinely lived under surveillance and lived under direct and indirect threats.[84] Even so, Lutheran communities endured behind the Iron Curtain, providing a great testimony to the faith and persistence of the people. Scholars like Helmar Junghans of the University of Leipzig, who edited the journal *Lutherjahrbuch* (Luther Year Book) from 1972 to 2009, and Bishop Zoltán Káldy, a Hungarian Lutheran who served as president of the Lutheran World Federation from 1984 to 1987, provided important perspectives and leadership.

By the late 1980s, people in the Soviet bloc were finding new ways to express their social and political hopes. Christians who had long been marginalized found allies for social change among fellow citizens who were passionate about denuclearization, international peace, environmental protection, and due process of law. Prayers for peace that started in November 1981 had continued at the St. Nicholas Church in Leipzig throughout the decade. In July 1989, the church informed the community and the government that these weekly services would continue with an increased emphasis on social reform. Similar events took place and continued to spread across East Germany.

In September 1989, eyewitness Katharina Führer reported that over a thousand people attended the prayer service inside the *Nikolaikirche*. Upon leaving the building and gathering in the courtyard, they were met by a riot squad that indiscriminately attacked and arrested people.[85] Despite this police opposition, the protests continued to grow. On October 9, 70,000 people attended the vigil in Leipzig, followed by 120,000 participants the next week, and 320,000 people after that. East German leader Erich Honecker resigned on October 18 and the Berlin Wall fell on November 9, 1989. Because most of the authoritarian regimes in Eastern Europe fell without violence, these dramatic events have been called the Peaceful Revolution.

There were many reasons for these dramatic changes.[86] Soviet policies of *perestroika* (restructuring) and *glasnost* (transparency) signaled an internal openness to change. In Poland, the underground Solidarity labor movement won new rights in 1989. Around the same time, the Hungarian government opened its border with Austria, providing an avenue through which people in the Soviet bloc might flee. Across Eastern Europe, calls for democratic reform grew louder and more effective. The prayer services that started at the *Nikolaikirche* joined with other powerful grassroots movements for peace and human rights.

While in many ways a much-desired end to the Cold War, the decades following the unification of Germany and the end of the Soviet bloc also brought new hardships for these countries and their Lutheran churches. In the former nation of East Germany, being a member of the Lutheran church had meant taking a clear position outside the power structures for the sake of Christian faith and social reform; it has been unclear what it means to continue those commitments from inside the dominant post–Cold War economic and political systems. Lutherans in Hungary and other nations have similarly had to keep working hard to find and claim their voice amid the contemporary realities of pluralism, secularism, and nationalism.[87] Having witnessed to Christ under the authoritarian regimes of the twentieth century, Lutherans in these lands continue to discern how best to engage today's struggles from a position of faith.

October 31, 2016: Pope Francis Worships with Lutheran Leaders

In anticipation of the five-hundredth anniversary of the Reformation, Lutheran and Catholic leaders met for an ecumenical prayer service in Lund, Sweden, on October 31, 2016. Worship was led by Pope Francis, LWF president Munib Younan, and LWF general secretary Martin Junge. Other participants included Sweden's first female archbishop, Rev. Antje Jackelén, and Bishop Anders Arborelius, the Roman Catholic bishop of Stockholm.

This prayer service was the fruit of decades of dialogue between Catholics and Lutherans, with important roots in **Vatican II** (1962–1965). At that council of the Roman Catholic Church, Eastern Orthodox and Protestant Christians had been invited to attend as observers. In the decrees of Vatican II, the Catholic Church recognized that the Holy Spirit works salvation among members of other "Churches and ecclesial communities" beyond the Church of Rome.[88] This openness to the gifts and perspectives of other Christians brought new energy and possibilities for ecumenical cooperation.

Addressing themes that had divided Catholics and Protestants since the Reformation, Vatican II promoted the translation of scripture and the liturgy into local languages. The council emphasized the role of the entire assembly in the Eucharistic liturgy and extended the communion cup to laypeople.[89] In the decades that

5.8 Pope Francis and Bishop Munib Younan, President of the Lutheran World Federation, sign a Joint Declaration in Lund, Sweden, in 2017. Photo © PHOTO.VA - Osservatore Romano.

followed, Lutherans and Catholics affirmed each other's common views of baptism and the ecumenical creeds.

Another centuries-old rift between Lutherans and Catholics had come from Luther's teaching that sinners are justified by faith alone in Christ alone, rather than by any human works, personal virtue, cooperation with grace, or ritual actions. After the council, therefore, international representatives of the Lutheran World Federation and the Roman Catholic Church began to discuss the doctrine of justification together. On October 31, 1999 in Augsburg, Germany, Pope John Paul II and then-President Christian Krause of the LWF signed the *Joint Declaration on the Doctrine of Justification*, a statement that intended "to show that on the basis of their dialogue the subscribing Lutheran churches and the Roman Catholic Church are now able to articulate a common understanding of our justification by God's grace through faith in Christ."[90] The document addresses both unity and difference by describing the views of each side, recognizing points of disagreement, and stating that these differences can coexist as Christian ways to understand Christ's reconciling, justifying, and saving grace.

A major milestone in ecumenical cooperation, the *Joint Declaration on the Doctrine of Justification* shows how Christians can work together to understand each other and set aside longstanding mutual condemnations for the sake of shared witness to Christ. That millions of Lutherans and Catholics can recognize each other as fellow Christians after centuries of official condemnation is a tremendously positive accomplishment.

Catholic and Lutheran theologians and church officials continue to engage in mutual dialogue, with recent joint statements such as *The Apostolicity of the Church* (2006) and *Declaration on the Way* (2015) focusing more on keeping the conversation going than on making official doctrinal pronouncements. Major points of disagreement—for instance, different views of the papacy, priesthood, and Eucharistic fellowship—probably will not be resolved any time soon. On the practical level, there also remains a gap between church officials meeting for ecumenical dialogue and the grassroots experiences of local congregations, who might not often learn about these discussions.

Although joint statements on major theological issues like justification might be rare, future ecumenical cooperation can continue to happen through a mutual appreciation of diversity in the one body of Christ. Trusting that the Holy Spirit works among Catholics and Protestants, Christians can cherish the gifts they see in others, claim their own unique perspectives on what it means to follow Jesus, and live out this faith in service to the world that God so loves.

That is the hope expressed in *Declaration on the Way*, the primary document behind the ecumenical prayer service held in Lund, Sweden, on October 31, 2016. That momentous occasion in the life of the global church brought an Argentinian pope together with Lutheran leaders from Chile and Palestine, who met in a cathedral led by a female archbishop. Indeed, five hundred years after Luther changed the world with his "love and zeal for the truth," inspiring and life-changing stories of gospel faith and service remain yet to be explored, lived out, and shared.

Questions

1. How have global relationships not only challenged earlier Lutheran perspectives but enriched how Lutherans understand their own theology and lives as Christians?
2. How have Lutherans adapted to or embraced changing social roles, including the leadership of women in the church? What aspects of the gospel of Jesus Christ most directly shape your response to continuing issues of faith and society?
3. What, if anything, have Lutherans you know learned from the wars and violent political struggles of the twentieth century?
4. What, if anything, have Lutherans you know learned from the racist views that undergirded dramatic horrors like the Holocaust and apartheid, as well as subtler—but still powerful—forms of discrimination and repression?
5. What have been some of your favorite examples of faith in action in this book? What examples lead you to grieve and lament?

6. How do you see the Holy Spirit at work in a church that is truly global?
7. What do you think about the agreements and discussions that have taken place between Lutherans and Catholics in recent decades? What do you think Luther and his colleagues would have said about these steps toward mutual understanding?
8. How do you imagine Lutherans will best use, share, or adapt their spiritual gifts for the next hundred years?

AFTERWORD

Introduction to Lutheranism in Its Sixth Century

This book presents a mosaic of global Lutheran history. Individual pieces have been gathered together to tell a bigger story. All of the pieces have made an important contribution to the whole. But as much as this work has shown that individual and communal "living stones" can move and change, rocks and stones are not the only metaphors we can use. Rocks don't feel joy or pain; people do. For that reason, this study concludes not with rocks but with another New Testament description for people and churches: we are bodies.

As the Easter story of John 20 tells us, the body of Christ bears wounds and painful memories, even as it lives the eternal life of resurrection. For this reason, the apostle Thomas courageously insisted that he meet the risen Christ in the flesh. He needed an encounter with the Messiah who truly had suffered and died because of love for a fallen world. A body of Christ without wounds would not have been the body of Jesus of Nazareth, God's Messiah, the one Thomas longed to know as "my Lord and my God!"

It is certainly tempting to imagine what great futures we could have if only we could free ourselves of the wounds and pain of the past, transcending the physical limits of our histories and contexts. Why worry about old theological fights, social struggles, or church controversies? Why not scrap it all and start fresh? In my time as a church member and pastor, I have heard this wish expressed countless times by people at all levels of church involvement, from all kinds of backgrounds, representing all manner of theological perspectives. I myself have often longed to be free of the hurts and mistakes of the past, both my own personal imperfections and those of the communities to which I belong.

Instead of running from the pain, however, the wounded hands, side, and feet of Christ bring us back to ourselves. Through his wounds and his resurrected body, we receive our whole selves again. Jesus Christ has not given us an ideal to achieve by escaping our pasts, but rather a real life to embrace and love in the here and now, scars and all. The Holy Spirit continues to work through ordinary people to bring peace, resist violence, serve our neighbors, and love the world the way God loves it: not abstractly or ideally but in the flesh of our actual embodied lives and complicated stories.

This immersion into real-life pains can be disappointing and terrifying. Disappointing, because troubles sometimes seem to multiply rather than end; Jesus's wounded hands can seem to excuse or minimize injustice rather than confront and resolve it. Terrifying, because the Way of Jesus is one that does not avoid sin, betrayal, and death but goes directly through them. Precisely in the fears and doubts of the apostles' locked room on that first Easter, Jesus showed his frightened friends that his life did not end with wounds, scars, and death. In the words of Desmond Tutu, the Anglican archbishop of South Africa, the resurrection of Christ proclaims:

> Goodness is stronger than evil;
> Love is stronger than hate;
> Light is stronger than darkness;
> Life is stronger than death;
> Vict'ry is ours, vict'ry is ours
> Through God who loves us.[1]

We may desire different, easier paths, and for good reason. But as St. Paul heard the risen Christ tell him, "My grace is sufficient for you, for power is made perfect in weakness" (2 Cor 12:9).

The body of Christ carries scars and wounds, some of which are still open. These injuries tell stories, often painful ones. The story of Lutheranism includes division, war, exile, colonialism, slavery, genocide, sexism, racism, and authoritarianism. It includes faithful people who suffered wrongly and wrong people who inflicted suffering in the name of God. Sometimes the lines between justice and injustice were clear, and sometimes they were excruciatingly blurry. Amid all that, the wounded hands, side, and feet of the risen Christ call us back to ourselves. We are individual bodies of Christ who belong to broken church bodies of Christ that themselves have their being in the one body of a crucified and risen Lord. We enact this repentance and faith, confession and forgiveness, brokenness and wholeness in Holy Communion and in the daily interactions we have as people who belong to Christ through grace.

Considering the many challenges and uncertainties that church communities have faced in the past and now face today, people sometimes ask me what I think the future of the church will look like. I reply with something I learned from Luther's explanation to the Lord's Prayer in the *Small Catechism*. Asking what it means to pray for God's kingdom to come, Luther answered, "In fact, God's kingdom comes on its own without our prayer, but we ask in this prayer that it may also come to us."[2] These words remind us that God's good reign appears where and when it will, whether or not we pray for it. Our prayer is not that we be the ones to create or find the kingdom; instead, we are praying that we get to keep being a part of it. Recalling the first of Luther's revolutionary *95 Theses*, praying for the kingdom to come among us is an invitation to repent, turn around, and follow Christ anew.

It does not take a prophet to know that the future of a healthy Lutheranism will include a loving embrace of global contexts and cultures, cooperation with secular and religious partners for the well-being of people and creation, and a conviction that the gospel of Jesus Christ truly transforms people for love and service. As clear as those points may be, we pray that such good signs of the kingdom continue to come to us, so that we truly live into our beautiful place in the beloved community of Christ's body.

The stories in this book have been shared to give a sense of the turning and following toward Christ that have happened in the past and that are still to come. Many other stories could have been included and many more are yet to be told. We belong to a beautiful mosaic that is still being pieced together. We are beloved bodies within the one body of Jesus Christ.

> Now thank we all our God with hearts and hands and
> voices,
> who wondrous things has done, in whom this world
> rejoices;
> who, from our mothers' arms, has blest us on our way
> with countless gifts of love, and still is ours today.[3]

Glossary

Accompaniment is a form of sharing the gospel built upon getting to know people and their customs rather than imposing a certain perspective or worldview.

Adiaphora is a word from Greek that means "undifferentiated." In the Lutheran tradition, it refers to things that the Bible neither approves nor forbids, and which can therefore be considered nonessential as matters of salvation. Early examples of adiaphora included what clergy ought to wear in worship and whether congregations could use organ music in worship. While this teaching about adiaphora has provided Lutherans with much freedom in worship and kept a focus on justification by faith alone, it has also led to controversy about who gets to decide what is essential for saving faith and what can be considered secondary.

The ***Augsburg Confession*** remains the primary expression of Lutheran faith and practice as based upon scripture and tradition. Presented to Emperor Charles V at the 1530 Diet of Augsburg by political leaders, it was composed mostly by Philip Melanchthon, who first prepared a German version and then wrote a Latin version. Because they were presented at the same time, they have been viewed as equally authoritative, even though they contain some differences. Melanchthon was asked by Elector John Frederick to revise the *Augsburg Confession* in 1540; because that revision (or *Variata*) later became controversial, Lutherans often refer to the *Unaltered Augsburg Confession* to indicate the version presented in 1530.

The **Augsburg Interim** was Emperor Charles V's attempt to bring German Protestants back to the Roman church. Introduced at the 1548 Diet of Augsburg, it would be a temporary—"interim"—religious policy in the Holy Roman Empire until the Council of Trent would make its more thorough conclusions. Although the Interim became a dead letter after the Princes' Revolt of 1552, divergent responses to the Interim launched generations of theological and political controversies among German Lutherans.

The ***Batak Confession*** is the statement of faith of the Batak Christian Protestant Church [HKBP] in Indonesia. A locally written confession, it is the doctrinal basis for the HKBP's membership in the Lutheran World Federation.

Bishops are described in the New Testament as ministers responsible for overseeing local churches (as in Phil 1:1; 1 Tim 3:1–2; and Titus 1:7). Because late-medieval bishops were often as much political rulers as church officials, Lutherans could not simply install their own new bishops without creating more political chaos. Instead, they filled the New Testament office of *episkopos* (overseer or bishop) by appointing superintendents, a Latin-based word that similarly refers to the work of overseeing faith and practices. In the Church of Sweden, however, the office of bishop was retained, giving Lutherans diverse approaches to the office of church oversight.

The ***Book of Concord*** is a collection of sixteenth-century Lutheran confessional writings that has often served as the basis for Lutheran preaching and teaching. It was first published in 1580 in Dresden and adopted as authoritative by numerous German cities and states. Because the controversies leading to its publication in Germany did not affect Scandinavian lands in the same way, Scandinavian Lutheran communities have been more content to base their teachings on the *Augsburg Confession* and Luther's catechisms. The *Book of Concord* remains a foundational text for many Lutheran communities around the world today.

Cantors are ministers of music in the Lutheran tradition, whose responsibilities since the early Reformation have often included directing choirs, providing musical education for youth, planning worship, and leading instrumental music.

Catechisms are handbooks for basic Christian instruction with roots in both early and medieval Christianity. While many reformers wrote catechisms and other resources, the ones that Martin Luther published in 1529 have remained central for Lutheran communities. The *Small Catechism* provides theological and devotional guidance for both adults and children. Started as sermons, the *Large Catechism* offers longer reflection on Christian lives of faith and love, rooted in scripture and the continuing work of the Holy Spirit.

Catechists are people who teach the basics of Christian faith. They have often served as nonordained evangelists and missionaries.

Christendom describes both the general religious unity of late-medieval Catholicism under the headship of the bishop of Rome and an idealized notion of religious and cultural unity among Europeans. The consistent presence of Jews, Muslims, and other religious groups in and around Europe shows that this idea was never true. Also, the constant warring of European states and the theological differences found among Christian teachers themselves reveals a far more divided and diverse Christianity in Western Europe than is often recognized. Nevertheless, the idea of a unified Christian church and culture was both powerful in its time and continues to influence people today.

Church orders served as early Lutheran church constitutions. They provided theological and practical foundations for local churches, including what pastors should preach and teach, when to hold worship services in cities and villages, how to establish local schools and pay the teachers, and how to organize and fund social services like midwives, doctors, and poor relief.

Colonialism is "the exploitation of a people by another nation for the purposes of gain."[1]

Communion in both kinds means that laypeople receive both the bread and the wine in the sacrament of Holy Communion. In the medieval church, it had become common for the laypeople to receive the bread and for only the priests to receive both the bread and wine. A hallmark of Jan Hus's fifteenth-century reform movement, communion in both kinds became a common reform advocated by Protestants in the sixteenth century.

The **Confessing Church** attempted to resist the Nazification of the Protestant church in Germany in the 1930s, especially in its Barmen Declaration (1934). Key leaders included Karl Barth and Dietrich Bonhoeffer. The movement splintered under internal and external pressure before World War II began.

Confessional theology in the Lutheran tradition refers not to penance or confessing sin but to the public confession—or profession—of faith, especially as expressed in works like the *Augsburg Confession* and the *Formula of Concord.*

Confessionalization is a historical label used to describe the process in which religious confessions of faith like the *Augsburg Confession* also served as political policy and law.

Consistories were local boards that oversaw cases of family law, marital cases, and social services. In early-modern lands where the church often served the public good in conjunction with the state, these boards were made up of a mix of clergy and secular officials.

Conventicles were small-group devotional meetings held by Pietists. Because they could not be easily controlled, the religious and secular authorities often viewed these gatherings with suspicion and passed laws against them, called **Conventicles Acts**.

The **Council of Trent**, held in three sessions from 1545 to 1563, was first called by Pope Paul III. It both responded to the Protestant Reformation and provided its own positive statements of church teachings and reforms. Its decisions shaped Roman Catholicism for centuries to come.

Creeds are communal statements of Christian belief. In the churches of Western Europe, the primary historical creeds have been the Apostles' Creed, the Nicene Creed, and the Athanasian Creed. The Apostles' Creed has origins in the baptismal liturgies of the Latin-speaking church. The Nicene Creed was composed by church councils held in the town of Nicaea in 325 CE and the capital city of Constantinople in 381 CE. The Athanasian Creed was long attributed to the influential fourth-century bishop Athanasius of Alexandria but was likely composed many years later in Gaul (modern-day France).

Cuius regio, eius religio—meaning "whose region, their religion"—summarizes the 1555 Peace of Augsburg, which legalized churches of the *Augsburg Confession* in the Holy Roman Empire. Communities could practice as Catholics or Lutherans, depending on the religious policies set by local authorities. In 1647, this legal protection was extended to Reformed Protestant communities.

Deacon is a New Testament office of ministry connected with serving the community. Early in the Reformation, deacons functioned as assistant pastors; later, they were officials elected and paid by the congregation to oversee the community chest and poor relief. At other points in history, deacons have been synonymous with church council members.

The **Deaconess** movement was started among Lutherans in the nineteenth century as a way for Lutheran women (at first, only unmarried women) to provide important social services like health care and education. Deaconesses also served as key leaders in international missions.

Diets were gatherings of leaders of the Holy Roman Emperor, often including the emperor (or his representative), imperial advisors and theologians, members of the nobility and their court advisors, church leaders, and representatives of city governments. Important diets in the history of early Lutheranism include those held in Worms (1521), Speyer (1526 and 1529), and Augsburg (1530, 1548, and 1555).

Ecumenism is the concern for Christian unity amid the reality of denominational difference. Its roots in Greek mean "one house."

The **Edict of Worms** was Holy Roman Emperor Charles V's verdict against Luther, his teachings, and his followers, published in the spring of 1521. This became the legal basis for the political suppression of Lutheran teachings in the decades that followed. It also served as the basis for legal and political negotiations that took place at imperial diets like those held in Speyer (1526 and 1529) and Augsburg (1530 and 1555).

Electoral Saxony was the land in which Wittenberg was located. In 1485, the Wettin dynasty divided Saxony between two heirs, Albrecht and Ernst. Duke Albrecht received the larger cities of Dresden and Leipzig in the territory of Ducal Saxony; Ernst received the title of Elector, which granted the important political right to have one of seven votes for the Holy Roman Emperor. Beginning with Frederick the Wise, the **electors of Saxony** supported the University of Wittenberg and gave essential political support to the Lutheran Reformation.

The **Enlightenment** refers to the scientific and philosophical movements of the 1600s and 1700s, in which traditional forms of study and governance were challenged by new questions and methods. In the natural sciences, this meant a new emphasis on repeatable experiments; in politics, Enlightenment thinking critiqued hereditary monarchies and aristocracies; in theology, the Enlightenment inspired new studies of biblical sources, morality, and comparative religion.

Eucharistic fellowship is an agreement in which church bodies agree on the meaning, practice, and administration of Holy Communion. It is also called "table fellowship," "altar and pulpit fellowship," or a "full communion agreement."

Eurocentrism is the prejudicial view that European ideas and cultures provide the proper way to evaluate all other human cultures.

Evangelical, meaning "from the gospel," became the preferred way for Lutherans and other Protestants in the Reformation era to describe their theology and church reforms. In contemporary English, this word commonly describes Protestants who focus strongly on personal belief and the conversion of the heart, traits related to—but somewhat distinct from—Lutheran teachings and faith experiences.

Faith in the Lutheran tradition primarily refers to the relationship of trust between God and people. Faith can also refer to what Christians believe (as in, we confess *the* faith) and it can mean personal commitment to God. Even so, for Lutherans faith describes the living relationship with God—a relationship itself initiated by

God—more than the content of religious belief or personal choices about believing in God.

Fifohazana is the spiritual awakening that took place in Madagascar and continues to shape the Malagasy Lutheran Church.

Fundamentalism is a movement that started in the 1800s in opposition to modern academic study of Christianity and scientific explanations of natural phenomena that differ from the Bible. The "Five Fundamentals" (first published in 1910) were: biblical inspiration and inerrancy, the virgin birth of Jesus, atonement by the payment of Christ's blood, bodily resurrection of Jesus, and the historical reality of Christ's miracles; belief in a six-day creation is now commonly included as a required point of belief for Christian fundamentalists. Most Lutheran churches do not require a fundamentalist approach to reading the Bible.

The **Hapsburg (or Habsburg) dynasty** was a powerful aristocratic family whose branches ruled both the Austro-Hungarian Empire and the Spanish Empire for centuries. Hapsburgs also ruled the Holy Roman Empire of the German Nation. Strongly Roman Catholic, Hapsburg dynastic concerns shaped the Reformation and European religious and political affairs in the early-modern era.

The **historic episcopate** describes the tradition of common Christian teachings as upheld by bishops who have been in historical and theological continuity with each other going back to the apostles. Because Catholic bishops in Sweden became Lutheran bishops in that country's Reformation, Swedish Lutheran communities claim participation in the historic episcopate. Other Lutherans, however, confident that continuity with ancient Christianity does not depend on structures like the consecutive consecration of bishops, took this to be a matter of freedom and appointed superintendents to oversee their churches outside the historic episcopate.

Holistic theology describes the teaching and practice of the Evangelical Ethiopian Church Mekane Yesus, especially as expressed by Bishop Gudina Tumsa.

The **Holy Roman Empire of the German Nation** of the medieval and early-modern eras was a vast conglomeration of cities and states in central Europe. Its name derived from the idea that this body was the political successor to the ancient Roman Empire and the Christian empire of Charlemagne (though direct connections were often extremely tenuous). It consisted of a variety of lands that had their own local laws, languages, and customs within the larger structure of the empire. It was feudal, as authority followed a pyramid structure from the peasantry to merchants, lesser nobility and vassals, to the higher nobility and an emperor, who was elected by seven members of the nobility. The empire also oversaw free cities that were governed independently, with oversight coming directly from the emperor. Members of the Hapsburg dynasty ruled as Holy Roman Emperors from the 1400s to the 1700s.

Humanists of the early-modern era were often independent scholars who studied and valued the writings of Greco-Roman civilization. It was marked by appreciation for *bona litera* (good writing) and by its freedom to read texts (including the Bible) in original languages, apart from the theological and philosophical systems of the Middle Ages. While some humanists like Erasmus of Rotterdam and Thomas More remained in the Church of Rome, reformers like Luther, Zwingli, Melanchthon, and Calvin were also deeply influenced by humanist ideas and used humanist methods in their biblical translations, exegetical works, and church reforms.

Iconoclasm means the destruction or prohibition of images, especially religious works of art that depict God and the saints. Among Protestants, this iconoclastic impulse came from a renewed emphasis on the biblical command "You shall not make for yourself an idol" (Exod 20:4) among Radical and Reformed Protestants. Rather than strictly enforcing this command, Lutherans generally followed more moderate interpretations of the religious use of images as expressed in the Roman Catholic and Eastern Orthodox traditions.

The **International Lutheran Council** is a global association of Lutheran churches, distinguished from the Lutheran World Federation by a strong stand on scriptural inerrancy and unconditional subscription to the *Book of Concord.*

Jesuits, or the Society of Jesus, have their foundation in the reforming ministry of Ignatius of Loyola and Francis Xavier in the 1530s.

Jesuits became leading opponents of the Protestant Reformation, while also becoming important missionaries and educational leaders in the Roman Catholic Church.

Justification refers to the theological teaching about how sinful people are made right or reconciled to a holy God. Lutheran theology has insisted that justification is entirely God's gracious action through Jesus Christ, received simply by trusting God's promises; that is, through faith alone. Luther wrote in his *Small Catechism* that even the reception of this grace is a work of the Holy Spirit in the heart.

Liberal theology is the attempt to integrate faith and reason, especially in light of the scientific revolution of the Enlightenment era.

Liberation theology describes contemporary theologies that emphasize human freedom from both spiritually and temporally oppressive structures.

Lutheran is a name for followers of the Reformation teachings of Martin Luther and his colleagues. It was first popularized by Luther's adversaries as an insulting heretical label. Luther preferred for his movement to be called Evangelical, meaning "from the gospel." In addition to describing themselves as Evangelical, Lutheran leaders of the sixteenth century also commonly referred to themselves as "theologians of the Augsburg Confession," identifying with a doctrinal tradition rather than the individual person of Martin Luther. But the name has stuck, especially in English-speaking communities where "evangelical" has come to be ascribed to other forms of Protestantism.

Lutheran Orthodoxy refers to the era (late 1500s to early 1700s) in which Lutheran theologians put great emphasis on "right doctrine," particularly to contrast Lutheran beliefs with Reformed and Catholic confessions. Although theologians of the period produced works of tremendous detail and precision, Lutheran Orthodox writers like Philipp Nicolai and Johann Gerhard also composed devotional and poetic works, revealing a simultaneous concern for lived spirituality.

Lutheran World Federation (LWF) is an international communion of Lutheran church bodies. Formed in 1947, its headquarters are in Geneva, Switzerland. The majority of the world's Lutherans belong to the LWF, which emphasizes human rights, religious dialogue, and common Christian witness.

Ministerium can refer either to a governing board of clergy or to an entire church body, as in the "Ministerium of Pennsylvania," which included nonclergy congregational representatives as voting members.

Modernism in theology describes an openness to modern academic study of the Bible, including a willingness to integrate scientific learning with religious belief. It has inspired opposition in the form of Protestant fundamentalism and Catholic anti-modernism.

Moravians are named after the central European region of Moravia. This Protestant church developed from the Bohemian Brethren of Jan Hus's reforms in the 1400s and from the Pietist renewal of the early 1700s, supported by Count Nicholas Ludwig von Zinzendorf. Because Zinzendorf supported Moravian refugees at his Herrnhut estate, they have also been called Herrnhuters. Moravians were important leaders in missionary work in the Americas and the Caribbean, promoting indigenous churches and local leadership.

Neocolonialism describes the reality that unequitable economic systems often persist after direct political colonialism has ended.

Offices, in the Lutheran tradition, refer to the roles that people have in life, usually in relationship to the wider community. For instance, civic leaders fulfill their office by caring for the common good. Church leaders hold offices that revolve around sharing the gospel and nurturing the community of faith. In Lutheran theology, family relationships like marriage, parenthood, and childhood are offices that set positive expectations for life together. Most of all, Christians share the same spiritual office as baptized believers, so that all have equal access before God and can equally pray to God, pray for each other, and share the gospel regardless of their age, employment, or social status.

The **Peace of Augsburg** was the 1555 decree that legalized the church of the *Augsburg Confession* for the first time in the Holy Roman Empire. Reformed Protestants or members of more radical

Reformation communities were not included in its protections. It operated under the principle *cuius regio, eius religio*: whose region, their religion.

Pentecostalism refers to a spiritual movement that emphasizes the outpouring of the Holy Spirit, as described in the Pentecost experience of Acts 2. With roots in revivalism and the Holiness Movement of the nineteenth century, modern Pentecostalism began with the Azusa Street Revival in Los Angeles in 1906. In the past century, Pentecostalism has become a major expression of global Christianity and has influenced many communities, including Lutherans.

Pietism is the name for the spiritual renewal movement that followed the publication of Philip Spener's *Pia Desideria* (Pious Desires). With a focus on personal conversion, works of love, and small-group devotions (meeting in conventicles), Pietism challenged many features of conventional Lutheran Orthodoxy. Its historical center became the Francke Foundations located in Halle, established by a younger colleague of Spener's named August Hermann Francke.

Protestant is a name that originally described those who disagreed with the religious policy of the Edict of Worms, especially as debated at the 1529 Diet of Speyer. It has come to refer to all Christian traditions that have roots in the Protestant Reformations of the 1500s.

Rationalism is an intellectual value that prioritizes knowledge that can be demonstrated over other forms of knowing such as experience, emotion, or tradition.

Real presence in Holy Communion refers to the teaching that Christ is truly present in the eating and drinking of the Eucharistic elements. Although the Lutheran reformers disagreed with the Catholic teaching of transubstantiation (which holds that the bread and wine of communion substantially become the body and blood of Christ), Lutherans believe with Catholics in the real physical presence of Christ in Holy Communion. This view contrasts with many Protestant communities that emphasize a spiritual or symbolic presence in the meal.

The **Reformation** is the era of history that started when Martin Luther's suggestions for church reforms started to inspire widespread change among Christian communities in Europe. The posting of Luther's *95 Theses* on October 31, 1517 is widely acknowledged as the symbolic start of the Reformation, which transformed Christianity over the following decades and centuries.

Reformed Protestants describes those communities who were influenced and led by reformers like Huldrych Zwingli, John Calvin, John Knox, and Heinrich Bullinger. Important early Reformed statements of faith include the Heidelberg Catechism (1563), the Scots Confession (1560), the Westminster Confession (1646), and Calvin's *Institutes of the Christian Religion.* Representing over one hundred million Christians today, the World Communion of Reformed Churches brings together global Reformed, Presbyterian, and United Church traditions.

Revivalism developed among Protestants in the early 1800s. With origins in the Presbyterian Eucharistic love feasts of rural Scotland, revivals came to emphasize charismatic preaching, inspiring music, and personal spiritual experience rather than traditional liturgical forms or the sacrament of Holy Communion.

Shoah is a Hebrew word meaning "destruction," describing the persecution and murder of millions of Jews, Poles, Romani, homosexuals, communists, disabled, and other people at the hands of the Nazi regime and their collaborators in Germany from 1933 to 1945. It is also called "the Holocaust," a word from Greek that means a burnt offering.

The **Smalcaldic League** was a political alliance organized in 1531 under the leadership of Elector John of Saxony and Philip of Hesse. It came to an end in 1547 when Emperor Charles V won the Smalcaldic War. Nevertheless, with its primary aim of mutual defense and its insistence on adherence to the *Augsburg Confession*, the Smalcaldic League served an important role in the institutional and political development of Protestantism.

Superintendents have filled the role of bishop in much of Lutheran history. Because late-medieval bishops were often political rulers as well as church officials, Lutherans could not always install their own bishops. Instead, they invented the office of superintendent (a Latin-based word that denotes the same office of oversight as the Greek *episkopos*—overseer or bishop). Superintendents functioned as head pastors and church administrators for cities and regions.

Synods in early Christian history were regional councils. Beginning in the 1700s, North American Lutherans came to use the word to describe both their regional and national church bodies. "Synod" comes from Greek and means "walking together."

Theology of the Cross refers to the conviction that God has revealed holiness, grace, and truth not through earthly ideas of power or purity but through Christ's self-giving, self-denying, and self-emptying love for sinners on the cross. In this way, the cross of Christ reveals that God's glory appears in the last place one would reasonably look.

Tolerance as a public religious policy became a way for nations to support a single church—for instance, the Dutch Reformed Church or the Church of England—while allowing individuals to practice their faith privately outside the established church.

Vatican II was a council of the Roman Catholic Church, which took place from 1962 to 1965. At the council, Catholics addressed issues of modernism and ecumenism in constructive new ways. The council also affirmed worship in local languages and communion in both kinds.

The **World Council of Churches** was formed in 1948 to promote Christian unity, common witness, and service. Its membership includes many worldwide Protestant and Orthodox churches—representing about half a billion Christians—and maintains a working relationship with the Roman Catholic Church. Its headquarters are in Geneva, Switzerland.

Notes

INTRODUCTION: LIVING STONES AND FAITH ROCKS

1. LW 31:350–51.
2. As in New Testament passages like 1 Cor 3:11 and Eph 2:19–22.
3. Jaroslav Pelikan, *Luther the Expositor* (St. Louis: Concordia, 1959), 115.
4. BC 334.25.
5. BC 440–441.2.
6. BC 174.10. See also the definition of the church in articles 7 and 8 of the *Augsburg Confession*, BC 42 and 43.
7. The Lutheran World Federation, https://tinyurl.com/zh6269y.
8. Paul Varo Martinson, "China," DLLT, 141.
9. *Lutheran Quarterly*, https://tinyurl.com/rao5u4a.
10. Psalm 22:29–31, ELW #22.

CHAPTER 1: 1517–1617

1. LW 25:238.
2. *Martin Luther's Ninety-Five Theses, with Introduction, Commentary, and Study Guide*, ed. Timothy J. Wengert (Minneapolis: Fortress Press, 2015), xviii–xxi.
3. LW 31:25. Luther sometimes spelled his last name with two t's at the time.
4. LW 31:25. Matt 4:17: "From that time Jesus began to proclaim, 'Repent, for the kingdom of heaven has come near.'"
5. LW 31:33. In ancient Rome, Marcus Licinius Crassus was famous for his wealth. The pope at the time of the indulgence controversy was Pope Leo X, a member of the wealthy and powerful Medici family. The indulgence being sold in Germany at the time was the St. Peter's

Indulgence; part of the income would go to rebuilding that basilica in Rome.

6. Volker Leppin and Timothy J. Wengert, "Sources for and against the Posting of the *Ninety-Five Theses*," *Lutheran Quarterly* 29 (2015): 373–98.
7. LW 31:40.
8. LW 31:225.
9. As in Mark 10:45; 2 Cor 5:21; Gal 3:13; and Phil 2:5–11.
10. LW 31:259–92. See also Martin Luther, *The Annotated Luther, Volume 1: The Roots of Reform*, ed. Timothy J. Wengert (Minneapolis: Fortress Press, 2015), 121–65.
11. Philip Melanchthon, *Loci Communes Theologici*, in *Melanchthon and Bucer*, ed. Wilhelm Pauck (Philadelphia: Westminster, 1969), 21.
12. In the Middle Ages, it became customary for only the priests to drink the wine and for the laypeople to receive only the bread in the sacrament of Holy Communion. Receiving both the bread and the wine is called "**communion in both kinds.**"
13. Heinz Scheible, "Luther and Melanchthon," *Lutheran Quarterly* 4 (1990): 325.
14. Clyde L. Manshrek, *Melanchthon: The Quiet Reformer* (Nashville: Abingdon, 1958), 143. See also Carl P. E. Springer, *Cicero in Heaven: The Roman Rhetor and Luther's Reformation* (Leiden: Brill, 2018), 140.
15. Martin Brecht, *Martin Luther: Shaping and Defining the Reformation, 1521–1532*, trans. James L. Schaaf (Minneapolis: Fortress Press, 1990), 107–12.
16. Martin Lohrmann, *Bugenhagen's Jonah: Biblical Interpretation as Public Theology* (Minneapolis: Lutheran University Press, 2012), 11.
17. LW 53:211–16. See also Robin A. Leaver, *The Whole Church Sings: Congregational Singing in Luther's Wittenberg* (Grand Rapids: Eerdmans, 2017), 55–64.
18. LW 44:127.
19. LW 45:63.
20. James Cone, *God of the Oppressed* (Maryknoll, NY: Orbis, 1997), 182–84.
21. Stephen G. Ray Jr., *Do No Harm: Social Sin and Christian Responsibility* (Minneapolis: Fortress Press, 2003), 128.
22. Martin Treu, "Katharina von Bora: The Woman at Luther's Side," *Lutheran Quarterly* 13 (1999): 158.
23. LW 34:291–97.
24. Kirsi Stjerna, "Katharina von Bora: Mother of the Lutheran Reformation," in *Together by Grace: Introducing the Lutherans*, ed. Kathryn A. Kleinhans (Minneapolis: Augsburg Fortress, 2016), 55–57.
25. ELW #309.
26. Mary Jane Haemig, "Cruciger, Elisabeth," DLLT, 181.
27. Marjorie Elizabeth Plummer, "Convents," DLLT, 166–67.

28. Kenneth G. Appold, "Taking a Stand for Reformation: Martin Luther and Caritas Pirkheimer," *Lutheran Quarterly* 32 (2018): 49–57.
29. Cited in Martin Marty, *Martin Luther: A Life* (New York: Penguin, 2004), 165.
30. For more on the Marburg Colloquy and ongoing Lutheran-Reformed discussions in the sixteenth century and beyond, see Gordon A. Jensen, *The Wittenberg Concord: Creating Space for Dialogue* (Minneapolis: Fortress Press, 2018), esp. 48–53.
31. Charles P. Arand, Robert Kolb, and James A. Nestingen, *The Lutheran Confessions: History and Theology of the Book of Concord* (Minneapolis: Fortress Press, 2012), 105.
32. Robert Kolb, *Confessing the Faith: Reformers Define the Church, 1530–1580* (St. Louis: Concordia, 1991), 57.
33. Philip Schaff, *History of the Christian Church, Volume 6* (New York: Scribner, 1892), 347. Describing the group that gathered in Wittenberg to work on Bible translation, Schaff wrote, "occasionally foreign scholars were admitted; and Jewish rabbis were freely consulted." For more on Luther and the Jews, see chapter 2.
34. LW 35:118.
35. LW 35:164–68.
36. BC 355.4.
37. LW 52:171–72.
38. Birgit Stolt, "Luther's Translation of the Bible," *Lutheran Quarterly* 28 (2014): 377–78.
39. LW 50:306.
40. Martin Brecht, *Martin Luther: The Preservation of the Church, 1532–1546*, trans. James Schaaf (Minneapolis: Fortress Press, 1993), 229–33.
41. LW 54:476.
42. Scott H. Hendrix, *Martin Luther: Visionary Reformer* (New Haven: Yale University Press, 2015), 231.
43. Martin Treu, *Katherine von Bora, Luther's Wife*, trans. Stephen P. Glinsky Jr. (Lutherstadt Wittenberg: Drei Kastanien, 2003), 82–86.
44. Arand, Kolb, and Nestingen, *The Lutheran Confessions*, 124.
45. Arand, Kolb, and Nestingen, *The Lutheran Confessions*, 173.
46. Lohrmann, *Bugenhagen's Jonah*, 34.
47. For more on these topics, see Brecht, *Martin Luther: The Preservation of the Church*, 205–15 and 320–23.
48. Johannes Bugenhagen, *Selected Writings, Volume 1*, trans. Kurt K. Hendel (Minneapolis: Fortress Press, 2015), 135–64, especially 153–60. See also Lohrmann, *Bugenhagen's Jonah*, 49.
49. Bugenhagen, *Selected Writings, Volume 1*, 163–64.
50. Robert Kolb and James A. Nestingen, eds., *Sources and Contexts of the Book of Concord* (Minneapolis: Fortress Press, 2001), 147.
51. Timothy Wengert, "Not by Nature *Philoneikos*: Philip Melanchthon's Initial Reactions to the Augsburg Interim," in *Politik und Bekenntnis:*

Die Reaktionen auf das Interim von 1548, ed. Irene Dingel and Günther Wartenberg (Leipzig: Evangelische Verlagsanstalt, 2006), 35.

52. Arand, Kolb, and Nestingen, *The Lutheran Confessions*, 181–82.
53. Arand, Kolb, and Nestingen, *The Lutheran Confessions*, 173–74.
54. Korey D. Maas, "Barnes, Robert," DLLT, 76–77.
55. Eric Lund, "Denmark," DLLT, 189.
56. Eric Lund, "Iceland," DLLT, 353.
57. Simo Heininen, "Finland," DLLT, 249.
58. Luka Ilić, "Primus Truber (1508–1586), the Slovenian Luther," *Lutheran Quarterly* 22 (2008): 270.
59. Ilić, "Primus Truber," 271–72.
60. David G. Truemper and Frederick A. Niedner Jr., *Keeping the Faith: A Guide to the Christian Message* (Philadelphia: Fortress Press, 1981), 14: "*Doctrine is what a Christian has to say in order that what gets heard will be the gospel*" [italics in the original].
61. Leaver, *The Whole Church Sings*, 15.
62. Robin A. Leaver, "Luther on Music," *Lutheran Quarterly* 20 (2006): 129.
63. BC 363.3.

CHAPTER 2: 1617–1717

1. Robert Kolb, *Martin Luther as Prophet, Teacher, and Hero: Images of the Reformer, 1520–1620* (Grand Rapids: Baker Academic, 1999), 126–34; and Michael J. Halvorson, "German Lutheran Centennial Dramas," *Lutheran Quarterly* 30 (2016): 279–83.
2. Margit Thøfner, "Framing the Sacred: Lutheran Church Furnishings in the Holy Roman Empire," in *Lutheran Churches in Early Modern Europe*, ed. Andrew Spicer (Routledge: London, 2016), 104.
3. Robert Kolb, "'So Much Began in Halle': The Mission Program That Sent Mühlenberg to America," *Concordia Historical Institute Quarterly* 84 (2011): 28–29.
4. William J. Layton, "If Theology Is Practical: Piety and Spirituality in Early Lutheran Orthodoxy" (master's thesis, Wartburg Theological Seminary, 2017).
5. Franz Hildebrandt, *Melanchthon: Alien or Ally?* (Cambridge: Cambridge University Press, 1946 [reprinted in New York, 1968]), and Richard R. Caemmerer, "The Melanchthonian Blight," *Concordia Theological Monthly* 18 (1947): 321–38.
6. For instance, Robert D. Preus, *The Theology of Post-Reformation Lutheranism: A Study of Theological Prolegomena* (St. Louis: Concordia, 1970), 157: "By the middle of the 17th century there are clearly discernible two different currents of theological thought within the Lutheran Church. The one, following Melanchthon, is humanistic, unionistic,

synergistic, catholic, and philosophically inclined. The other, in the footsteps of Luther and Chemnitz, is confessional and monergistic, but also catholic and not averse to the adventitious help of philosophy in presenting theology."

7. See Bodo Nischan, *Prince, People, and Confession: The Second Reformation in Brandenburg* (Philadelphia: University of Pennsylvania Press, 1994).
8. Hajo Holborn, *A History of Modern Germany: The Reformation* (Princeton: Princeton University Press, 1959), 288–89, 299–301.
9. Holborn, *A History of Modern Germany*, 291, 304.
10. Defenestration means "throwing out of the window." The defenestrated officials seem to have survived their fall, which Catholics explained as divine intervention and Protestants said happened because they landed in a manure pile; see Diarmaid MacCulloch, *The Reformation* (New York: Viking, 2003), 477.
11. Holborn, *A History of Modern Germany*, 320–26.
12. Holborn, *A History of Modern Germany*, 338.
13. Michael J. Halvorson, "Thirty Years' War," DLLT, 740.
14. Bo Andersson, "Sweden, the Elect Nation," *Lutheran Quarterly* 13 (1999): 305–14.
15. Holborn, *A History of Modern Germany*, 341–42.
16. Steven Ozment, *A Mighty Fortress: A New History of the German People* (New York: HarperCollins, 2004), 121.
17. Ted Peters, "Natural Science," DLLT, 533–34.
18. C. F. v. Weizsäcker, "Kepler, Johannes," *Die Religion in Geschichte und Gegenwart*, vol. 3, 3rd ed. (Tübingen: Mohr Siebeck, 1959), 1247.
19. Joyce Irwin, "Celestial Harmony in Baroque Lutheran Writings," *Lutheran Quarterly* 3 (1989): 288–89.
20. Irwin, "Celestial Harmony," 281.
21. Irwin, "Celestial Harmony," 285.
22. "O Lord, How Shall I Meet You," stanza 1, ELW #241.
23. Variations on this spelling include Jiří, Jiřik, or Jur Třanovský; it is Latinized as Georg Tranoscius. Some sources indicate a birth year of 1591.
24. Janka Krivošová, "Witnesses to the Lutheran Faith in Bratislava," *Lutheran Quarterly* 16 (2002): 422.
25. Marilyn Kay Stulken, *Hymnal Companion to the Lutheran Book of Worship* (Philadelphia: Fortress Press, 1981), 196–97.
26. John Clapham, "Tranovský, Juraj," *The New Grove Dictionary of Music and Musicians*, Vol. 16, ed. Stanley Sadie (London: Macmillan, 1980), 116.
27. Hellmuth Christian Wolff, "Tranoscius," *Die Musik in Geschichte und Gegenwart*, Band 13 (Kassel: Bärenreiter, 1966), 623.
28. Clapham, "Tranovský, Juraj," 116.
29. "Your Heart, O God, Is Grieved," stanza 1, ELW #602.

30. Kenneth G. Appold, "Early Lutheran Perspectives on the Council of Trent," *Lutheran Quarterly* 32 (2018): 151.
31. Bengt Hägglund, "Polemics and Dialogue in John Gerhard's *Confessio Catholica*," *Lutheran Quarterly* 14 (2000): 160.
32. LW 40:231–32.
33. Timothy J. Wengert, *Priesthood, Pastors, Bishops: Public Ministry for the Reformation & Today* (Minneapolis: Fortress Press, 2008), 91.
34. Hägglund, "Polemics and Dialogue," 161.
35. Klaus P. Fischer, *The History of an Obsession: German Judeophobia and the Holocaust* (New York: Continuum, 1998), 28.
36. Fischer, *The History of an Obsession*, 30. The modern prejudice of anti-Semitism added unscientific (or pseudo-scientific) racial theories to justify the discrimination and hatred of anti-Judaism.
37. LW 47:268.
38. Kirsi I. Stjerna, in *The Annotated Luther, Volume 5: Christian Life in the World*, ed. Hans J. Hillerbrand (Minneapolis: Fortress Press, 2017), 391.
39. Darrel Jodock, "Holocaust," DLLT, 334.
40. Craig L. Nessan, "Bonhoeffer, Dietrich, Influence on," *Encyclopedia of Martin Luther and the Reformation, Volume 1: A-L*, ed. Mark A. Lampport (Lanham, MD: Rowman & Littlefield, 2017), 83.
41. Heiko Oberman, *The Roots of Anti-Semitism in the Age of Renaissance and Reformation*, trans. James I. Porter (Philadelphia: Fortress Press, 1984), 47–48.
42. Brooks Schramm, in *The Annotated Luther, Volume 5: Christian Life in the World*, ed. Hans J. Hillerbrand (Minneapolis: Fortress Press, 2017), 612.
43. Martin Brecht, *Martin Luther: The Preservation of the Church, 1532–1546* (Minneapolis: Augsburg Fortress, 1993), 349.
44. Kenneth G. Appold, "Early Lutheran Attitudes toward Jews," *Lutheran Quarterly* 20 (2006): 173.
45. Appold, "Early Lutheran Attitudes toward Jews," 178.
46. Appold, "Early Lutheran Attitudes toward Jews," 179.
47. George Orwell, *Animal Farm* (London: Secker & Warburg, 1945; New York: Harcourt, Brace & Co., 1946), 148. Orwell's original phrase is "All animals are equal, but some animals are more equal than others."
48. LW 31:25.
49. LW 31:351 and BC 362.5–63.8, respectively.
50. BC 127.45.
51. Philipp Jakob Spener, *Pia Desideria*, ed. and trans. Theodore G. Tappert (Philadelphia: Fortress Press, 1964), 29.
52. Spener, *Pia Desideria*, 92–95.
53. Jonathan Strom, "Conventicles," DLLT, 165.
54. Strom, "Conventicles," 165.

55. Timothy Maschke, "Philipp Spener's Pia Desideria," *Lutheran Quarterly* 6 (1992): 196.
56. Klaus vom Orde, "Spener, Philipp Jakob," DLLT, 700.
57. Peter James Yoder, "Francke, August Hermann," DLLT, 265.
58. Thomas Müller Bahlke, "Francke Foundations," DLLT, 266–67.
59. W. Gordon Marigold, "Opera, Politics, and Religion in Hamburg 1678–1715," *Lutheran Quarterly* 3 (1989): 67. The opera controversy [*die Operstreit*] is also known as the Hamburg theater controversy [*die Theaterstreit*].
60. Marigold, "Opera, Politics, and Religion," 70.
61. Bernhard Lohse, "Hamburg," *Theologische Realenzyklopädie*, Volume 15 (Berlin: De Gruyter, 1985), 408.
62. Lohse, "Hamburg," 409: "*Schutzpatron aller Schwärmer.*"
63. Marigold, "Opera, Politics, and Religion," 73.
64. Lohse, "Hamburg," 409.
65. Marigold, "Opera, Politics, and Religion," 79.
66. Mark Granquist, *Lutherans in America: A New History* (Minneapolis: Fortress Press, 2015), 33–34.
67. Kim-Eric Williams, "Laughing with the Lenape: Swedes and Native Americans in Colonial Delaware," *Journal of the Lutheran Historical Conference* 1 (2011): 79.
68. Trygve Skarsten, "Johan Campanius, Pastor in New Sweden," *Lutheran Quarterly* 2 (1988): 57.
69. Isak Collijn, "The Swedish-Indian Catechism, Some Notes," *Lutheran Quarterly* 2 (1988): 89.
70. Williams, "Laughing with the Lenape," 86.
71. Williams, "Laughing with the Lenape," 89.
72. Justo González, *The Story of Christianity, Volume 1: The Early Church to the Dawn of the Reformation*, revised and updated (New York: HarperOne, 2010), 75–81.
73. Daniel Brunner, "Anglican Perceptions of Lutheranism in Early Hanoverian England," *Lutheran Quarterly* 20 (2006): 63–82.
74. Luther D. Reed, *The Lutheran Liturgy*, revised edition (Philadelphia: Muhlenberg, 1947), 168; see also E. Clifford Nelson, *The Lutherans in America* (Philadelphia: Fortress Press, 1975), 44, 63.

CHAPTER 3: 1717–1817

1. David Bosch, *Transforming Mission: Paradigm Shifts in Theology of Mission*, 20th anniversary ed. (Maryknoll, NY: Orbis, 2011), 233.
2. Richard J. Boles, "African Americans and Northern Lutherans in the Eighteenth Century," *Lutheran Quarterly* 33 (2019): 153–79.
3. US Declaration of Independence, 1776, https://tinyurl.com/h2zqchv.

4. Christoph Wolff, *Johann Sebastian Bach: The Learned Musician* (New York: Norton, 2000), 50–51.
5. *The Bach Reader: A Life of Johann Sebastian Bach in Letters and Documents*, rev. ed., ed. Hans T. David and Arthur Mendel (New York: Norton, 1966), 42.
6. LW 15:273–74; cited in Robin A. Leaver, "Johann Sebastian Bach and the Lutheran Understanding of Music," *Lutheran Quarterly* 16 (2002): 29–30.
7. Leaver, "Johann Sebastian Bach and the Lutheran Understanding of Music," 27.
8. Leaver, "Johann Sebastian Bach and the Lutheran Understanding of Music," 37.
9. Paul Westermeyer, "Bach, Johann Sebastian," DLLT, 69–70.
10. Wolff, *Johann Sebastian Bach*, 426–28.
11. Wolff, *Johann Sebastian Bach*, 462.
12. Todd Green, "Swedish Pietism (1700–1727) as Resistance and Popular Religion," *Lutheran Quarterly* 21 (2007): 67–68.
13. Green, "Swedish Pietism (1700–1727) as Resistance and Popular Religion," 64.
14. Green, "Swedish Pietism (1700–1727) as Resistance and Popular Religion," 69–70.
15. Green, "Swedish Pietism (1700–1727) as Resistance and Popular Religion," 65.
16. Mark Granquist, ed., *Scandinavian Pietists: Spiritual Writings from 19th-Century Norway, Denmark, Sweden, and Finland* (Mahwah, NJ: Paulist, 2015), 147.
17. See Ann Öhrberg, "'A Threat to Civic Coexistence': Forbidden Religious Literature and Censorship in Eighteenth-Century Sweden," in *Religious Reading in the Lutheran North: Studies in Early Modern Scandinavian Book Culture*, ed. Charlotte Appel and Morton Fink-Jensen (Newcastle: Cambridge Scholars, 2011), 112–32.
18. John C. England, *The Hidden History of Christianity in Asia: The Churches of the East before 1500* (Delhi: Indian Society for Promoting Christian Knowledge and Christian Conference of Asia, 1996 and 2002), 59.
19. *The Travels of Marco Polo* (New York: Orion, 1985), 293–94 [book 3, chapter 20].
20. England, *The Hidden History of Christianity in Asia*, 64.
21. J. Paul Rajashekar, "India," DLLT, 363–64.
22. P. Daniel Jeyaraj, "Lutheran Churches in Eighteenth-Century India," *Lutheran Quarterly* 17 (2003): 84–85, 92–93.
23. Kolb, "'So Much Began in Halle,'" 32.
24. Rajashekar, "India," 365.

25. J. Paul Rajashekar, "Lutheranism in Asia and the Indian Subcontinent," in *The Future of Lutheranism in a Global Context*, ed. Arland Jacobson and James Aageson (Minneapolis: Fortress Press, 2008), 70.
26. Wolfgang Splitter, "Jewish Support of the Salzburg Lutheran Refugees in 1732/33," *Lutheran Quarterly* 27 (2013): 143–66.
27. Russell Kleckley, "Ebenezer Community," DLLT, 200.
28. Jeff G. Johnson, *Black Christians: The Untold Lutheran Story* (St. Louis: Concordia, 1991), 58.
29. Kleckley, "Ebenezer Community," 201.
30. J. G. Johnson, *Black Christians*, 234–37.
31. Craig D. Atwood, "Zinzendorf, Nikolaus Ludwig von," DLLT, 810–12.
32. J. G. Johnson, *Black Christians*, 38.
33. John M. Jensen, "Egede, Hans Poulsen," TELC 1, 768.
34. J. G. Johnson, *Black Christians*, 38.
35. J. G. Johnson, *Black Christians*, 39.
36. J. G. Johnson, *Black Christians*, 49–50, 158–59.
37. Atwood, "Zinzendorf, Nikolaus Ludwig von," 811.
38. Kim-Eric Williams, "Justus Falckner," DLLT, 245.
39. Mark Granquist, *Lutherans in America: A New History* (Minneapolis: Fortress Press, 2015), 62–64.
40. *The Journals of Henry Melchior Muhlenberg*, vol. 1, trans. Theodore Tappert and John Doberstein (Philadelphia: Muhlenberg Press, 1942), 74.
41. *The Journals of Henry Melchior Muhlenberg*, 1, 76–84.
42. BC 47.3.
43. Kim-Eric Williams, "Ministerium of Pennsylvania," DLLT, 501.
44. *The Journals of Henry Melchior Muhlenberg*, 1, 102. Grammatically, *ecclesia plantanda* can be translated as a command—"the church must be planted"—but in the context of the 1745 report, the more pragmatic "planting the church" is clearly meant.
45. Immanuel Kant, "What Is Enlightenment?" in *The Enlightenment: A Brief History with Documents*, ed. Margaret C. Jacob (Boston: Bedford/St. Martin's, 2001), 203.
46. Voltaire (François-Marie Arouet), "Letters concerning the English Nation," in *The Enlightenment: A Brief History with Documents*, ed. Margaret C. Jacob (Boston: Bedford/St. Martin's, 2001), 119.
47. Mark A. Noll, *A History of Christianity in the United States and Canada* (Grand Rapids: Eerdmans, 1992), 134.
48. Immanuel Kant, *Religion within the Limits of Reason Alone*, translated with an introduction and notes by Theodore M. Greene and Hoyt H. Hudson (New York: Harper, 1960), 7–9.
49. Kant, *Religion within the Limits of Reason Alone*, 99.
50. James O'Flaherty, "Language and Reason in the Thought of Johann Georg Hamann," *Lutheran Quarterly* 2 (1988): 471–74.

51. Mark C. Mattes, "Hamann, Johann Georg," DLLT, 311–12.
52. Søren Kierkegaard, *For Self-Examination / Judge for Yourself!*, ed. and trans. Howard V. Hong and Edna H. Hong (Princeton: Princeton University Press, 1990), 209.
53. Ibram X. Kendi, *Stamped from the Beginning: The Definitive History of Racist Ideas in America* (New York: Nation Books, 2016), 44–46.
54. Karl Krueger, "Mary Mühlenberg Speaks," *Lutheran Quarterly* 31 (2017): 397.
55. Paul A. Baglyos, "The Muhlenbergs Become Americans," *Lutheran Quarterly* 19 (2005): 47.
56. Krueger, "Mary Mühlenberg Speaks," 405–6.
57. *The Correspondence of Heinrich Melchior Mühlenberg, Volume 4: 1757–1762*, ed. Wolfgang Splitter and Timothy J. Wengert (Rockland, ME: Picton, 2010), 98–99.
58. Baglyos, "The Muhlenbergs Become Americans," 52–53.
59. Baglyos, "The Muhlenbergs Become Americans," 55.
60. Karl Krueger, "Mühlenberg, Heinrich (Henry) Melchior," DLLT, 521.
61. Baglyos, "The Muhlenbergs Become Americans," 58.
62. J. C. Jensson, *American Lutheran Biographies* (Milwaukee: Hautkamp & Son, 1890), 697.
63. Christine Helmer, "Schleiermacher for Lutherans," *Lutheran Quarterly* 29 (2015): 172.
64. Helmer, "Schleiermacher for Lutherans," 174–75.
65. Justo González, *The History of Theological Education* (Nashville: Abingdon, 2015), 110.
66. González, *The History of Theological Education*, 110–13.
67. Hans Nielsen Hauge, *Autobiographical Writings of Hans Nielsen Hauge*, trans. Joel M. Njus (Minneapolis: Augsburg, 1954), 42–43. The language of Hauge's vision recalls Isaiah 55:6–7.
68. BC 352.6.
69. Hauge, *Autobiographical Writings of Hans Nielsen Hauge*, 8, 12.
70. Granquist, *Scandinavian Pietists*, 16.
71. Inger Furseth, "The Role of Women in the Hauge Movement," *Lutheran Quarterly* 13 (1999): 396.
72. Furseth, "The Role of Women in the Hauge Movement," 397.
73. Furseth, "The Role of Women in the Hauge Movement," 400.
74. Furseth, "The Role of Women in the Hauge Movement," 403.
75. Furseth, "The Role of Women in the Hauge Movement," 395.
76. Hauge, *Autobiographical Writings of Hans Nielsen Hauge*, 144.

CHAPTER 4: 1817–1917

1. Donald McKim, ed., *The Westminster Dictionary of Theological Terms* (Louisville: Westminster John Knox, 1996), 53.
2. Justo González, *The Story of Christianity, Volume One: The Early Church to the Dawn of the Reformation* (New York: HarperCollins, 2010), 487.
3. Cited in DHL 2, 54.
4. See Bodo Nischan, *Prince, People, and Confession: The Second Reformation in Brandenburg* (Philadelphia: University of Pennsylvania Press, 1994).
5. Martin J. Lohrmann, "Prussian Union," DLLT, 626.
6. Claus Harms, *Fünf und neunzig Sätze* (Jena: Schmid, 1818), 6. This provocative version of Harms's theses was published with anonymous commentary by "an enlightened, thinking theologian," who included a quotation from Cervantes's tragedy *La Numancia* on the title page: "Que la oblacion mejor y la primera / Que se debe ofrecer al alto cielo / Es alma limpia y voluntad sincera." This translates to: "The greatest and first duty that we owe to highest heaven is a clean heart and an honest will." This edition also includes an ironic dedication to leading proponents of rational Christianity, namely, "the worthy doctors of theology Ammon, Gabler, and Schleiermacher." The word *Zeitgeist* is German for "the spirit of the time."
7. Harms, *Fünf und neunzig Sätze*, 48.
8. Harms, *Fünf und neunzig Sätze*, 105–11.
9. J. G. Johnson, *Black Christians*, 29.
10. J. G. Johnson, *Black Christians*, 30.
11. Mark Granquist, *Lutherans in America: A New History* (Minneapolis: Fortress Press, 2015), 102.
12. J. G. Johnson, *Black Christians*, 116.
13. Walter A. McDougall, *Throes of Democracy: The American Civil War Era 1829–1877* (New York: Harper, 2008), 14, 64.
14. J. G. Johnson, *Black Christians*, 121.
15. Karl E. Johnson Jr. and Joseph A. Romeo, "Jehu Jones (1786–1852): The First African American Lutheran Minister," *Lutheran Quarterly* 10 (1996): 425.
16. Johnson and Romeo, "Jehu Jones (1786–1852)," 427–28.
17. J. G. Johnson, *Black Christians*, 122.
18. Johnson and Romeo, "Jehu Jones (1786–1852)," 429.
19. Richard O. Johnson, "Fliedner, Theodore," DLLT, 258.
20. Jonathan Strom and Louise Williams, "Deaconesses," DLLT, 185.
21. Florence Nightingale, *The Institution of Kaiserswerth on the Rhine . . .* (London: Inmates of the London Ragged Colonial School, 1851). Available online: books.google.com.
22. *Diakonissen für Amerika: Sozialer Protestantismus in internationaler Perspektive im 19. Jahrhundert, Quellenedition*, ed. Roland Liebenberg,

Klaus Raschzok, Gury Schneider-Ludorff, and Matthias Hanold (Leipzig: Evangelische Verlagsanstalt, 2013), 28.

23. L. DeAne Lagerquist, *From Our Mother's Arms: A History of Women in the American Lutheran Church* (Minneapolis: Augsburg, 1987), 68.
24. Lagerquist, *From Our Mother's Arms*, 69.
25. Justo González, *The Story of Christianity, Volume 1*, 199. González writes of Athanasius: "Among those who were present at the Council of Nicaea there was a young man, so dark and short that his enemies would later call him 'the black dwarf.'"
26. Justo González, *The Mestizo Augustine: A Theologian between Two Cultures* (Downers Grove, IL: InterVarsity, 2016), 39–32.
27. Shekutaamba Nambala, "Namibian Churches under Colonialism," *Lutheran Quarterly* 2 (1988): 246.
28. Nambala, "Namibian Churches under Colonialism," 247–54. See also "Berlin streets to lose links with brutal colonial past," April 12, 2018, https://tinyurl.com/qp7c2u8.
29. E. Theodore Bachmann and Mercia Brenne Bachmann, *Lutheran Churches in the World: A Handbook* (Minneapolis: Augsburg, 1989), 100.
30. Nambala, "Namibian Churches under Colonialism," 257.
31. Ludwig Fischer, *Das falsche Märtyrertum oder die Wahrheit in der Sache der Stephaniter* (Leipzig: Künzel, 1839), 53–54; Walter O. Forster, *Zion on the Mississippi* (St. Louis: Concordia, 1953), 100–104; Mary Todd, *Authority Vested: A Story of Identity and Change in the Lutheran Church—Missouri Synod* (Grand Rapids: Eerdmans, 2000), 30–32, 37.
32. Forster, *Zion on the Mississippi*, 390–98; Todd, *Authority Vested*, 46–50; Marvin Huggins, "Lutheran Church—Missouri Synod," DLLT, 448.
33. BC 43.1: "The church is the assembly of saints in which the gospel is taught purely and the sacraments are administered rightly."
34. Huggins, "Lutheran Church—Missouri Synod," 448.
35. Todd, *Authority Vested*, 77.
36. Richard O. Johnson, "Ohio/Buffalo/Iowa Synods," DLLT, 561.
37. R. O. Johnson, "Ohio/Buffalo/Iowa Synods," 561.
38. J. G. Johnson, *Black Christians*, 151–81.
39. Susan Wilds McArver, "American Civil War," DLLT, 7.
40. Richard N. Stewart, "Race/Minorities," DLLT, 630.
41. Ibram X. Kendi, *Stamped from the Beginning: The Definitive History of Racist Ideas in America* (New York: Nation Books, 2016), 6. "During America's first century, racist theological ideas were absolutely critical to sanctioning the growth of American slavery and making it acceptable to the Christian churches. These ideas were featured in the sermons of early America's greatest preacher and intellectual, Boston divine Cotton Mather (1663–1728)." See also Granquist, *Lutherans in America*, 175–76.
42. Abdel Ross Wentz, *Pioneer in Christian Unity: Samuel Simon Schmucker* (Philadelphia: Fortress Press, 1967), 317.

43. Wentz, *Pioneer in Christian Unity*, 324.
44. Cited in DHL 2, 153–54.
45. Cited in DHL 2, 153.
46. Cited in DHL 2, 154.
47. Cited in Richard C. Wolf, *Documents of Lutheran Unity in America* (Philadelphia: Fortress Press, 1966), 121–22.
48. For Lincoln's first inaugural address, see https://tinyurl.com/mcqjcs; for the "Cornerstone" speech of Alexander H. Stephens, see https://tinyurl.com/lxepaeq.
49. Wentz, *Pioneer in Christian Unity*, 326–31.
50. J. C. Jensson, *American Lutheran Biographies* (Milwaukee: Hautkamp & Son, 1890), 51.
51. McArver, "American Civil War," 8.
52. J. G. Johnson, *Black Christians*, 227.
53. J. G. Johnson, *Black Christians*, 16.
54. Cited in DHL 2, 367–68.
55. James B. Vigen, "*Fifohazana* Movement," DLLT, 247–48.
56. Hans Austnaberg, *Shepherds and Demons: A Study of Exorcism as Practiced and Understood by Shepherds in the Malagasy Lutheran Church* (New York: Peter Lang, 2008), 54.
57. Samuel Yonas Deressa, "Onesimus Nesib, Ethiopian Evangelical Pioneer," *Lutheran Quarterly* 32 (2018): 164.
58. Deressa, "Onesimus Nesib, Ethiopian Evangelical Pioneer," 165.
59. Gudina Tumsa, "Memorandum: Some Issues Requiring Discussions and Decisions," in *The Life, Works, and Witness of Tsehay Tolessa and Gudina Tumsa, the Ethiopian Bonhoeffer*, ed. Samuel Yonas Deressa and Sarah Hinlicky Wilson (Minneapolis: Fortress Press, 2017), 87.
60. Victor Tinambunan, "Nommensen, Ludwig Ingwer," DLLT, 549.
61. Cited in DHL 2, 344.
62. Fridz Pardamean Sihombing and Jubil Raplan Hutauruk, "Church in the Archipelago: Stories of Lutherans in Indonesia," in *Abundant Harvest: Stories of Asian Lutherans*, edited and compiled by Edmond Yee and J. Paul Rajashekar (Minneapolis: Lutheran University Press, 2012), 100.
63. Sihombing and Hutauruk, "Church in the Archipelago," 96.
64. Victor Tinambunan, "Batak Confession," DLLT, 79. The confession can be found in full in *Creeds of the Churches*, 3rd edition, ed. John H. Leith (Louisville: John Knox, 1982), 556–66; and can be found in part in DHL 2, 384–85.
65. Binsar Pakpahan, "Sharing a Common Story for an Indonesian Context," cited in DHL 2, 386–87.
66. Pakpahan, "Sharing a Common Story for an Indonesian Context," 387.
67. Sihombing and Hutauruk, "Church in the Archipelago," 112.

68. Luther D. Reed, *The Lutheran Liturgy*, rev. ed. (Philadelphia: Muhlenberg, 1947), 152.
69. Lorraine S. Brugh and Gordon W. Lathrop, *The Sunday Assembly* (Minneapolis: Augsburg Fortress, 2008), 33.
70. Bethany Kilcrease, "Luther as Mirror, Hammer, and 'Other' among Victorian Britons," *Lutheran Quarterly* 24 (2010): 394.
71. Kilcrease, "Luther as Mirror, Hammer, and 'Other' among Victorian Britons," 405–10.
72. Dean Zweck, "Australia," DLLT, 62.
73. Dean Zweck, "Australian Aboriginal People," DLLT, 64.
74. Hermann Vorländer, *Church in Motion: The History of the Evangelical Lutheran Mission in Bavaria* (Eugene, OR: Pickwick, 2018), 96.
75. Vorländer, *Church in Motion*, 102.
76. Vorländer, *Church in Motion*, 104.
77. Vorländer, *Church in Motion*, 105.
78. Dean Zweck, "Papua New Guinea," DLLT, 574.
79. Vorländer, *Church in Motion*, 105–6.
80. Vorländer, *Church in Motion*, 111.
81. Zweck, "Papua New Guinea," 574.
82. Lutheran Church of Australia, "Our People," https://tinyurl.com/st3u8eu.
83. Vorländer, *Church in Motion*, 108; see also the website of the Evangelical Lutheran Church of Papua New Guinea: https://tinyurl.com/uva5nay.

CHAPTER 5: 1917–2017

1. BC 174.10. See also the definition of the church in articles 7 and 8 of the *Augsburg Confession*, BC 42 and 43.
2. Lagerquist, *From Our Mother's Arms*, 50–66.
3. Lagerquist, *From Our Mother's Arms*, 37.
4. Lagerquist, *From Our Mother's Arms*, 37.
5. Peter Vethanayagamony, "St. Anna Sarah Kugler," *Lutheran Forum* 44 (Winter 2010): 40–49.
6. Vethanayagamony, "St. Anna Sarah Kugler," 46–47; and Julianna Frost, "The Education of Hidden Women: Dr. Anna S. Kugler and the Zenana Missions," *Journal of the Lutheran Historical Conference* 2 (2012): 188–89.
7. Cited in Julianna Frost, "Helen C. Frost's Missionary Images of the Inupiaq (Eskimos)," *Lutheran Quarterly* 23 (2009): 300.
8. Lagerquist, *From Our Mother's Arms*, 63–65.
9. Dietz Lange, "Nathan Söderblom (1866–1931)," *Lutheran Quarterly* 29 (2015): 40.

10. Jonas Jonson, *Nathan Söderblom: Called to Serve*, trans. Norman A. Hjelm (Grand Rapids: Eerdmans, 2016), 130.
11. Jonson, *Nathan Söderblom*, 137–41.
12. Jonson, *Nathan Söderblom*, 363–64.
13. Jonson, *Nathan Söderblom*, 405–7.
14. Jonson, *Nathan Söderblom*, 408.
15. Jonson, *Nathan Söderblom*, 209.
16. The Mission of the Norman Borlaug Heritage Foundation, https://tinyurl.com/v24zree.
17. Leymah Gbowee, *Mighty Be Our Powers: How Sisterhood, Prayer, and Sex Changed a Nation at War* (New York: Beast, 2011); and *Pray the Devil back to Hell*, directed by Abigail Disney and Gini Reticker (Fork Films, 2008).
18. Jonson, *Nathan Söderblom*, 3.
19. *Creeds of the Church*, 517–22.
20. Victoria Barnett, "The Confessing Church," DLLT, 156–57.
21. Eric W. Gritsch, *A History of Lutheranism* (Minneapolis: Fortress Press, 2002), 224–25.
22. Reggie L. Williams, *Bonhoeffer's Black Jesus: Harlem Renaissance Theology and an Ethic of Resistance* (Waco, TX: Baylor University Press, 2014), 20–33.
23. Dietrich Bonhoeffer, *Life Together / Prayerbook of the Bible*, English edition, ed. Geffrey B. Kelly and trans. Daniel W. Bloesch and James H. Burtness (Minneapolis: Fortress Press, 2005), 101.
24. Matthew L. Becker, "Bonhoeffer, Dietrich," DLLT, 97.
25. Williams, *Bonhoeffer's Black Jesus*, 140.
26. Jens Holger Schjørring, Prasanna Kumari, and Norman A. Hjelm, eds., *From Federation to Communion: The History of the Lutheran World Federation* (Minneapolis: Fortress Press, 1997), 6.
27. Schjørring, Kumari, and Hjelm, eds., *From Federation to Communion*, 14.
28. Short biographies appear in *From Federation to Communion*, 28–32, and in *The Encyclopedia of the Lutheran Church*. The title of executive secretary was later changed to general secretary.
29. Schjørring, Kumari, and Hjelm, eds., *From Federation to Communion*, 28.
30. Musimbi Kanyoro, ed., *The Continuing Journey: Women's Participation in the Lutheran World Federation* (Geneva: Lutheran World Federation Department for Mission and Development, 1992), 6.
31. Kanyoro, ed., *The Continuing Journey*, 24.
32. Abdel Ross Wentz, "Lutheran World Federation," TELC 2, 1429.
33. Schjørring, Kumari, and Hjelm, eds., *From Federation to Communion*, 161–62.
34. Schjørring, Kumari, and Hjelm, eds., *From Federation to Communion*, 382–89.

35. Kathryn L. Johnson, "Lutheran World Federation," DLLT, 465.
36. The Lutheran World Federation, "Women in Church and Society," https://tinyurl.com/shtkzka.
37. The Lutheran World Federation, "Churches," https://tinyurl.com/zh6269y. In order, as of this writing.
38. K. L. Johnson, "Lutheran World Federation," 462.
39. K. L. Johnson, "Lutheran World Federation," 462.
40. Evangelische Kirche in Deutschland, "Leuenberg Agreement," https://tinyurl.com/tu6ucv4.
41. K. L. Johnson, "Lutheran World Federation," 464. See also the Lutheran World Federation, "Theology, Mission and Justice," https://tinyurl.com/sevyu5y.
42. *The Martyrdom of Perpetua*, ed. Sara Maitland (Evesham, UK: Arthur James, 1996).
43. Gregory of Nyssa, *The Life of Saint Macrina*, trans. Kevin Corrigan (Toronto: Peregrina, 1998).
44. Barbara J. MacHaffie, *Her Story: Women in Christian Tradition* (Philadelphia: Fortress Press, 1986), 27.
45. Mary Todd, *Authority Vested: A Story of Identity and Change in the Lutheran Church—Missouri Synod* (Grand Rapids: Eerdmans, 2000), 143.
46. Mary Devers, "Woman in the Pulpit," *Lutheran Quarterly* 34 [earlier series] (April 1904): 287; see also Martin J. Lohrmann, "Lutherans and the Nineteenth Amendment," *Journal of the Lutheran Historical Conference* 5 (2015): 51–61.
47. Andreas H. Wöhle, "Tribute to a Pioneering Woman in the Ordained Ministry," https://tinyurl.com/y8lskh6s.
48. TELC 2, 1722.
49. This history has come from the published recollections of Bishop Øllgaard; Hans Øllgaard, "Women as Clergymen in Denmark," *Lutheran Quarterly* [earlier series] 18 (1966): 163–67.
50. Gracia Grindal, "How Lutheran Women Came to Be Ordained," in *Lutheran Women in Ordained Ministry 1970-1995: Reflections and Perspectives*, ed. Gloria E. Bengtson (Minneapolis: Augsburg, 1995), 37.
51. Nona M. Diehl, Dorothy E. L. Haas, and Lieselotte Nold, "Woman's Place," TELC 3, 2496.
52. For a multimedia online resource about women's ordination in the United States, assembled by L. DeAne Lagerquist and Erin Magoon, "50 Years On: A Half Century of Ordaining Lutheran Women," https://tinyurl.com/w9agj3l.
53. DHL 2, 384; and Godson S. Maanga, "The Evangelical Lutheran Church in Tanzania, 1963-2013," *Lutheran Quarterly* 28 (2014): 187.
54. The Lutheran World Federation, "Women's Pre-Assembly Message to the Twelfth Assembly" (May 10, 2017), https://tinyurl.com/utvzupb.

55. Ricardo W. Rieth, "Luther in Portuguese, in Brazil," *Lutheran Quarterly* 30 (2016): 430.
56. Paulo Wille Buss, "Brazil," DLLT, 101–4.
57. Rieth, "Luther in Portuguese, in Brazil," 435.
58. E. Clifford Nelson, *The Lutherans in America* (Philadelphia: Fortress Press, 1975), 281.
59. This is a current research interest of Dr. José David Rodriguez of the Lutheran Theological Seminary at Chicago.
60. Mytch Pierre-Noel Dorvilier, "Lutheranism in Haiti: The Birth of a Church in Exile," in *Journal of the Lutheran Historical Conference 2016*, ed. Mark Granquist (Minneapolis: Lutheran University Press, 2018), 94–99.
61. Dorvilier, "Lutheranism in Haiti," 98.
62. Nelson Rivera, "Luther in Spanish," *Lutheran Quarterly* 30 (2016): 60.
63. See Fundación Federico Fliedner, "Fritz Fliedner," https://tinyurl.com/wezdo9x.
64. Rivera, "Luther in Spanish," 61.
65. Maanga, "The Evangelical Lutheran Church in Tanzania, 1963–2013," 179.
66. Maanga, "The Evangelical Lutheran Church in Tanzania, 1963–2013," 183.
67. The Lutheran World Federation, "LWF Twelfth Assembly," https://tinyurl.com/vhvj7ra.
68. Walter Altmann, *Luther and Liberation: A Latin American Perspective*, trans. Mary M. Solberg (Minneapolis: Fortress Press, 1992), 55.
69. Vítor Westhelle, *The Scandalous God: The Use and Abuse of the Cross* (Minneapolis: Fortress Press, 2006), 105.
70. Victoria Cortez Rodríguez, "A Church of Faith and Hope," in *The Future of Lutheranism in a Global Context*, ed. Arland Jacobson and James Aageson (Minneapolis: Fortress Press, 2008), 94.
71. Makito Masaki, "Japan," DLLT, 377.
72. Kazoh Kitamori, *Theology of the Pain of God* (Richmond, VA: John Knox, 1958), 7.
73. Toshihiro Takamura, "Discerning the Spirit in the Double Life of the Church: The Japanese Context," conference paper available online: https://tinyurl.com/r4q5hvx.
74. Munib Younan, "The Future of the Lutheran Reformation Tradition: From the Perspective of Palestinian Christians," in *The Future of Lutheranism in a Global Context*, 103.
75. Monica Melanchthon, "The Grace of God and the Equality of Human Persons," in *The Gift of Grace: The Future of Lutheran Theology*, ed. Niels Henrik Gregersen, Bo Holm, Ted Peters, and Peter Widmann (Minneapolis: Fortress Press, 2005), 58.
76. BC 515.6.

77. Trevor Noah, *Born a Crime: Stories from a South African Childhood* (New York: Spiegel & Grau, 2016), 19.
78. Cited in DHL 2, 349.
79. Schjørring, Kumari, and Hjelm, eds., *From Federation to Communion*, 400.
80. Cited in DHL 2, 351.
81. Elelwani Bethuei Farisani, "The Challenges Facing Lutherans in South Africa," in *The Future of Lutheranism in a Global Context*, 40.
82. Farisani, "The Challenges Facing Lutherans in South Africa," 44.
83. Tibor Fabiny Jr., "The Testimony of Bishop Lajos Ordass during Communism in Hungary," *Lutheran Quarterly* 19 (2005): 435–54.
84. See DHL 2, 214–20.
85. DHL 2, 219–20.
86. US Department of State's Office of the Historian, "Fall of Communism in Eastern Europe, 1989," https://tinyurl.com/k6ujho2.
87. Tibor Fabiny Jr., "The Captivity of Our Church Today: A Letter to the National Council of the Lutheran Church in Hungary and All Her Members," *Lutheran Quarterly* 18 (2004): 325–32.
88. *Catechism of the Catholic Church*, 2nd ed. (Washington, DC: Libreria Editrice Vaticana, 2000), 216.
89. *Catechism of the Catholic Church*, 340, 351.
90. Cited in DHL 2, 420–21. The full document is available online in many places, including the websites of the Evangelical Lutheran Church in America (www.elca.org), Lutheran World Federation (www.lutheranworld.org), and the Vatican (www.vatican.va).

AFTERWORD: INTRODUCTION TO LUTHERANISM IN ITS SIXTH CENTURY

1. "Goodness Is Stronger Than Evil," ELW #721.
2. BC 356.4 and 357.10.
3. "Now Thank We All Our God," ELW #840.

GLOSSARY

1. Donald McKim, ed., *The Westminster Dictionary of Theological Terms* (Louisville: Westminster John Knox, 1996), 53.

Bibliography

Altmann, Walter. *Luther and Liberation: A Latin American Perspective*. Translated by Mary M. Solberg. Minneapolis: Fortress Press, 1992.

Andersson, Bo. "Sweden, the Elect Nation." *Lutheran Quarterly* 13 (1999): 305–14.

Appold, Kenneth G. "Early Lutheran Attitudes toward Jews." *Lutheran Quarterly* 20 (2006): 170–89.

———. "Early Lutheran Perspectives on the Council of Trent." *Lutheran Quarterly* 32 (2018): 146–59.

———. "Taking a Stand for Reformation: Martin Luther and Caritas Pirkheimer." *Lutheran Quarterly* 32 (2018): 40–59.

Arand, Charles P., Robert Kolb, and James A. Nestingen. *The Lutheran Confessions: History and Theology of the Book of Concord*. Minneapolis: Fortress Press, 2012.

Austnaberg, Hans. *Shepherds and Demons: A Study of Exorcism as Practiced and Understood by Shepherds in the Malagasy Lutheran Church*. New York: Peter Lang, 2008.

Bachmann, E. Theodore, and Mercia Brenne Bachmann. *Lutheran Churches in the World: A Handbook*. Minneapolis: Augsburg, 1989.

Baglyos, Paul A. "The Muhlenbergs Become Americans." *Lutheran Quarterly* 19 (2005): 43–62.

Bonhoeffer, Dietrich. *Life Together / Prayerbook of the Bible*. English edition edited by Geffrey B. Kelly. Translated by Daniel W. Bloesch and James H. Burtness. Minneapolis: Fortress Press, 2005.

The Book of Concord: The Confessions of the Evangelical Lutheran Church. Edited by Robert Kolb and Timothy J. Wengert. Minneapolis: Fortress Press, 2000.

Bosch, David J. *Transforming Mission: Paradigm Shifts in Theology of Mission, 20th Anniversary Edition.* Maryknoll, NY: Orbis, 2011.

Brecht, Martin. *Martin Luther: The Preservation of the Church, 1532–1546.* Translated by James L. Schaaf. Minneapolis: Fortress Press, 1993.

———. *Martin Luther: Shaping and Defining the Reformation, 1521–1532.* Translated by James L. Schaaf. Minneapolis: Fortress Press, 1990.

Brugh, Lorraine S., and Gordon W. Lathrop. *The Sunday Assembly.* Minneapolis: Augsburg Fortress, 2008.

Brunner, Daniel. "Anglican Perceptions of Lutheranism in Early Hanoverian England." *Lutheran Quarterly* 20 (2006): 63–82.

Bugenhagen, Johannes. *Selected Writings, Volume 1 and 2.* Edited and translated by Kurt K. Hendel. Minneapolis: Fortress Press, 2015.

Caemmerer, Richard R. "The Melanchthonian Blight." *Concordia Theological Monthly* 18 (1947): 321–23.

Catechism of the Catholic Church. Second edition. Washington, DC: Libreria Editrice Vaticana, 2000.

Clapham, John. "Tranovský, Juraj." In *The New Grove Dictionary of Music and Musicians*, volume 16. Edited by Stanley Sadie. London: Macmillan, 1980.

Collijn, Isak. "The Swedish-Indian Catechism, Some Notes." *Lutheran Quarterly* 2 (1988): 89–98.

Cone, James. *God of the Oppressed.* New revised edition. Maryknoll, NY: Orbis, 1997.

David, Hans T., and Arthur Mendel, eds. *The Bach Reader: A Life of Johann Sebastian Bach in Letters and Documents.* Revised edition. New York: Norton, 1966.

Deressa, Samuel Yonas. "Onesimus Nesib, Ethiopian Evangelical Pioneer." *Lutheran Quarterly* 32 (2018): 160–72.

Deressa, Samuel Yonas, and Sarah Hinlicky Wilson, eds. *The Life, Works, and Witness of Tsehay Tolessa and Gudina Tumsa, the Ethiopian Bonhoeffer.* Minneapolis: Fortress Press, 2017.

Dever, Mary. "Woman in the Pulpit." *Lutheran Quarterly* 34 [earlier series] (April 1904): 284–87.

Disney, Abigail, and Gini Reticker, directors. *Pray the Devil back to Hell* [DVD]. Fork Films, 2008.

England, John C. *The Hidden History of Christianity in Asia: The Churches of the East before 1500.* Delhi and Hong Kong: Indian Society for Promoting Christian Knowledge and Christian Conference of Asia, 1996 and 2002.

Evangelical Lutheran Worship. Minneapolis: Augsburg Fortress, 2006.

Fabiny Jr., Tibor. "The Captivity of Our Church Today: A Letter to the National Council of the Lutheran Church in Hungary and All Her Members." *Lutheran Quarterly* 18 (2004): 325–32.

———. "The Testimony of Bishop Lajos Ordass during Communism in Hungary." *Lutheran Quarterly* 19 (2005): 435–54.

Fischer, Klaus P. *The History of an Obsession: German Judeophobia and the Holocaust.* New York: Continuum, 1998.

Fischer, Ludwig. *Das falsche Märtyrertum oder die Wahrheit in der Sache der Stephaniter.* Leipzig: Künzel, 1839.

Forster, Walter O. *Zion on the Mississippi: The Settlement of the Saxon Lutherans in Missouri 1839–1841.* St. Louis: Concordia, 1953.

Frost, Julianna. "The Education of Hidden Women: Dr. Anna S. Kugler and the Zenana Missions." *Journal of the Lutheran Historical Conference* 2 (2012): 175–92.

———. "Helen C. Frost's Missionary Images of the Inupiaq (Eskimos)." *Lutheran Quarterly* 23 (2009): 296–313.

Furseth, Inger. "The Role of Women in the Hauge Movement." *Lutheran Quarterly* 13 (1999): 395–422.

García, Alberto, and John Nunes. *Wittenberg Meets the World: Reimagining the Reformation at the Margins.* Grand Rapids: Eerdmans, 2017.

Gbowee, Leymah. *Mighty Be Our Powers: How Sisterhood, Prayer, and Sex Changed a Nation at War.* New York: Beast, 2011.

González, Justo. *The History of Theological Education.* Nashville: Abingdon, 2015.

———. *The Mestizo Augustine: A Theologian between Two Cultures.* Downers Grove, IL: InterVarsity, 2016.

———. *The Story of Christianity, Volume 1: The Early Church to the Dawn of the Reformation.* Revised and updated edition. New York: HarperOne, 2010.

Granquist, Mark. *Lutherans in America: A New History.* Minneapolis: Fortress Press, 2015.

———, ed. *Scandinavian Pietists: Spiritual Writings from 19th-Century Norway, Denmark, Sweden, and Finland.* Mahwah, NJ: Paulist, 2015.

Green, Todd. "Swedish Pietism (1700–1727) as Resistance and Popular Religion." *Lutheran Quarterly* 21 (2007): 59–77.

Gregory of Nyssa. *The Life of Saint Macrina.* Translated by Kevin Corrigan. Toronto: Peregrina, 1998.

Grindal, Gracia. "How Lutheran Women Came to Be Ordained." In *Lutheran Women in Ordained Ministry 1970–1995: Reflections and Perspectives.* Edited by Gloria E. Bengtson. Minneapolis: Augsburg, 1995.

Gritsch, Eric W. *A History of Lutheranism.* Minneapolis: Fortress Press, 2002.

Grosshans, Hans-Peter, and Martin L. Sinaga, eds. *"Like Living Stones": Lutheran Reflections on the One, Holy, Catholic and Apostolic Church.* Minneapolis: Lutheran University Press, 2011.

Hägglund, Bengt. "Polemics and Dialogue in John Gerhard's *Confessio Catholica.*" *Lutheran Quarterly* 14 (2000): 159–72.

Halvorson, Michael J. "German Lutheran Centennial Dramas." *Lutheran Quarterly* 30 (2016): 276–306.

Harms, Claus. *Fünf und neunzig Sätze.* Jena: Schmid, 1818.

Hauge, Hans Nielsen. *Autobiographical Writings of Hans Nielsen Hauge.* Translated by Joel M. Njus. Minneapolis: Augsburg, 1954.

Helmer, Christine. "Schleiermacher for Lutherans." *Lutheran Quarterly* 29 (2015): 162–83.

Hendrix, Scott H. *Martin Luther: Visionary Reformer.* New Haven: Yale University Press, 2015.

Hildebrandt, Franz. *Melanchthon: Alien or Ally?* Cambridge: Cambridge University Press, 1946 [reprinted in New York, 1968].

Holborn, Hajo. *A History of Modern Germany: The Reformation.* Princeton: Princeton University Press, 1959.

Ilić, Luka. "Primus Truber (1508–1586), the Slovenian Luther." *Lutheran Quarterly* 22 (2008): 268–77.

Irwin, Joyce. "Celestial Harmony in Baroque Lutheran Writings." *Lutheran Quarterly* 3 (1989): 281–97.

Jacobson, Arland, and James Aageson, eds. *The Future of Lutheranism in a Global Context*. Minneapolis: Fortress Press, 2008.

Jensen, Gordon A. *The Wittenberg Concord: Creating Space for Dialogue*. Minneapolis: Fortress Press, 2018.

Jensson, J. C. *American Lutheran Biographies*. Milwaukee: Hautkamp & Son, 1890.

Jeyaraj, P. Daniel. "Lutheran Churches in Eighteenth-Century India." *Lutheran Quarterly* 17 (2003): 77–97.

Johnson, Jeff G. *Black Christians: The Untold Lutheran Story*. St. Louis: Concordia, 1991.

Johnson Jr., Karl E., and Joseph A. Romeo. "Jehu Jones (1786–1852): The First African American Lutheran Minister." *Lutheran Quarterly* 10 (1996): 425–43.

Jonson, Jonas. *Nathan Söderblom: Called to Serve*. Translated by Norman A. Hjelm. Grand Rapids: Eerdmans, 2016.

Kant, Immanuel. *Religion within the Limits of Reason Alone*. Translated with an introduction and notes by Theodore M. Greene and Hoyt H. Hudson. New York: Harper, 1960.

———. "What Is Enlightenment?" In *The Enlightenment: A Brief History with Documents*. Edited by Margaret C. Jacob. Boston: Bedford/St. Martin's, 2001.

Kanyoro, Musimbi, ed. *The Continuing Journey: Women's Participation in the Lutheran World Federation*. Geneva: Lutheran World Federation Department for Mission and Development, 1992.

Kendi, Ibram X. *How to Be an Antiracist*. New York: One World, 2019.

———. *Stamped from the Beginning: The Definitive History of Racist Ideas in America*. New York: Nation Books, 2016.

Kierkegaard, Søren. *For Self-Examination / Judge for Yourself*. Edited and translated by Howard V. Hong and Edna H. Hong. Princeton: Princeton University Press, 2008.

Kilcrease, Bethany. "Luther as Mirror, Hammer, and 'Other' among Victorian Britons." *Lutheran Quarterly* 24 (2010): 394–423.

Kitamori, Kazoh. *Theology of the Pain of God.* Richmond, VA: John Knox, 1958.

Kleinhans, Kathryn A., ed. *Together by Grace: Introducing the Lutherans.* Minneapolis: Augsburg Fortress, 2016.

Kolb, Robert. *Confessing the Faith: Reformers Define the Church, 1530–1580.* St. Louis: Concordia, 1991.

———. *Martin Luther as Prophet, Teacher, and Hero: Images of the Reformer, 1520–1620.* Grand Rapids: Baker Academic, 1999.

———. "'So Much Began in Halle': The Mission Program That Sent Mühlenberg to America." *Concordia Historical Institute Quarterly* 84 (2011): 28–29.

Kolb, Robert, and James A. Nestingen, eds. *Sources and Contexts of The Book of Concord.* Minneapolis: Fortress Press, 2001.

Krivošová, Janka. "Witnesses to the Lutheran Faith in Bratislava." *Lutheran Quarterly* 16 (2002): 415–32.

Krueger, Karl. "Mary Mühlenberg Speaks." *Lutheran Quarterly* 31 (2017): 396–423.

Lagerquist, L. DeAne. *From Our Mother's Arms: A History of Women in the American Lutheran Church.* Minneapolis: Augsburg, 1987.

Lange, Dietz. "Nathan Söderblom (1866–1931)." *Lutheran Quarterly* 29 (2015): 33–61.

Layton, William J. "If Theology Is Practical: Piety and Spirituality in Early Lutheran Orthodoxy." Unpublished master's thesis submitted to Wartburg Theological Seminary, Spring 2017.

Leaver, Robin A. "Johann Sebastian Bach and the Lutheran Understanding of Music." *Lutheran Quarterly* 16 (2002): 21–47.

———. "Luther on Music," *Lutheran Quarterly* 20 (2006): 125–45.

———. *The Whole Church Sings: Congregational Singing in Luther's Wittenberg.* Grand Rapids: Eerdmans, 2017.

Leith, John H., ed. *Creeds of the Churches.* Third Edition. Louisville: John Knox, 1982.

Leppin, Volker, and Timothy J. Wengert. "Sources for and against the Posting of the *Ninety-Five Theses.*" *Lutheran Quarterly* 29 (2015): 373–98.

Liebenberg, Roland, Klaus Raschzok, Gury Schneider-Ludorff, and Matthias Hanold, eds. *Diakonissen für Amerika: Sozialer Protestantismus in internationaler Perspektive im 19. Jahrhundert, Quellenedition.* Leipzig: Evangelische Verlagsanstalt, 2013.

Lohrmann, Martin J. *Bugenhagen's Jonah: Biblical Interpretation as Public Theology*. Minneapolis: Lutheran University Press, 2012.

———. "Lutherans and the Nineteenth Amendment." *Journal of the Lutheran Historical Conference* 5 (2015): 51–61.

Lohse, Bernhard. "Hamburg." In *Theologische Realenzyklopädie*, Volume 15. Berlin: De Gruyter, 1985.

Long, Roy. *Martin Luther and His Legacy: A Perspective on 500 Years of Reformation*. London: Council of Lutheran Churches, 2017.

Lund, Eric, ed. *A Documentary History of Lutheranism, Volume 1: From the Reformation to Pietism*. Edited by Eric Lund. Minneapolis: Fortress Press, 2017.

Lund, Eric, and Mark Granquist, eds. *A Documentary History of Lutheranism, Volume 2: From the Enlightenment to the Present*. Minneapolis: Fortress Press, 2017.

Luther, Martin. *The Annotated Luther, Volume 1: The Roots of Reform*. Edited by Timothy J. Wengert. Minneapolis: Fortress Press, 2015.

———. *Luther's Works, American Edition*, 55 vols. Edited by J. J. Pelikan, H. C. Oswald, and H. T. Lehmann. Philadelphia: Fortress Press and St. Louis: Concordia, 1955–86.

———. *Martin Luther's Ninety-Five Theses, with Introduction, Commentary, and Study Guide*. Edited by Timothy J. Wengert. Minneapolis: Fortress Press, 2015.

Maanga, Godson S. "The Evangelical Lutheran Church in Tanzania, 1963–2013." *Lutheran Quarterly* 28 (2014): 179–93.

MacCulloch, Diarmaid. *The Reformation*. New York: Viking, 2003.

MacHaffie, Barbara J. *Her Story: Women in Christian Tradition*. Philadelphia: Fortress Press, 1986.

Maitland, Sara, ed. *The Martyrdom of Perpetua*. Evesham, UK: Arthur James, 1996.

Manschreck, Clyde. *Melanchthon: The Quiet Reformer*. Nashville: Abingdon, 1958.

Marigold, W. Gordon. "Opera, Politics, and Religion in Hamburg 1678–1715." *Lutheran Quarterly* 3 (1989): 65–90.

Marty, Martin. *Martin Luther: A Life*. New York: Penguin, 2004.

Maschke, Timothy. "Philipp Spener's Pia Desideria," *Lutheran Quarterly* 6 (1992): 187–204.

McDougall, Walter A. *Throes of Democracy: The American Civil War Era 1829–1877*. New York: Harper, 2008.

McKim, Donald, ed. *The Westminster Dictionary of Theological Terms*. Louisville: Westminster John Knox, 1996.

Melanchthon, Monica. "The Grace of God and the Equality of Human Persons." In *The Gift of Grace: The Future of Lutheran Theology*. Edited by Niels Henrik Gregersen, Bo Holm, Ted Peters, and Peter Widmann. Minneapolis: Fortress Press, 2005.

Melanchthon, Philip. *Loci Communes Theologici*, in *Melanchthon and Bucer*. Edited by Wilhelm Pauck. Philadelphia: Westminster, 1969.

Muhlenberg, Henry Melchior. *The Correspondence of Heinrich Melchior Mühlenberg, Volume 4: 1757–1762*. Edited by Wolfgang Splitter and Timothy J. Wengert. Rockland, ME: Picton, 2010.

———. *The Journals of Henry Melchior Muhlenberg*. Three volumes. Edited and translated by Theodore Tappert and John Doberstein. Philadelphia: Muhlenberg Press, 1942.

Nambala, Shekutaamba. "Namibian Churches under Colonialism." *Lutheran Quarterly* 2 (1988): 245–69.

Nelson, E. Clifford. *The Lutherans in America*. Philadelphia: Fortress Press, 1975.

Nessan, Craig L. "Bonhoeffer, Dietrich, Influence on." In *Encyclopedia of Martin Luther and the Reformation, Volume 1: A-L*. Edited by Mark A. Lamport. Lanham, MD: Rowman & Littlefield, 2017.

Nightingale, Florence. *The Institution of Kaiserswerth on the Rhine: for the practical training of deaconesses, under the direction of the Rev. Pastor Fliedner, embracing the support and care of the hospital, infant, and industrial schools, and a female penitentiary*. London: Inmates of the London Ragged Colonial School, 1851.

Nischan, Bodo. *Prince, People, and Confession: The Second Reformation in Brandenburg*. Philadelphia: University of Pennsylvania Press, 1994.

Noah, Trevor. *Born a Crime: Stories from a South African Childhood*. New York: Spiegel & Grau, 2016.

Noll, Mark A. *A History of Christianity in the United States and Canada*. Grand Rapids: Eerdmans, 1992.

Oberman, Heiko A. *The Roots of Anti-Semitism in the Age of Renaissance and Reformation*. James I. Porter, translator. Philadelphia: Fortress Press, 1984.

O'Flaherty, James. "Language and Reason in the Thought of Johann Georg Hamann." *Lutheran Quarterly* 2 (1988): 457–75.

Öhrberg, Ann. "'A Threat to Civic Coexistence': Forbidden Religious Literature and Censorship in Eighteenth-Century Sweden." In *Religious Reading in the Lutheran North: Studies in Early Modern Scandinavian Book Culture*. Edited by Charlotte Appel and Morton Fink-Jensen. Newcastle: Cambridge Scholars, 2011.

Øllgaard, Hans. "Women as Clergymen in Denmark." *Lutheran Quarterly* [earlier series] 18 (1966): 163–67.

Orwell, George. *Animal Farm*. London: Secker & Warburg, 1945; New York: Harcourt, Brace and Co., 1946.

Ozment, Steven. *A Mighty Fortress: A New History of the German People*. New York: HarperCollins, 2004.

Pelikan, Jaroslav. *Luther the Expositor: Introduction to the Reformer's Exegetical Writings. Luther's Works*: Companion Volume. St. Louis: Concordia, 1959.

Polo, Marco. *The Travels of Marco Polo*. New York: Orion, 1985.

Preus, Robert D. *The Theology of Post-Reformation Lutheranism: A Study of Theological Prolegomena*. St. Louis: Concordia, 1970.

Rajashekar, J. Paul. "Lutheranism in Asia and the Indian Subcontinent." In *The Future of Lutheranism in a Global Context*. Edited by Arland Jacobson and James Aageson. Minneapolis: Fortress Press, 2008.

Ray Jr., Stephen G. *Do No Harm: Social Sin and Christian Responsibility*. Minneapolis: Fortress Press, 2003.

Reed, Luther D. *The Lutheran Liturgy*. Revised edition. Philadelphia: Muhlenberg, 1947.

Rieth, Ricardo W. "Luther in Portuguese, in Brazil." *Lutheran Quarterly* 30 (2016): 430–35.

Rivera, Nelson. "Luther in Spanish." *Lutheran Quarterly* 30 (2016): 60–67.

Schaff, Philip. *History of the Christian Church, Volume 6*. New York: Scribner, 1892.

Scheible, Heinz. "Luther and Melanchthon." *Lutheran Quarterly* 4 (1990): 317–39.

Schjørring, Jens Holger, Prasanna Kumari, and Norman A. Hjelm, eds. *From Federation to Communion: The History of the Lutheran World Federation*. Minneapolis: Fortress Press, 1997.

Schramm, Brooks. "Introduction to *On the Schem Hamphoras* and *On the Lineage of Christ*." In *The Annotated Luther, Volume 5: Christian Life in the World*. Edited by Hans J. Hillerbrand. Minneapolis: Fortress Press, 2017.

Skarsten, Trygve. "Johan Campanius, Pastor in New Sweden." *Lutheran Quarterly* 2 (1988): 47–87.

Spener, Philipp Jakob. *Pia Desideria*. Edited and translated by Theodore G. Tappert. Philadelphia: Fortress Press, 1964.

Splitter, Wolfgang. "Jewish Support of the Salzburg Lutheran Refugees in 1732/33." *Lutheran Quarterly* 27 (2013): 143–66.

Springer, Carl P. E. *Cicero in Heaven: The Roman Rhetor and Luther's Reformation*. Leiden: Brill, 2018.

Stjerna, Kirsi I. "Introduction to *That Jesus Christ Was Born a Jew*." In *The Annotated Luther, Volume 5: Christian Life in the World*. Edited by Hans J. Hillerbrand. Minneapolis: Fortress Press, 2017.

———. *Lutheran Book: Orientation and Sources*. London: T & T Clark, 2021.

Stolt, Birgit. "Luther's Translation of the Bible." *Lutheran Quarterly* 28 (2014): 373–400.

Stulken, Marilyn Kay. *Hymnal Companion to the Lutheran Book of Worship*. Philadelphia: Fortress Press, 1981.

Takamura, Toshihiro. "Discerning the Spirit in the Double Life of the Church: The Japanese Context." Conference paper presented at the 2016 Crossings Convention. Available online: https://tinyurl.com/r4q5hvx.

Thøfner, Margit. "Framing the Sacred: Lutheran Church Furnishings in the Holy Roman Empire." In *Lutheran Churches in Early Modern Europe*. Edited by Andrew Spicer. Routledge: London, 2016.

Todd, Mary. *Authority Vested: A Story of Identity and Change in the Lutheran Church—Missouri Synod*. Grand Rapids: Eerdmans, 2000.

Treu, Martin. "Katharina von Bora: The Woman at Luther's Side." *Lutheran Quarterly* 13 (1999): 156–78.

———. *Katherine von Bora, Luther's Wife*. Translated by Stephen P. Glinsky Jr. Wittenberg: Drei Kastanien, 2003.

Truemper, David G., and Frederick A. Niedner Jr. *Keeping the Faith: A Guide to the Christian Message*. Philadelphia: Fortress Press, 1981.

Vethanayagamony, Peter. "St. Anna Sarah Kugler." *Lutheran Forum* 44 (Winter 2010): 40–49.

Vethanayagamony, Peter, and F. Volker Greifenhagen, eds. *Global Lutheranism: Vitality and Challenges*. Minneapolis: Lutheran University Press, 2018.

Vogt, Karl August Traugott. *Johannes Bugenhagen Pomeranus: Leben und ausgewälte Schriften*. Elberfeld: Friederichs, 1867.

Voltaire (François-Marie Arouet). "Letters concerning the English Nation." In *The Enlightenment: A Brief History with Documents*. Edited Margaret C. Jacob. Boston: Bedford/St. Martin's, 2001.

Vorländer, Hermann. *Church in Motion: The History of the Evangelical Lutheran Mission in Bavaria*. Eugene, OR: Pickwick, 2018.

Weizsäcker, C. F. v. "Kepler, Johannes." In *Die Religion in Geschichte und Gegenwart*. Vol. 3, 3rd ed. Tübingen: Mohr Siebeck, 1959.

Wengert, Timothy J. "Not by Nature *Philoneikos*: Philip Melanchthon's Initial Reactions to the Augsburg Interim." In *Politik und Bekenntnis: Die Reaktionen auf das Interim von 1548*. Edited by Irene Dingel and Günther Wartenberg. Leipzig: Evangelische Verlagsanstalt, 2006.

———. *Priesthood, Pastors, Bishops: Public Ministry for the Reformation & Today*. Minneapolis: Fortress Press, 2008.

———, general editor. *Dictionary of Luther and the Lutheran Traditions*. Grand Rapids: Baker Academic, 2017.

Wentz, Abdel Ross. *Pioneer in Christian Unity: Samuel Simon Schmucker*. Philadelphia: Fortress Press, 1967.

Westhelle, Vítor. *The Scandalous God: The Use and Abuse of the Cross*. Minneapolis: Fortress Press, 2006.

Williams, Kim-Eric. "Laughing with the Lenape: Swedes and Native Americans in Colonial Delaware." *Journal of the Lutheran Historical Conference* 1 (2011): 79–92.

Williams, Reggie L. *Bonhoeffer's Black Jesus: Harlem Renaissance Theology and an Ethic of Resistance*. Waco, TX: Baylor University Press, 2014.

Wolf, Richard C., ed. *Documents of Lutheran Unity in America*. Philadelphia: Fortress Press, 1966.

Wolff, Christoph. *Johann Sebastian Bach: The Learned Musician*. New York: Norton, 2000.

Wolff, Hellmuth Christian. "Tranoscius." In *Die Musik in Geschichte und Gegenwart*, Vol. 13. Kassel: Bärenreiter, 1966.

Yee, Edmond, and J. Paul Rajashekar, eds. *Abundant Harvest: Stories of Asian Lutherans*. Minneapolis: Lutheran University Press, 2012.

Index

Lutheran Quarterly Books

Living by Faith: Justification and Sanctification, by Oswald Bayer (2003).

Harvesting Martin Luther's Reflections on Theology, Ethics and the Church, essays from *Lutheran Quarterly*, edited by Timothy J. Wengert, with foreword by David C. Steinmetz (2004).

A More Radical Gospel: Essays on Eschatology, Authority, Atonement, and Ecumenism, by Gerhard O. Forde, edited by Mark Mattes and Steven Paulson (2004).

The Role of Justification in Contemporary Theology, by Mark C. Mattes (2004).

The Captivation of the Will: Luther vs. Erasmus on Freedom and Bondage, by Gerhard O. Forde (2005).

Bound Choice, Election, and Wittenberg Theological Method: From Martin Luther to the Formula of Concord, by Robert Kolb (2005).

A Formula for Parish Practice: Using the Formula of Concord in Congregations, by Timothy J. Wengert (2006).

Luther's Liturgical Music: Principles and Implications, by Robin A. Leaver (2006).

The Preached God: Proclamation in Word and Sacrament, by Gerhard O. Forde, edited by Mark C. Mattes and Steven D. Paulson (2007).

Theology the Lutheran Way, by Oswald Bayer (2007).

A Time for Confessing, by Robert W. Bertram (2008).

The Pastoral Luther: Essays on Martin Luther's Practical Theology, edited by Timothy J. Wengert (2009).

Preaching from Home: The Stories of Seven Lutheran Women Hymn Writers, by Gracia Grindal (2011).

The Early Luther: Stages in a Reformation Reorientation, by Berndt Hamm (2013).

The Life, Works, and Witness of Tsehay Tolessa and Gudina Tumsa, the Ethiopian Bonhoeffer, edited by Samuel Yonas Deressa and Sarah Hinlicky (2017).

The Wittenberg Concord: Creating Space for Dialogue, by Gordon A. Jensen (2018).

Luther's Outlaw God: Volume 1: Hiddenness, Evil, and Predestination, by Steven D. Paulson (2018).

Lutheran Quarterly Books

The Essential Forde: Distinguishing Law and Gospel, by Gerhard O. Forde, edited by Nicholas Hopman, Mark C. Mattes, and Steven D. Paulson (2019).

Luther's Outlaw God: Volume 2: Hidden in the Cross, by Steven D. Paulson (2019).

The Augsburg Confession: Renewing Lutheran Faith and Practice, by Timothy J. Wengert (2020).

Luther's Outlaw God: Volume 3: Sacraments and God's Attack on the Promise, by Steven D. Paulson (2020).

Stories from Global Lutheranism: A Historical Timeline, by Martin J. Lohrmann (2021).